50 Hikes in the Adirondacks

50 *Hikes*

In the Adirondacks

Short Walks, Day Trips, and
Backpacks throughout the Park

Fourth Edition

BARBARA McMARTIN

BACK COUNTRY

Backcountry Guides

Woodstock, Vermont

AN INVITATION TO THE READER

Over time trails can be rerouted and signs and landmarks altered. If you find that changes have occurred on the routes described in this book, please let us know so that corrections may be made in future editions. The author and publisher also welcome other comments and suggestions. Address all correspondence to:

Editor, 50 Hikes™ Series
Backcountry Guides
P.O. Box 748
Woodstock, VT 05091

Library of Congress
Cataloging-in-Publication Data
has been requested.

Copyright © 1980, 1988, 1997, 2003 by
Barbara McMartin

Fourth Edition

Published by Backcountry Guides, a division of The Countryman Press, P.O. Box 748, Woodstock, VT 05091

Distributed by W.W. Norton & Company, Inc., 500 Fifth Avenue, New York, NY 10110

Series design by Glenn Suokko

Cover photograph of Lake George, Adirondack Park & Preserve by Carr Clifton
Maps by Richard Widhu and Mapping Specialists Ltd., Madison, WI

Hike 47 was written with the assistance of Lee M. Brenning

Hikes 6, 7, 15, 20, and 26, and parts of Hikes 27 and 34 were written by Bill Ingersoll.

Printed in the United States of America

10 9 8 7 6 5 4 3 2 1

Acknowledgments

I find it hard to believe that I began writing *50 Hikes in the Adirondacks* almost a quarter century ago and that this is its fourth edition. Over the years many friends have helped me with revisions or accompanied me on long walks. Two of my best companions have died: Erwin Miller, who walked with me on most of the hikes in the first edition, and Lee Brenning, who did so much for my *Discover the Adirondacks* series. I miss them both very much.

Jim Dawson, Dennis Conroy, Scott Gray, Peter O'Shea, Chuck Bennett, and especially Edythe Robbins have helped with revisions. My husband, W. Alec Reid, not only continues to walk with me, he still prints our black-and-white photographs and oversees the maps.

Many rangers and foresters at DEC and several who have retired have given me advice, told me about new state acquisitions, and alerted me to trail changes.

The highlight of this fourth edition is the addition of the work of Bill Ingersoll. For the past three years Bill has assisted me in walking, scouting, writing, and revising my *Discover the Adirondacks* guides. His keen observation, attention to detail, and work with maps are outstanding. He is gradually taking over that series and it was logical that he contribute the five new hikes included in this edition, plus the necessary updates on a few trail descriptions.

Bill, a graduate of Rochester Institute of Technology, lives in Barneveld, hikes every weekend, and works in Utica. He sketches Adirondack scenes with pen and ink, some for himself, some for my canoe book. We occasionally hike together, and I will depend on him for future revisions of all my guides.

50 Hikes in the Adirondacks at a Glance

Region	Hike	Nearest Town
Lake George	1. Buck Mountain	Lake George Village
Lake George	2. Black Mountain	Whitehall
Lake George	3. Tongue Mountain Range	Bolton
Southeast	4. Hadley Mountain	Hadley/Lake Luzerne
Southeast	5. Murphy, Middle, Bennett Lakes	Northville
Southwest	6. Ice Cave Mountain	Forestport
West Central	7. Ross, Whortleberry, and Big Bad Luck Ponds	Indian Lake
Southern	8. Falls on the West Branch Sacandaga	Wells
Southern	9. Good Luck Cliffs	Caroga Lake
Southeast	10. Pine Orchard	Wells
West Central	11. Echo Cliffs on Panther Mountain	Piseco
Southern	12. Goldmine Stream Waterfall	Stratford/Piseco
South Central	13. Peaked Mountain	North Creek
West Central	14. Moose River Plains	Indian Lake/Inlet
West Central	15. Brooktrout Lake and Falls Pond	Speculator
West Central	16. John Brown's Tract	Thendara
West Central	17. Vista Trail and Bald Mountain	Old Forge/Eagle Bay
West Central	18. Cascade and Queer Lakes	Eagle Bay
Southwest	19. Gleasmans Falls	Lowville
Northwest	20. Grass River Waterfalls	Fine/Newton Falls
Northern	21. Jenkins Mountain	Paul Smiths
Northern	22. Saint Regis Mountain	Paul Smiths
Northern	23. Debar Mountain	Meacham Lake
Northern	24. Catamount Mountain	Wilmington
Northeast	25. Pokamoonshine Mountain	Keeseville

DISTANCE (miles)	RISE	DIFFICULTY	GOOD FOR KIDS	CAMPING	VIEWS	Notes
6.6	2,000	3	★	★	★	Great views and excellent trail
8.5	1,100	3	★	★	★	Great views and nature walk
12.4	3,000	5			★	Be sure to have water
4	1,550	2	★	★	★	Fire tower
7.2	500	2	★	★		Great camping opportunities
3.8	494	4		★		Amazing fissures
8.1	1,080	2	★	★		Good fishing on Big Bad Luck
6	–	4		★		Some bushwhacking involved, beautiful waterfalls
4.4	700	3		★	★	Part of route is unmarked
4.8	–	1–2	★	★		Spectacular stand of old-growth pine
1.4	600	1	★	★	★	Three state campgrounds nearby
2.6	–	1	★	★		Unmarked path, virgin spruce stands, charming waterfall
8.2	1,245	4		★	★	Shorten by canoe trip on Thirteenth Lake
5.4	–	1	★	★		Explore many lakes from long dirt road
10	2,244	3		★		Remote and wild
9.6	–	3	★	★		Explore wilderness lakes
8.1	1,300	3	★	★	★	Distant views
9.7	–	3–4	★	★		Walk through great forests
6	–	2	★	★		Dramatic waterfalls
4.4	–	1	★			Very easy, series of wonderful waterfalls
8.2	780	2	★	★	★	Take in the Visitors Center as well
6	1,235	2	★		★	Views of lakes and high peaks
7	1,600	3	★	★	★	Remote peak with views
3.8	1,568	2	★	★	★	Great rocky summit
2	1,260	2	★	★	★	Easy climb for views

– = minimal

✳ = yet to do   • = do again

50 Hikes in the Adirondacks at a Glance

Region	Hike	Nearest Town
Eastern	26. Treadway Mountain	Schroon Lake
Eastern	27. Pharaoh Ponds Loop	Schroon Lake
Eastern	28. Severance Hill	Schroon Lake
Southeast	29. Crane Mountain	Johnsburg
South Central	30. Siamese Ponds	Bakers Mills
South Central	31. Chimney Mountain	Indian Lake
West Central	32. Pillsbury Mountain	Speculator
West Central	33. Snowy Mountain	Indian Lake
West Central	34. Wakely Mountain	Indian Lake
Central	35. Rock, Cascade, and Stephens Ponds	Blue Mountain Lake
Central	36. Blue Mountain	Blue Mountain Lake
Central	37. Owls Head Mountain	Long Lake
Northern	38. Nehasane Preserve	Tupper Lake
Northern	39. Ampersand Mountain	Tupper Lake/Saranac Lake
Northern	40. McKenzie Mountain	Ray Brook
Northern	41. Pitchoff Mountain	Keene
Central	42. Blue Ledge on the Hudson	Minerva
Central	43. Vanderwhacker Mountain	Minerva/Newcomb
Central	44. Goodnow Mountain	Newcomb
Central	45. Santanoni Preserve	Newcomb
Central	46. Hoffman Notch	Schroon Lake/North Hudson
Northwest	47. Bear Mountain and Boardwalk Nature Trail	Cranberry Lake
Northeast	48. Giant Mountain	Keene Valley
High Peaks	49. Indian Pass	Lake Placid/Newcomb
High Peaks	50. Algonquin Peak in the MacIntyre Mountains	Lake Placid

great hike! (handwritten note by #44. Goodnow Mountain)

DISTANCE (miles)	RISE	DIFFICULTY	GOOD FOR KIDS	CAMPING	VIEWS	Notes
8	1,026	2–3		★	★	Lovely lakes on the way to fine views
19.4	1,000	5	★	★		Best as a 2- or 3-day hike
2	880	1	★	★	★	Short and easy, rewarding climb
4.8	1,300	3	★		★	If wet, be careful on open rock
13.2	600	3		★		Great camping destination
2.5	900	2	★		★	Use care on rocks and near cave openings
5.6	1,677	3	★		★	More views
7.5	2,100	4	★		★	Tallest mountain in the southern Adirondacks
6.4	1,636	3	★	★	★	Tallest fire tower in the Adirondacks
7.5	370	2	★	★		Good for a winter cross-country ski trip
4	1,560	3	★		★	Very popular!
7.2	1,060	3	★	★	★	Nice bare summit, swimming
9.4	460	3	★	★	★	Canoeing, too
5.6	1,790	3	★		★	Improved trail
10.6	1,221	3–4		★	★	Not hard, but long
5.2	1,440	3	★		★	Extraordinary rocks and small summits
5	230	1	★			Dramatic cliffs, rapids, and small falls
5.8	1,700	3	★		★	A favorite for views north to the High Peaks
3.4	1,030	2	★	★	★	Near the Newcomb Visitor Center
10.2	–	2	★			Good cross-country ski route
7.5	300	3		★		Long car shuttle to make one-way walk
8.3	540	2	★	★	★	Views of the lake and wilderness to the south
6.6	3,000	4	★		★	One of the best climbs
10.6	674	4		★		Long shuttle, but great one-way walk
8	2,936	4	★	★	★	History and views

– = minimal

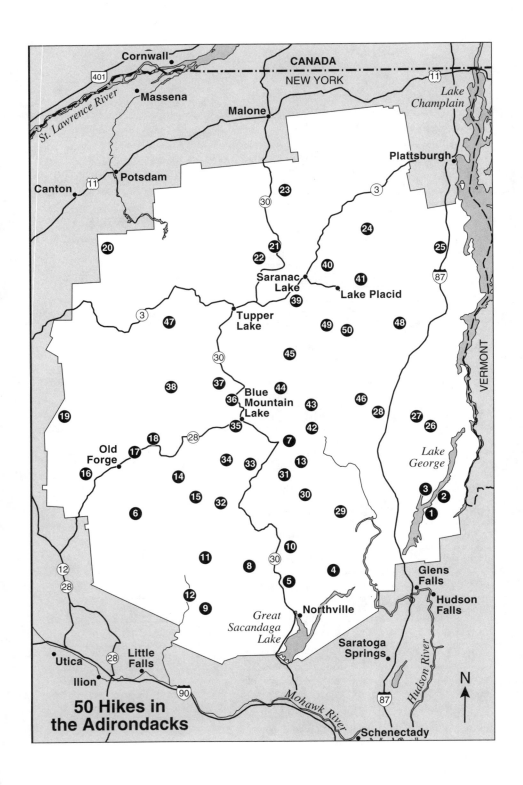

50 Hikes in
the Adirondacks

O – Do again (after 2006)

CONTENTS

2012
2012

2012
2012

Introduction

The first edition of *50 Hikes in the Adirondacks* was written as an introduction to the many different areas of the Adirondack Park. It has been updated repeatedly. In this fourth edition, Bill Ingersoll has added five new hikes.

In addition to representing almost all the Wild Forest and Wilderness Areas of the park, the 50 hikes sample each of the geographical areas now described in depth in the *Discover the Adirondacks* series. This series of 11 regional guides is published by Lake View Press and distributed by North Country Books, 311 Turner Street, Utica, NY 13501; 315-735-4877. This book is a companion to that series in that it will not only introduce you to the different parts of the park, but it will also help you find the Discover guide that will allow you to explore your favorite regions in depth. Each of the 50 hikes here is typical of the region covered in the Discover guides, but the latter contain every hiking trail and path and most of the exciting bushwhacks of each region.

The Adirondack Park is surrounded by a magical Blue Line that sets it apart from the rest of New York State. With nearly 6 million acres, this park is almost as large as the state of Vermont. Calling the area a park is confusing, for the Blue Line in fact delineates a hodgepodge of public and private lands.

The public lands inside the park's boundary have been gradually incorporated into a body known as the Forest Preserve, which was established in 1885 and given the protection of the state constitution in 1894. The Forest Preserve was initially intended to protect forever the state's water resources. At present, the Adirondack Park Agency oversees all of the land within the park, both public and private.

Forest Preserve lands, roughly 45 percent of the area inside the Blue Line, are managed by the Department of Environmental Conservation (DEC), which has responsibility for all public trails. The Forest Preserve is managed in a way that permits hunting throughout but prohibits any cutting of timber. According to the State Land Master Plan that was prepared by the Adirondack Park Agency, the public lands are divided into Wilderness, Wild Forest, Primitive, Canoe, and Intensive Use Areas.

The 50 hikes represent as many of the Adirondacks' regions, both political and natural, as possible. The guide describes every type of hiking route, from those well known to those unmarked paths visited by only a few people. The trails lead you up the tall peaks of the northern mountain ranges as well as up the gentler mountains surrounding the central Adirondack dome. They follow abandoned logging roads and chains of uninhabited lakes. On them you meet wild rivers and distant waterfalls, discover caves and cliffs, and reach a few of the fire towers that still survive. In short, this guide acquaints you with a cross-section of adventures available to Adirondack hikers.

Of course, I hope this guidebook does more than introduce you to the 360 miles of trails and 60,000 feet of climbing outlined in the 50 hikes. It should make you aware of the geological structures that underlie the trails and their relation to the various types of forest vegetation. It should lead you to observe alpine summits and broad plains, virgin forests and quaking bogs, ferns and wildflowers, and birds and wild animals.

Equally important, you should become acquainted with a few of the early settlers who pioneered in the mines and forests, the trappers, lumbermen, and guides whose footsteps echoed on the woodland routes that are today's hiking trails. The Discover series treats each of these themes in greater depth. This guide and all the others contain a list of books that can increase your knowledge and appreciation of the trails' history. These books are chosen not necessarily because they are the most scholarly, but because they have most vividly re-created the past for me. I want this guide to pinpoint where specific historical events occurred.

All the details I have tried to weave into this trail guide are still no more than hints of what you will find. Enrichment is the most important part of this guide and the Discover series. If you let them take you on a true voyage of discovery, you will enjoy much more than the pleasures of hiking. You will come to know the land and to develop a sense of love and reverence for all that it embraces. That is what I want to share with you.

BEFORE YOU START
The majority of these 50 hikes are just that—hikes. This guide is designed to acquaint you with extended walks throughout the Adirondacks. Strenuous hikes are usually associated with the High Peaks Region in the northeastern part of the park, but you can also find them throughout the Forest Preserve. To give everyone a chance to discover the wonders of this vast area, however, I have included a few shorter, easy walks. Many more exist, and are described in the Discover guides.

While all these excursions are day hikes, you should be well equipped before starting the longer walks. If you are new to hiking, it will be best to join a hiking group and learn from those with experience. Or you may want to consult two of my guides for young people, *Adventures in Hiking* and *Adventures in Backpacking*. The more experience you have in the woods, the greater will be your enjoyment and your safety. Do not count on this summary of what you need to know to prepare you for every situation you are likely to encounter. This guide was not written primarily for novices, and this introduction is not a primer for beginning hikers. Treat it as a checklist and a set of reminders.

SAFETY IN THE WOODS
This guide does offer routes for which there are no marked state trails. Four hikes are included where you should be able to use map and compass and common sense in navigating. Numerous cautions have been added to the trail descriptions. Stay on the trail and be aware of your progress. Remember, only your preparedness and caution can make you safe.

THE WEATHER
Whenever possible, wait for a sunny day. The pleasures are much greater, and the problems more predictable. But even on sunny days, prepare for the worst; downpours and cold fronts can occur almost unannounced. The hiking season in the Adirondacks generally extends from May through October, but this does not mean

you cannot see snowflakes in July. In May, for instance, the temperature may range from a sweltering 92 degrees Fahrenheit on a trail not yet sheltered by leaf cover to a frigid 22 degrees Fahrenheit on a mountain path smothered in a foot of new snow. June is no less variable, and by then the blackflies, scourge of the North, are out in full force. July and August can be severe on the tops of the higher mountains, and by mid-September you should again be prepared for snow. Of course, preparing for the worst does not mean the worst will happen. Remember, the greatest advantage in planning day trips is that you can wait until a good day comes before setting out.

PREPARATIONS

Even with the best of forecasts, your watchword should be to *plan for the unexpected.* Possible changes in temperature mean you should take extra clothing, of which at least one layer should be wool—yes, wool, even in the heat of summer. It is the one material that keeps you warm when wet. In addition to changes of warm clothing, you may also want to carry a change of socks and a shirt, even on a day hike. Experiment with a combination of layers of light waterproof gear, warm wool shirts, thermal underwear, and cool, long-sleeved cotton shirts. Your pants should be sturdy and comfortable. If you are modest, you might want to carry a bathing suit in your pack. Gloves and a hat usually also find their way into my pack.

Changes in terrain mean you should have a sturdy, lightweight, waterproof, over-the-ankle pair of boots. And you need a pair that fits perfectly and is well broken-in. You ought to wear two pairs of socks, an inner lightweight pair and a heavy outer pair that is at least partly wool.

Of course you want a sturdy daypack, large enough to hold your needs. The separate pouch along the side of my pack always contains a whistle, a case with dry matches, a jackknife, a small can opener, lip balm, and a space blanket. I have used them all.

Carry a map and compass (more on that later), a flashlight in case you are delayed beyond dusk, and a watch so you do not panic if that happens. You also need a small first-aid kit, containing a few bandages, first-aid cream, and moleskin for the unexpected blister.

Buy a small squeeze bottle of insect repellent. Carry it all summer long, for the blackfly season in spring stretches into the mosquito season of early summer, deerflies and horseflies follow, and many years see a resurgence of blackflies in autumn. If you plan ahead, the bugs are not all that bad. If it is warm and dry enough to walk in early May, you can enjoy a few weeks before the bugs start. They first appear at lower elevations and in the south, so try a few higher or more northern hikes until the blackflies catch up with you. Most years there is about a week in early June—the timing and length may vary—when you should simply stay home. That week invariably occurs when the trout fishing is best. Although modern science has made great improvements in repellents, nothing really seems to work during this one short period.

I fill a Ziploc® bag with toilet paper so that it will stay dry. I also throw in a few moist towelettes to use before lunch on those dry mountaintops.

All wise hikers are likely to carry these basic items, but my personal list has additional items you should consider. I always wear unbreakable glasses. Overhanging twigs and branches have a way of poking eyes. Even if you do not need them for vi-

A typical Adirondack landscape from the summit of Ampersand Mountain

sion, carry dark sunglasses for bright days and a lightly tinted pair for the duller light.

There is always a magnifying glass in my pack for resolving the contour lines on maps and for identifying plant specimens. I would not be without my lightweight pair of binoculars. Distant mountaintops and birds are an important part of what I see. For pure fun I carry an altimeter that works according to barometric pressure. On relatively stable days, it provides a good clue to my progress up a mountain, and on an unstable day it can alert me to sudden changes in the weather.

Managing water has become a problem in the Adirondacks. The appearance of *Giardia* cysts in once pure mountain streams means that the hiker can no longer drink with impunity. As a general rule, the day hiker ought to carry enough water for his needs. The camper must use other methods, and though there is a variety of opinions about the best methods of water purification, certain filters do work.

I prefer to use lightweight aluminum fuel bottles (used, of course, only for drinking purposes) as I have found they are the most indestructible and leakproof water carriers. Individual cardboard juice cartons solve the pick-me-up problem for me. They are sturdy, safe, and offer a variety of natural juices, perfect for the hiker.

Remember, hiking should be fun. If you are uncomfortable with the weather or tired, turn back and make the complete hike another day. Do not create a situation in which you risk yourself or your companions.

And *never walk alone*. Be sure someone knows your intended route and expected return time. Always sign in at the DEC trailhead registers where they are available. The unexpected can occur. Weather can change, trail markings can become obscured, you can fall, and you can get lost. But you will not be in real danger if you have anticipated the unexpected.

BEHAVIOR IN THE WOODS

So now you are safe in the woods, but what about the woods? The Adirondack environment that can threaten you may be just as fragile as you are, and you are the only one who can protect it.

Walk dry. Wet soil is more easily compacted, making roots more susceptible to damage, so try to hike when the trails are dry. Stay on trails or rock surfaces, especially on higher summits. Avoid wet places, or walk through them with extreme care. This guide does point out a few bogs; enjoy them without altering them.

Camp at designated areas where they exist or in places where a campsite will leave no trace. Regulations require that you camp 150 feet from water or trailsides and at elevations below 4,000 feet.

Bury your wastes at least 200 feet from water and from a trail or path. If possible, select a leaf- or duff-covered area where a suitable hole can be easily scraped aside. With the appearance of *Giardia* in some locations, it is imperative that hikers manage human wastes to prevent the spread of this hikers' scourge.

Do not bathe with soap in lakes or streams; when picnicking or camping, carry wash water as well as dishwater back from the shore. Keep lake or running water pure for drinking and swimming.

If you are camping, carry a stove for cooking, and do not build fires except in an emergency. Then use only dead downed wood, and build your fire on dry stone or on gravelly or sandy soil surfaces, surrounded by a fire ring of stones to protect duff, leaf mold, or organic soils from burning.

Burn organic trash if you can. Otherwise, carry out everything you carry into the woods.

Respect the rights of others—the property rights of private landholders, as well as the privacy of fellow hikers and the wilderness rights of future hikers.

NOTES FOR USING THIS GUIDE

Summaries at the beginning of each hike list the hiking distance, vertical rise, time on the trail, and the United States Geological Survey (USGS) topographical map or maps for the area the hike traverses. If the hike is in one of the official Wilderness Areas, that fact is mentioned. The guide notes where fire towers still stand on mountaintops.

Unless otherwise indicated, distances are for the round-trip or circuit. Distances have been derived from either state trail markings or measurements made from the USGS sheets. The latter are correct to within 10 percent. Errors and inconsistencies in the state signing system are described in the text.

Distances are given in miles, feet, and yards. Unless you are an experienced hiker, you probably have little sense of distance. You might want to practice "guesstimating" 100-yard intervals on the level and pacing them out to check. Because the difficulty of a hike can be so affected by elevation changes and the condition of the trail, time is as important as distance in estimating a segment of a trip.

Vertical rise refers to the total rise in elevation for the hike. In cases where the terrain is relatively level, a numerical figure has not been used.

Hiking time is given for the total time for a leisurely pace, but it is simply the minimum needed to walk and enjoy the trail as described. The text often tells you to allow more time for sightseeing, and the difference is a good indication of the special things you might encounter on the way.

The *maps,* the USGS topographical sheets mentioned in each heading, are not absolutely necessary equipment, because the maps in this guide are based on them. (The hike route is shown by a solid line, and the walking direction of any loop by an arrow.) However, you will have more fun on a mountaintop if you can identify some of the surrounding countryside, and the USGS maps enable you to do this.

If you do not know how to read a map, you should learn to do so before hiking all but a half dozen of the simplest trails in this guide. Spend time walking with someone who does know how to read a map. The same instructions are appropriate for the use of a compass. If you are not proficient in the use of a compass, get help. Or work with a good book on compass reading or orienteering. The skillful use of maps and a compass is developed only with practice.

This book is a guide to 50 great hikes, not a course in using map and compass. Almost all of the routes described are on marked trails, but markings have a way of changing. You cannot always depend on them. Furthermore, bridges wash out, beaver build new ponds, and mountaintops become so clouded in fog that visibility beyond your fingertips is impossible. None of this should bother you if you have developed map and compass skills.

NEW WILDERNESS REGULATIONS FOR THE HIGH PEAKS

The regulations called for by the Unit Management Plan (UMP) for the High Peaks Wilderness Complex (HPWC) were adopted in 2000. Special regulations apply to the eastern HPWC, as defined by DEC map to be the area east of the line north from Tahawus to the HPWC boundary, including Street and Nye. While these regulations were not applicable to the Dix and Giant Wilderness Areas, many are being considered for inclusion in those UMPs, due in 2003. The following is a summary.

1. All hikers in the Eastern Zone HPWC must fill out and possess a self-issuing trip ticket. The reverse of the trip ticket details regulations and gives safety tips.

2. All hikers are also required to sign in the registers at trailheads to facilitate search and rescue.

3. Group size: Overnight camping groups may not exceed 8 individuals; Day-hiking groups may not exceed 15 individuals.

4. Campfires: Campfires are prohibited throughout the Eastern HPWC Zone;

5. Camping: Camping is prohibited above 4,000 feet, at any time of year. Camping between 3,500 and 4,000 feet is permitted at designated sites only. Camping in the South Meadows–Lake Colden corridor is restricted to designated sites only. Contact DEC for current status before beginning your trip.

6. Glass containers, except those containing prescription medicines, are prohibited, throughout the HPWC.

7. Pets must be leashed on DEC-marked trails in the eastern zone, at all lean-tos and designated campsites, in congregated areas, and above 4,000 feet.

8. Stay on marked trails and on bare rock on alpine summits in order to protect the fragile alpine plants.

9. Winter visitors must possess and use skis or snowshoes when the terrain is snow-covered.

OTHER HELPFUL INFORMATION

New York State Atlas and Gazetteer, DeLorme Mapping Co., $19.95. This book shows all Adirondack roads. It is especially helpful in locating trailheads.

The New York State Department of Environmental Conservation (DEC) is the source of all DEC booklets, trail maps, and campsite information. Some specific titles are "Nordic Skiing Trails in New York State," "Lake George Islands Map," "Moose River Recreation Area," "Pharaoh Lake Trails Map," "Trails in the Lake George Region," "Trails in the Cranberry Lake Region," "Trails in the Old Forge–Big Moose Region," and "Trails in the Schroon Lake Region."

The DEC operates regional offices throughout New York State. Addresses and telephone numbers for offices in Region 5: Regional Headquarters, Route 86, Ray Brook, NY 12977, 518-891-1200 (covering Clinton, Essex, and Franklin Counties); Saratoga, Warren, and Washington Counties Sub-Office, Hudson Street, Warrensburg, NY 12885, 518-623-3671; Fulton and Hamilton Counties Sub-Office, Main Street Extension, Northville, NY 12134, 518-863-4545.

For Region 6, which also extends into the Adirondack area: Regional Headquarters, 317 Washington Street, Watertown, NY 13601, 315-785-2239; Lewis and Jefferson Counties Sub-Office, Route 26A, P.O. Box 3, Lowville, NY 13367, 315-785-3521; Herkimer and Oneida Counties Sub-Office, 225 North Main Street, Herkimer, NY 13350, 315-866-6330; St. Lawrence County Sub-Office, 30 Court Street, Canton, NY 13617, 315-386-4546.

New York State
Department of Commerce
Office of Tourism
99 Washington Avenue
Albany, NY 12245

Among the publications this office issues are the "I Love New York" brochures, camping guides, a tourism map, and the "State Travel Guide."

UNITED STATES GEOLOGICAL SURVEY MAPS

Maps are available from many local stores. Jimapco of Clifton Park, NY, 518-899-5091, is a good supplier.

Key to Maps	
——	MAIN TRAIL
● ● ●	SIDE TRAIL
Ⓟ	PARKING
⌂	SHELTER
↑↑	VIEW

1

Buck Mountain

Distance (round-trip): 6.6 miles

Vertical rise: 2,000 feet

Hiking time: 4½ hours

Maps: USGS 7.5' Bolton Landing; USGS 7.5' Shelving Rock

Buck Mountain lies on the southeast shore of Lake George, and it is a perfect introduction to the Adirondacks. Pick a bright day in May and start your Adirondack hiking with a great climb.

The views from Buck Mountain's summit encompass thousands of square miles of the Adirondacks to the north and west, parts of Vermont's Green Mountains to the east, and two large bodies of water that have figured significantly in the settlement and military histories of this region and indeed the United States. Lake Champlain and Lake George were major water highways connecting the Hudson and its river settlements to the south with the St. Lawrence and its settlements in French Canada to the north. Both lakes were important military routes, as the number of old forts and battlefields along their shores attest.

Lake George was christened Lac du St. Sacrement by its European discoverer, Father Jogues, in 1609. From that date until the end of the War of 1812, the lake was the scene of many bloody battles among the Native Americans, French, English, and American patriots. During that entire period, no peaceful settlement graced its shores, although there was a military presence after 1755, when Fort William Henry was erected on its southern shore. Much of the lake is still bordered with stands of solemn evergreens, so that in places it looks very much as it did to the first white men who visited it.

Buck Mountain is only one of Lake George's mountains. Those planning additional hikes in this long-favorite resort region

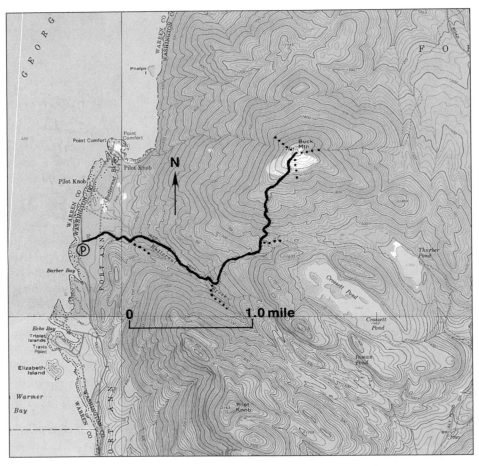

should investigate some of the area's state campgrounds. The Lake George Beach State Campground has picnic facilities only. Both the Hearthstone Point State Campground, 2 miles north of Lake George Village, and Rogers Rock State Campground, near the north end of the lake, have good camping facilities. Perhaps the most beautiful campsites are those scattered among the many state-owned islands in the lake. All of these campsites are accessible only by water. The required permits may be obtained from island caretakers on Glen, Long, and Narrow Islands. You will also want the campsite recreation circular, avail-

able from the DEC (see introduction).

Like Buck Mountain, many of Lake George's other mountains are within the public lands of the New York State Forest Preserve, and several have excellent trails, the majority of which were constructed as horse trails in the 1930s by the Civilian Conservation Corps. The trail on Buck Mountain is one of the best-designed in the Adirondacks. Spring comes early here, so any of these mountains is ideal for that first spring hike. Fires have swept most of the summits, leaving bare rock promontories with great views. Because of the sparseness of the cover near the summits, the trails are hot and dry in summer, so you will probably find spring or fall preferable for hiking here. You must be sure to carry water. Finally, rattlesnakes inhabit the rock crevices on many of Lake George's mountains. Their infrequent presence on trails should not deter you, but do wear sturdy, high boots, and watch where you place your hands.

How to Get There

Take the Adirondack Northway (I-87) to either exit 21 or exit 22, head into Lake George Village, and pass Fort William Henry and the Minnehaha Boat Landing. Continue east around the south end of the lake 0.4 mile to NY 9L. Turn left on that highway, which follows the eastern shore of Lake George north for 6.8 miles and then forks. The way left is marked PILOT KNOB, 4 MILES. The state parking turnout for the Buck Mountain trailhead is 3.3 miles along this dead-end road on your right, and is well marked.

The Trail

You begin walking along an abandoned roadway at the east end of the parking lot. The trail is marked with yellow DEC hiking trail signs and light blue horse trail signs. The trail is raised and dry as it immediately plunges into a hemlock bog with many osmunda ferns, their huge root clump masses rising from the soggy ground. As the forest changes to tall hardwoods, the heavy vines of fox grapes are reminiscent of typical Hudson Highland cover.

At this lower elevation, the trail intersects several logging roads: At the first fork turn right, and at the second, at 0.3 mile, turn left. You cross Butternut Brook, then begin to climb the deep, hemlock-covered slopes that shelter the brook. You pass another old woods road forking left, then cross Butternut Brook again and continue beside

it, climbing a slope beneath a deep, hemlock-covered ledge. The trail zigzags as it climbs seriously, and if you look down on your right, you should see a picnic table beneath the hemlock and beside the stream.

Another indistinct woods road coming from the left will remind you that this area was once farmed and logged. You are now climbing moderately and are already high enough to see the blue water of Lake George through the trees. Rock ledges rise on your left where the trail has been carved into the hillside. After walking for about a half hour, you pass an old stone fence. It leads to a promontory with a small opening and a view of mountains to the south. Beyond that you walk through an open field and cross a small stream on a slippery log. The stream cascades in a pretty series of small waterfalls down to Butternut Brook. Follow the stream for 100 yards to an intersection, where a sign says it is 1.5 miles back to Pilot Knob trailhead. (Pilot Knob itself is privately owned and inaccessible.) You probably walked that distance in 40 minutes.

At the intersection, the blue trail bears right to Inman Pond, 3.1 miles away. Take the left fork, which heads north to the summit of Buck Mountain, 1.8 miles distant. Here the trail is deeply cut into the hillside, with high banks on either side, and the route is somewhat boulder strewn. You begin a gradual but steady climb with gentle switchbacks into a scrubby deciduous forest. Refreshing level stretches curve between the steepest segments. About 20 minutes from the intersection, a logging road joins from the left, and you turn sharply right, uphill. At this point there are so few trail markers that you may be misled.

A couple of hundred yards past the logging road, water pours from a spring-fed pipe to the right and spills across the trail to join the small stream on the left. About 20

The view south from Buck Mountain toward Lake George Village

minutes beyond the logging road you cross the stream again. The forest cover of small maple, beech, and birch is home to a multitude of birds, and you may even spot a nesting pair of scarlet tanagers. About 10 minutes from the second stream crossing, in a level between climbs, the trail has been widened to avoid a wet seep. This is the only place where the route might be confusing. Look for the yellow markers on your left to show you where to begin the climb again, the steepest grades so far encountered. Even the stretches between switchbacks seem steeper now. The forest is more open, with scrubby oak indicating that the summit is near.

You soon reach the first real overlook, with views southeast to Crosset Pond. Beyond it the trail climbs and then flattens out, heading north across a shoulder of the mountain. Pine, hemlock, and tall birch fill the level ground below the last rise. The path, narrow here, crosses a boggy area lush with wild iris, clintonia, spring anemones, bunchberry, goldthread, putty root orchid, *Corallorhiza trifida,* and huge clumps of *Polygala*, or gaywings. As open rock and the summit appear ahead, you realize you still have a way to walk. Yellow arrows painted on the bare rock direct you among scrubby patches of cherry, maple, birch, aspen, and blueberry. The view begins to unfold, and after 2½ hours of walking, you reach the summit. In a cleft filled with garnet sand near the summit, a sign indicates that the trail continues northeast toward Shelving Rock Road, 2.5 miles away.

Buck Mountain rises steeply from the deepest part of Lake George. From the 2,330-foot summit you will not only enjoy views of the lake, which lies in a deep fault valley whose ends are blocked by glacial debris, but you will also meet some of the other peaks described in this guide. Crane Mountain lies almost due west, and Gore Mountain with its tower and ski slopes is to the north. Just north of Gore on the horizon is the distinctive, flat-topped hump of Blue Mountain. In the distance between Crane and Blue lies Snowy Mountain. It is 43 miles away and distinguished by the jagged knob whose cliff face reflects white, prompting the name.

To the north-northeast beyond Little Buck Mountain lies Sleeping Beauty, with Erebus to its left and Black Mountain just peeping up behind. If it is a clear day in summer, when there is little definition between rocks and trees, the cliffs on Sleeping Beauty may show up in such a way that they reveal the form of a reclining female stretched like a romantic billboard across that mountain's southwestern slopes. Pharaoh Mountain rises almost 21 miles away in the direction of magnetic north. Beyond it, and more than 40 miles distant, range the Adirondacks' High Peaks, with Giant Mountain to the right of Pharaoh, and the cluster that includes Nippletop and Marcy to the left.

Northwest of Buck, lying against the western shore of Lake George, is Green Island, with the rebuilt Hotel Sagamore. Look beyond it to the hills on the horizon. South of a line to Green are the cliffs on Moxon Mountain, which mark the route toward Vanderwhacker Mountain. Sight above the middle of the island to Hoffman Mountain, whose western notch makes a great day's trek. From the eastern promontories you can enjoy the sweep of the Champlain Valley with the Green Mountains behind.

When you start the return, retrace your footsteps, being careful to follow the designated route on the open summit. That way you will not disturb the fragile plants that have managed to find niches in cracks along the open rock.

The long sweep of the shoulder you traverse points to Pilot Knob Mountain to the south. Your zigzag descent to the shoulder and the trek across it should take no more than 20 minutes; you then begin the series of switchbacks that will bring you within 45 minutes to the piped spring. When you reach the trail intersection, less than a half hour beyond, most of the steep descent is finished. Native columbine and sweetfern shrub edge the route. The rest of the walk is so easy that a half hour will suffice for the last 1.5 miles, unless you pause to look at wildflowers.

➤ Adirondack Roads

Old road, woods road, tote road, and logging road are all terms for the abandoned roads you will see in the Forest Preserve. They once led to settlements, logging camps, hunting lodges, isolated farms, and sugarbushes. Many Adirondack trails now follow these old routes. No motorized vehicles are permitted on them, except in winter, when snowmobiles can use those that are designated for snowmobile use.

2

Black Mountain

Distance (around loop): 8.5 miles

Vertical rise: 1,100 feet

Hiking time: 6 hours

Map: USGS 7.5' Shelving Rock and Whitehall

Fire tower

Black Mountain, at 2,646 feet, is the highest peak in the two ranges of mountains that shelter Lake George. It lies about halfway along the lake's eastern shore, and the views from the summit are more than proportional to its height. One of the trails to its summit rises steeply from the shore of Lake George, but it is accessible only by water. Your route on Black Mountain is a loop that requires a bit less climbing, but it still traverses part of the reputedly more handsome trail from the lake. This loop also allows you to visit a series of charming ponds that lie south and east of the summit.

There is a fire tower on Black Mountain, and although you might appreciate climbing it to identify distant mountains, Black's summit is mostly open rock, so overlooks in every direction can be found at ground level.

How to Get There

From the north and west, take exit 28 off the Adirondack Northway (I-87) to NY 74, and follow that route east to NY 22 at Ticonderoga. Head south on NY 22 to Clemons. From the south, take NY 149 to Fort Ann and turn north on NY 22/US 4. At Whitehall stay north on NY 22 to Clemons. This latter route takes you on a beautiful drive through the Champlain Valley and across the South Bay of Lake Champlain above Whitehall. At Clemons, drive 2.6 miles west toward Huletts Landing on County Road 6, and then bear south (left) on Pike Brook Road for 0.8 mile to the trailhead. You will have views of Black Mountain as well as Knob Hill and Sugarloaf, two unusual small moun-

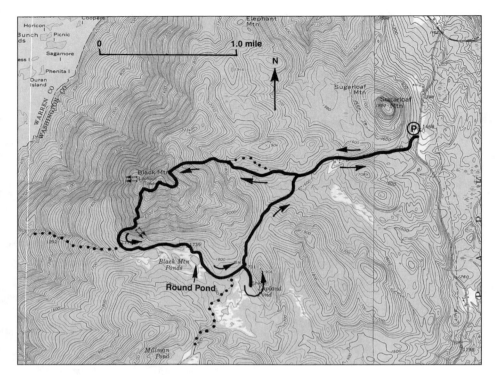

tains whose distinctive shapes you will be able to identify again clearly from Black's summit. Signs at the trailhead indicate that the Black Mountain Fire Tower is 2.8 miles away, and that the Lapland Pond Lean-to, which you pass on your return leg, is 2.5 miles distant.

The Trail

The trail begins along a gravel road that leads to a private residence. Red trail disks on telephone poles, which you will follow all the way to the summit, mark the route. A splash of the wildflowers that make every walk in the Lake George region special brightens this otherwise dull roadway. Trillium, blue cohosh, crinkleroot, twisted stalk, Solomon's seal, and clintonia are only a few of the flowers you may see.

You reach an intersection in 0.9 mile. Across the field of the nearby farmhouse,

the tower still looks a long way off. The trail follows the right side of the field and continues gently uphill through a more mature and taller woods, making pleasanter walking. You should spot the rattlesnake fern, which will remind you to be watchful of rattlesnakes on this mountain, as on all of Lake George's mountains.

After a half hour or so, in just over 1.2 miles, the trail to the Lapland Pond Lean-to and the ponds to the south forks left, marked with blue disks. You take the right-hand trail, still marked with red disks. The sign indicates it is 1.6 miles to the tower. The trail continues to follow an old roadway, which has stretches of corduroy. Look to the edges for trailing arbutus and foam-flower. A snowmobile trail forks right at a second intersection. It winds toward the summit by a more circuitous route, with a lower grade than the hiking trail. You will meet it again just below the last pitch on the summit.

For the hiking trail, go left, on the less obvious route. Fortunately, a plethora of red disks marks the intersection. The trail quickly takes you across a little stream where water falls over a series of small horizontal ledges.

The trail turns sharply left uphill and really begins to climb, following the little watercourse to a rock ledge. The trail heads straight up the ledge, so steeply that you will probably have to pause and catch your breath. Beyond, the trail, wide enough that vehicles once used it, is worn to bedrock. The forest is fairly open, and within an hour you can look back toward Knob Hill. You pass through an area of heavy blowdowns where winter has taken its toll of many treetops, leaving a scene of destruction. Then you continue climbing through red spruce forests with some hemlock, low balsam, and striped maple. The underbrush becomes thick before finally opening by moss-covered ledges near the summit.

It will probably take you a little over 90 minutes to reach the open, windswept summit, shared by picnic tables, two cabins, and the tower. A sign points south where the red-marked trail continues to Black Mountain Point on Lake George, some 2.7 miles away.

From the tower you can't help noticing first the Tongue Mountain Range on the opposite shore of Lake George. The Range Trail and Fivemile Mountain, Fifth Peak, and French Point Mountain are easily identified. You will appreciate from this vantage the lumps and valleys on the Range Trail that make it so challenging and difficult: The deep valley to the south of Fifth Peak, the height of the two unnamed knobs to its south, and the deep valley between French Point Mountain and First Peak reveal how much climbing there is.

Elephant Mountain lies northeast of Black on the east shore of Lake George. Sabbath Day Point, Silver Bay, and The Hague stretch north on the lake's western shore, with the slopes of Rogers Rock silhouetted beyond. Slightly south of Rogers Rock, on the west shore, Anthony's Nose raises its unmistakable profile. In the distance to the northeast Lake Champlain is visible, with the Green Mountains beyond.

If it is a really clear day, you can identify the mountains on the horizon that lie between the northern end of the Tongue Mountain Range and Catamount, the long mountain northwest of Sabbath Day Point. Sight beyond Catamount to Giant Mountain. Dix rises directly over Fivemile Mountain, and continuing to the left you see Macomb, Nippletop, Basin, Haystack, Marcy, Skylight, and Redfield. Pharaoh Mountain, just to the left of Nippletop, is much nearer. Still in the closer range, Hoffman Mountain is farther left, with Santanoni to its left on the horizon. Vanderwhacker is next left, its steep cone standing isolated. This panorama occupies the skyline defined by Fivemile Mountain and the valley between it and Fifth Peak. Over that valley is the flat top of Blue Mountain.

Once you have climbed back down the tower, the views south are best as you begin your descent, continuing along the red trail. At the end of the promontory, ledges to the right overlook Erebus Mountain and the islands that fill the narrows of Lake George. This is the best place from which to appreciate the deep trench of the down drop fault, or *graben,* that forms the lake. Here the bent forms of wind-shaped trees frame the views, and clusters of misshapen cherries, maples, and elderberries provide little shelter from the sun. The trail, built up with rock, hugs the steep slopes and begins its twisting, turning descent, dropping rapidly and without views below many cliffs and ledges. The switchbacks (I lost track of the count after 20) allow you to descend quickly to a magnificent lookout southeast to the chain of ponds you are about to visit, as well as southwest to Lake George.

Below the overlook, the trail becomes less steep and the woods become deeper, changing to a high, open forest of huge birch. You have passed the imaginary line that separates the sharp knob of Black Mountain's summit and the valley below. On the upper slopes, which rise 800 feet in 0.5 mile, rockwork was necessary to build the trail against the mountain, but here it is beautiful, soft, and wide. After walking only a few minutes on the wider trail, a total descent of 40 minutes (if you did not pause too long for views), you reach an intersection. The well-used, red-marked trail turns right toward Black Mountain Point, but you turn left on the yellow-marked trail. This intersection 200 yards below the lookout is not obvious. If you are still on the red trail heading downhill when it crosses the outlet of Black Mountain Pond, you have followed it about 200 yards too far. Retrace your steps and look for the intersection with the yellow trail. It is easier to spot when walking in this direction. This little-used route will take you 0.3 mile to Black Mountain Pond, 0.7 mile to Round Pond, and a bit over 1 mile to Lapland Pond.

Your walk on the yellow trail begins beside a boggy swale with handsome birch. Next, climb to a hemlock knoll above Black Mountain Pond, which is hardly visible at first below the ledge on which you are walking. Descend to the muddy shore of the marshy little body of water, complete with beaver house and bog plants. Continue up another knoll topped with huge paper birch and walk on high ground to Round Pond. The trail dips

to its shore beside a hemlock-covered hillside that makes a great place to camp.

Just east of Round Pond you intersect a snowmobile trail. Your yellow-marked route continues east, winding alongside a hemlock marsh, and reaches a three-way junction 15 minutes from Round Pond. (The sign indicates it is 0.77 mile from Black Mountain Pond. You will notice that distances vary in the Adirondacks sign to sign; the sum of the mileages rarely adds up to the totals given at the trailheads.) The entire walk between intersections takes no more than 30 minutes, unless, of course, you could not resist stopping at one of the ponds. The yellow-marked route heads right (south) toward Millman and Fishbrook Ponds. You take the blue-blazed trail left, which the sign indicates heads toward Pike Brook Road. Walk along it for no more than five minutes, about 0.2 mile, to another intersection, where a spur trail heads back southeast along Lapland Pond's eastern shore to a lovely lean-to high on a rock slide.

Lapland is the largest and deepest of the three ponds and has beautiful shores. You will surely stop here for a rest or swim before continuing north. The trail north is marked both with blue hiking trail disks and orange snowmobile trail disks. It follows a long level valley on an old road, and although the woods are handsome, the walking is not good. The level roadway may be flooded, even in dry times. Within 10 minutes you begin a long descent, first following a stream and then continuing through the saddle high and dry above the stream, which you ultimately cross. Thirty minutes probably suffices for the walk from Lapland Pond to the last trail intersection and the end of the blue-marked trail. You fork right on the red trail to retrace your steps for the final 1.2 miles to your car.

3

Tongue Mountain Range

Distance (around loop): 12.4 miles

Vertical rise: 3,000 feet

Hiking time: 8 hours

Map: USGS 7.5' Shelving Rock and Silver Bay

The Tongue Mountain Range is a great block fault thrust up in the midst of the fault valley that Lake George has filled. On this loop hike you first climb its ridge, then follow the backbone of the Tongue, which thrusts south into the lake, and conclude with a walk back north along the shore of Northwest Bay. From countless vantage points along the ridge, views of Lake George and The Narrows are superb. French Point Mountain, halfway along the portion of the Range Trail you hike here, lies just far enough out of line with the rest of the Tongue Range to have long, uninterrupted views both north and south. Because the lack of tree cover on the ridge permits a completely different range of flowers from those found in the deep woods that fill the slopes along Northwest Bay, this hike also introduces you to an amazing variety of Adirondack flora.

The Tongue Mountain Range is a good choice for spring hiking. The trail is among the first to dry out enough to walk, and in May the cover of wildflowers is magnificent. The long stretches of open ridge that are a plus in spring discourage hiking in summer months, when a canopy of shade trees is more desirable. The abundance of hardwoods makes it a spectacular fall hike.

This is a most strenuous trip, however, so if you plan to go in early spring, be sure you are up to it. The hike is long, and the vertical rise is equivalent to that on Giant Mountain or Algonquin Mountain, the two highest peaks described in this guide. You rise 1,560 feet directly from lake level to

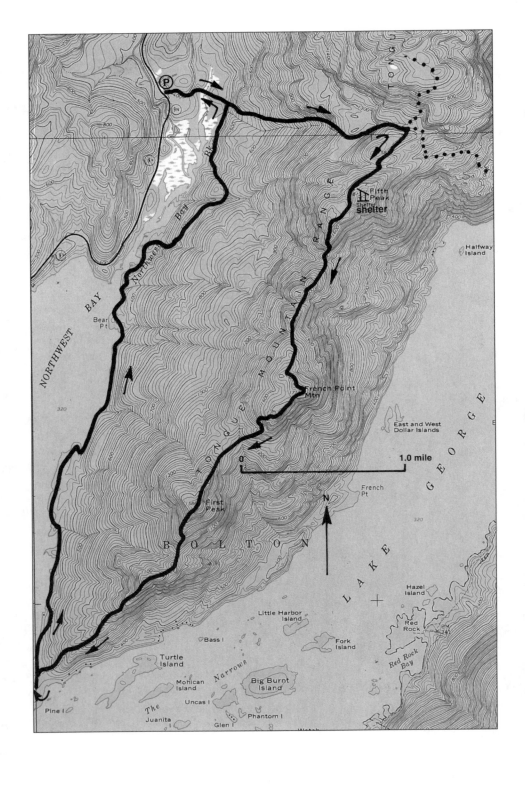

Fifth Peak, and then snake across the peaks to the south as if you were following the Great Wall of China, soaring to each summit from a deep intervening valley.

How to Get There

For the easiest route to the trailhead from the Adirondack Northway (I-87), take exit 24 and follow County Road 11 east, toward Bolton Landing and NY 9N. After descending the long hill toward the lake, head north on NY 9N. From the intersection you will see the Tip of the Tongue and a portion of the ridge you will walk. Drive north on NY 9N for 4 miles, past signs for a boat-launching site and the Tongue Mountain–Clay Meadows trailhead, to a parking area beside an old quarry on the east side of the road.

The Trail

If you have allowed enough time for a full day of hiking, take a few minutes now to cross the road just south of the parking area and walk about 100 yards along the evergreen-covered promontory above Northwest Bay Brook to a handsome little falls in the deep, hemlock-shrouded gorge.

Signs at the trailhead direct you east toward the Tongue Mountain Range. You begin at the blue markers by walking through a tall red pine reforestation stand—the site of the old farm that gave the area the name Clay Meadows—and then crossing the marsh beside a small inlet of Northwest Bay. The marsh sports many ferns, and in spring, brilliant yellow clumps of marsh marigold.

Within 10 minutes and 0.3 mile, you reach a junction. You will return later in the day by way of the trail to the right. For now, go straight ahead on the red-marked trail (there are few visible markers). The trail follows a small stream that flows from Fifth Peak on your right. Although you hardly ever

see it, you can almost always hear it. Five minutes from the intersection you may want to leave the trail to walk right toward the stream at the top of its plunge down a deep, shaded gorge.

The well-worn trail climbs steeply, crossing three bridges, two over intermittent streams. Watch as ledges appear along the trail on your left; one of these is man-made and is the cue to turn sharply left for a switchback that covers the last steep pitch before a plateau. This is the only place where the relative absence of trail markers might cause confusion. You then round the hemlock marsh that fills the plateau and cross the stream that feeds it, here without benefit of a bridge. You climb steeply again, a pitch covering about 160 vertical feet, before reaching a second plateau and the major intersection with the Range Trail. It is 1.9 miles from Clay Meadows to this spot, and the climb should take nearly 1 hour and 15 minutes.

Here the red route continues straight ahead and down to the shore of Lake George. The left, or north, branch of the blue trail leads to Fivemile Mountain and Deer Leap. (A trailhead farther north on NY 9N offers easier access to these peaks in the Tongue Mountain Range and is described in *Discover the Eastern Adirondacks*.) Your route is right on the blue trail, south to the Tip of the Tongue.

The roller-coaster trip along the ridge begins mildly enough with a 0.5-mile climb of under 300 feet toward Fifth Peak. You leave the blue trail on a yellow-marked, 0.2-mile-long spur to reach the actual peak and its nearby lean-to. Note that there is no water at all on the peak. Hikers who detour to the peak often bushwhack southwest from there, descending a few tricky ledges to intersect the blue trail farther along, rather than retrace steps along the spur.

The view from French Point Mountain across Lake George

W. ALEC REID

Beyond Fifth Peak, the trail shows much less use, and the trail markers are more numerous and definitely necessary. In places under the leaf cover the footpath is hardly visible, although the trail shows signs of its superior Civilian Conservation Corps construction.

There is a second lookout on Fifth Peak from a shoulder 0.2 mile south of the summit. In 1985, in the area of the second lookout on Fifth Peak, a forest fire burned many acres on the east flank of the mountain, a reminder that this area is very prone to fire damage. Only a small portion of the trail was affected by the fire, however. Just beyond, the trail crosses the ridge to afford a view straight down Northwest Bay. Then it starts to drop into the valley south of the peak. "Drop" is scarcely the word for the long rock slide with several extremely steep pitches. You will lose almost 350 feet in elevation in 0.2 mile. As you descend, look

back to the cliffs behind you. And while you are grappling for handholds on the descent, you might be amused to think that Robert Moses, the master roadbuilder, had plans to build a highway that would encircle Lake George's shores. The prospect always conjures images of a huge flying span across the gulf between Fifth Peak and the unnamed knob to its immediate south.

You no sooner hit bottom than you immediately start climbing again, heading up that knob. It is just short of 1 mile from Fifth Peak to the top of the first knob. There is a view back to the cliffs on Fifth Peak, but the trail leads you immediately on, plunging down the next southern slope. Here you turn sharply, below the cliff, and head away from the lake. Another steep drop takes you to a hemlock swale where you must look carefully for the turn left to head up a second knob.

Again, you will make a short, sharp

descent before continuing on the ridge, without the aid of many trail markers. Your route gradually heads southeast to French Point Mountain. It takes a good hour to walk from the south shoulder of Fifth Peak to the summit of French Point Mountain, because of the scramble over and around the unnamed knobs.

Your hike has lasted about three hours so far, and you have covered 4.6 miles. That makes French Point Mountain (elevation: 1,739 feet) the perfect place to stop for lunch. You will find a perch suspended almost 1,400 feet above the lake, with fantastic views northeast up the lake and south toward The Narrows, which are choked with tiny islands, just a few of the 200 that grace Lake George. The DEC map for the island campsites of Lake George (see introduction), which shows the campsites and dayuse areas on the islands below you, is the best guide to their names. Opposite your perch lies Paradise Bay, whose deep green, gem-clear waters are visited by the steamer *Mohican* on its regular trips on the lake. During your lunch stop you will certainly see one of the steamers, successors to those that plied the lake as long ago as 1817. Black Mountain is a little north of east across the lake, and Erebus, Sleeping Beauty, and the Buck Range are to the south.

After leaving French Point Mountain, cross over the ridge, guided by blue daubs on the bare rock, for another view of Northwest Bay. You can now almost see the Tip of the Tongue, or Montcalm Point. Imagine the scene during the French and Indian War when Montcalm's army of attacking French rounded the tip toward Northwest Bay. You head down toward the bay in as steep a descent as that which followed Fifth Peak. Walk along the vertical side of the mountain with cliffs below, and then turn away from the bay still descend-

ing, in a switchback heading toward Lake George. The scrub cover of beech, butternut, shadblow, white pine, ash, oak, and hop hornbeam is not thick enough to block the views. The drier, sparser cover contrasts with the deep, rich woods of the western slopes. Most of the time now you are walking right at the exposed edge of the cliffs overlooking Lake George.

After climbing another small promontory, you will see that First Peak, your next destination, is maddeningly far away on the opposite side of another deep valley. Here, the talus slopes make rugged walking.

When you reach First Peak, a 45-minute walk after lunch, you are rewarded with a view back to French Point Mountain. You can appreciate the magnificence of the cliff that falls away from it, dropping to water level. The reason for your difficult walk is clear, for looking back north is like viewing the ridges of a dragon's back. Someone said the trail was laid out along the teeth of a giant saw.

The saw blade continues southwest to the very Tip of the Tongue. Green Island is opposite the Tip, and Dome Island lies farther south in the middle of the lake. From First Peak the trail drops steeply at first and then levels out, as it twists and turns along the top of the ridge on a fairly well-marked route. From an outcrop a spectacular cliff drops away to Turtle Bay, and you overlook Turtle Island and Shelving Rock across The Narrows. The trail continues into a narrow slot between ledges, where the talus makes for very difficult footing.

You have been walking for almost two hours since lunch, and you haven't reached the Tip yet. After still more rock outcrops with views and one last knoll to climb, you descend nearly to lake level and reach a junction. Continue straight ahead on a 0.2-mile spur to the Tip and a well-earned rest soaking your feet in the cooling waters of the lake. The sign says you have traveled 2.5 miles from French Point Mountain, descending 1,426 feet. It doesn't say how much you climbed in that "descent." After returning from your detour to the Tip, you will have walked 7.6 miles, but you still have 4.8 miles left to reach Clay Meadows again.

The blue trail along the shores of Northwest Bay is level at first, but before you have time to enjoy the flatness, you have to climb around a small piece of private land. Beyond it, the trail continues at lake level, sometimes wet underfoot, and usually close to the water, but shortly the steepness of the shoreline forces you to climb again.

You cross a small creek and then turn sharply left, to edge a small bay. About 40 minutes from the intersection, you cross a stream with a waterfall; ledges beside it drip with mosses and maidenhair spleenwort. For those who count ferns, this could be the 20th species of fern you have seen along the hike.

Rockwork lines the trail, which was originally constructed as a bridle path. The walking is easier as you cross two bridges in a beautiful deep hemlock stand, but only briefly. You climb again, now around the marshes that border Northwest Bay Brook.

When you reach a final bridge, you are just 200 feet short of the trail intersection you passed at the outset. Here you head left to the highway and your car.

By the end of your trip you will certainly have walked for 8 hours, but if you have paused to enjoy the spectacular scenery, you will probably have been on the trail for at least 10 hours.

Look up at the range when you leave to drive south along the highway. You will have a great respect for the sinuous route that the trail takes along the bumps and ridges of the Tongue Mountain Range.

➤ Adirondack Wildflowers

A May count of blooming wildflowers on Tongue Mountain always exceeds 30. It includes pale corydalis, four kinds of violets, twisted stalk, red trillium, dwarf ginseng, wild oat, foamflower and miterwort, toadflax and Canada mayflower, lady's slipper, clintonia, Dutchman's-breeches, bluets, saxifrage, early buttercup, cucumber root, pipsissewa, three-toothed cinquefoil, wood betony or lousewort, and the amazing fields of trailing arbutus for which the Tongue Mountain Range is famous.

4

Hadley Mountain

Distance (round-trip): 4 miles

Vertical rise: 1,550 feet

Hiking time: 2½–3 hours

Map: USGS 7.5' Conklingville and Stony Creek

Fire tower: Private sources fund staffing of the tower

With a summit of only 2,700 feet, half the height of Mount Marcy, Hadley might not sound like much of a mountain. This just proves how little elevation can figure in the true pleasures of mountain climbing. Views from the fire tower on Hadley or from its open summit are among the most spectacular in the Adirondacks. In the north, you can see many of the eastern High Peaks; in the south, the major summits of the Catskills; and in the east, an open panorama of the hills beyond Lakes George and Champlain ranging to Vermont's Green Mountains and the edges of the Berkshires in Massachusetts. The view southwest is across Great Sacandaga Lake and northwest to a multitude of southern Adirondack mountains. Once I climbed Hadley on a perfectly clear day, and I remember the trip as one of the most beautiful I have ever had in the mountains.

Hadley is near the southern end of a chain of summits that together comprise West Mountain, a ridge in the southeast corner of the Adirondacks. There are many open spots along the ridge's north-northeast to south-southwest axis, and you should plan to extend your visit to Hadley by walking along it, watching the perspectives change. The lichens growing in niches between open rock make a multicolored carpet and easy, crunchy walking through the scrub. Here, moving from open rock ledges to scrubby promontories can hardly be called bushwhacking.

At the trailhead a sign states: SUCCESSIVE FIRES IN 1903, 1908, 1911, AND 1915 SE-

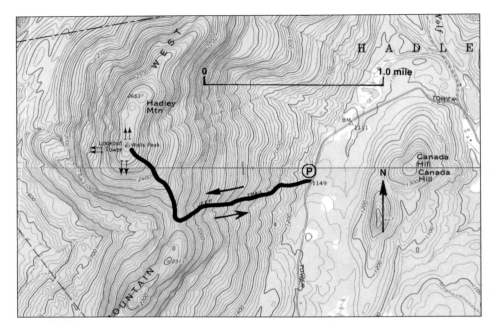

VERELY BURNED 12,000 ACRES OF THE SUR-
ROUNDING FOREST LAND. Fires alone did not
create the bare peaks. As recently as
10,000 years ago, retreating glaciers
scraped the mountaintops and left huge
boulders and glacial erratics perched precariously on even the highest summits. What
little organic soil had accumulated in the ge-
ologically short interval since the last glacier
was quickly consumed by the raging fires.

What caused these great fires? When
settlers first advanced into the Adirondacks, cutting the towering pine, red spruce,
and hemlock for building lumber and later
harvesting hardwoods for pulp, little thought
was given to the methods of harvesting timber. Tops and slashes were left in huge,
loose piles across the once forested hills
and valleys. The early years of the 20th
century were unusually dry, and the tinder
piles were easily ignited by lightning and
careless sparks. Nearly a million acres of
New York's forest land were burned.
Charred stumps and bare soil can still be

found on many mountains, and the soil's
ability to retain water has been completely
disrupted. Only the vigilance of fire observers prevented further burning, and although many dry, bare summits persist, the
forests have begun to recover.

How to Get There

The only difficult part about climbing Hadley
is locating the trailhead; no markers point
the way, and there are few road names to
assist in the search. If you are driving from
the west, along the shores of Great
Sacandaga Lake, the signs are pretty clear.
The north shore road is County Road 4. Just
before the Paul River Hardware Store, turn
north onto Hadley Hill Road. The intersection is in Day Center, almost a 30-minute
drive east of Northville. Follow Hadley Hill
Road for 5.2 miles to Tower Road, on your
left. The parking turnout for the tower is 1.4
miles north on Tower Road.

From the south, east, or north, take NY
9N, which passes through Lake Luzerne.

Turn left in Lake Luzerne to Hadley, then go north on Stony Creek Road. Hadley Hill Road is a left turn at a marked intersection just over 3 miles north of Hadley. Drive west on Hadley Hill Road for nearly 3 miles and turn right on an unmarked road (Eddy Road). Follow the road for 0.8 mile to a Y where the macadam road bears right. Go straight ahead on the dirt road (Tower Road). After 1.7 miles, a small sign on your right indicates the parking lot for the Hadley Tower. This will probably be the first sign you see for the tower.

The Trail

The directions along the trail are quite simple, and the trail needs almost no description, even though it is marked sparsely by red disks. It is simple and direct and wide and open. Much of the route is over exposed bedrock. The high cover of beech and birch soon gives way to smaller trees. The route is fairly consistently steep.

Three-quarters of the way to the summit, the road turns sharply left. Telephone lines angle right through a cliff-lined draw. Those with youngsters may prefer to scramble to the summit under the telephone lines, the little ledges and cliffs providing a bit of sport. Going down, though, it is safer along the road.

On the 2,700-foot summit you can spend hours playing "name that peak." Among the features you should spot is the edge of the Helderberg escarpment over Great Sacandaga Lake. North beyond Roundtop, which is a part of West Mountain, you can see Baldhead, Moose, and Crane Mountains. To their left lie Bearpen and Mount Blue. Farther left, the knob of Snowy's summit rises above the line of mountains on the horizon. Nippletop and Dix are easily identified in the High Peaks 50 miles away. Pharaoh Mountain can be spotted in the north-northeast, and the peaks surrounding Lake George in the northeast. You will have no trouble at all filling a day with things to do on this lovely mountaintop.

➤ Adirondack Fires and Fire Towers

In response to fires in the late 19th and early 20th centuries, the state erected a series of fire towers across the Adirondacks. From early spring to snowfall, these towers were manned by dedicated observers who often trudged long distances with heavy packs to supply their weeklong stays on the mountaintop. The men were dependent on fragile telephone lines for communication and usually had to maintain both the lines and the trails to their towers. Most of the southern Adirondack mountaintops are heavily wooded, so the towers provide the only opportunities for views from their summits. The fire towers have long been favorite hiking destinations, and the recent closing of a substantial number is mourned by many. The daily plane flights that took their place may provide adequate fire surveillance, but they deprive hikers of many fine views. Fortunately, Hadley's tower remains open, although there are great views from the summit even without the tower.

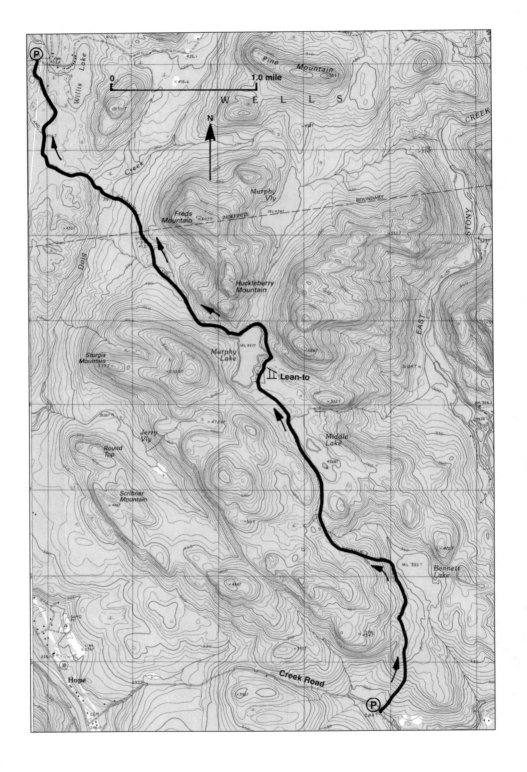

5

Murphy, Middle, and Bennett Lakes

Distance (one-way): 7.2 miles

Vertical rise: 500 feet

Hiking time: 4 hours

Map: USGS Metric Hope Falls

During the early 19th century, settlers traced a network of roads into the valleys of the southern Adirondacks. These routes were used after the Revolutionary War to reach the rich stands of timber in the northern wilderness and to establish new settlements in the Adirondack interior.

Today some of these old roads are the routes of modern highways. Others remain concealed in the wilderness, completely forgotten. And a few are the trails we now follow. The hamlets of Hope, Hope Falls, and Pumpkin Hollow, on the Sacandaga River and East Stony Brook, were established by settlers who built roads north from Northville immediately after 1800.

One such road started near Hope Falls and headed north past several homesteads, a paint mine, and a string of small lakes. Today that road is a fine trail, short enough for a one-day, one-way trek if you leave a car at each end, and interesting enough for an extended camping expedition. There are several good camping sites and a lean-to near the lakes.

How to Get There

The northern end of the trail is the easiest to find; I suggest you arrange to leave a car there. Distances are given from the NY 30 bridge over the Sacandaga River, about 3.5 miles north of the fork to Northville. From the bridge, drive north on NY 30 for 7.2 miles to Pumpkin Hollow Road, which is on the right, or east. A snowmobile trail signboard also marks the turn. The northern end of the trail is 1.6 miles along Pumpkin

Murphy Lake

Hollow Road and marked. There is parking off the road near the trailhead.

There are two ways to reach the southern end of the trail by Hope Falls. Just over 3 miles north of the Sacandaga Bridge, turn right, or east, from NY 30 onto Creek Road and drive east for 2.5 miles to the trailhead, which is on the north side of the road and marked. A prettier approach is from Northville on Hope Falls Road, which approximates the route used by early settlers. Follow Hope Falls Road north to Creek Road and then bear left for 0.5 mile to the trailhead. Hope Falls Road and its extension north make a nice drive along East Stony Creek.

The Trail

The trail has been marked with both yellow hiking and orange snowmobile disks, although the colors are worn. The old road is so easy to follow that you should not be bothered by the indistinct markings. The first mile north skirts private land along a road that has been recently used for logging, with hemlock, sugar maple, and beech remaining. The route is uphill, and the road has eroded and washed out. As you approach a height-of-land, white pine and yellow and gray birch appear. After about 25 minutes, you will notice that the forest cover changes to a small, dense population of pine, birch, and beech. You can see the old stone wall of one of the 19th-century farm sites on your left. Just beyond, a cable marks the boundary of state land.

No more than five minutes beyond the cable you arrive at the old paint mine, now hardly more than a depression in the ground. The red-stained rocks and soil indicate a low-grade hematite, the mineral that made barns and homes deep red. Imagine using this road to walk to school, as children did in the late 1800s, and coming home by lantern light after dark every evening.

The trail continues through a mature mixed forest around the side of the hill. Less than 1.5 miles and 40 minutes from your start, you will glimpse Bennett Lake down through the trees on your right. Within 200 yards an unmarked path forks right toward the lake. Follow it down a relatively steep grade for 150 yards to a flat place along the shore, where there are several good camping spots, an outhouse, a fireplace, and a sandy beach.

Returning to the main trail, continue west, climbing a small hill. You will pass an unmarked loop that quickly rejoins the main route and reach a small brook at the top of the rise.

Approximately 10 minutes after you pass the creek, you will have your first glimpse of Middle Lake. The distance between Bennett and Middle Lakes is 1.6 miles, and the walk between them should take about 40 minutes. The trail continues on the hillside, about 540 feet above the lake. The lake is 0.6 mile long and very narrow, with steep, evergreen-covered shores and several small islands. One side path leads 100 feet to a camping spot, and shortly beyond that fork the main trail approaches the lakeshore and follows it past many campsites. The remains of an old foundation are visible on the lakeshore. There are impressive views of the cliffs on the mountain to the north.

At the northern end of Middle Lake the trail turns left and enters a small, thick, wet forest. Only 15 minutes is required for the 0.5-mile walk between Middle and Murphy Lakes. The approach to the latter is signaled by a mature hemlock stand. As you come to the lake, there are spectacular views of cliffs on the small knob to the north as well as those on the mountain to the east. Adventurous bushwhackers will want to find a route to these cliffs for a view of the lake (see *Discover the Southeastern Adirondacks* for a description).

A lean-to and several campsites border the trail at its southern approach to the lake. Continue north along the trail to a huge boulder on the shore. You can enjoy both a great view of the lake and a swim from the boulder.

The footpath around the lake is not always easy to follow, but for 0.6 mile you stay close to the shore until you reach the northern inlet, crossing that small brook on a log bridge. Continue along the shore, heading southwest, for 0.2 mile to the outlet. From here it is 2.8 miles northwest to the northern trailhead via the snowmobile trail. The first part of the route beside Murphy Lake outlet is the prettiest. Then you cross the creek, pass a beaver flow with views east to the cliff-faced knob, recross the creek, cross Doig Creek, and end with a rather ordinary and level stretch on the old logging road.

6

Ice Cave Mountain

Distance (round-trip): 3.8 miles

Vertical rise: 494 feet

Hiking time: 90 minutes

Map: USGS Metric Honnedaga Lake

The low foothills of the southwestern Adirondacks rise gradually to the central mountain dome. It is a region of sandy plains—the borders of ancient glacial lakes. Flat logging roads crisscross the lower slopes. There are few mountains in the region, mostly low-rising ridges of little distinction. Were it not for its unique topographical features, Ice Cave Mountain would be a rarely visited bump on the landscape.

The "caves" on the mountain are actually deep fissures on one of the summit knobs, as if the mountain were splitting open. The two fissures are so deep and sheltered from the sun that you may find snow and ice in their depths well into the summer months. You do not need ropes or caving equipment to enjoy the fissures, but *only* people so equipped should consider entering into them. Because some of the openings are not very obvious or are partly concealed by vegetation, this is not a good place for children or pets.

Another consideration is the fact that the DEC does not currently maintain a trail on Ice Cave Mountain. Reaching the summit requires the ability to navigate a system of old logging roads and herd paths without the benefit of markers and signs. It is not a difficult route, but it is not for novice hikers.

Ice Cave Mountain rises over North Lake, which was dammed to provide water to New York's canal system. The original dam was finished in 1856, creating North Lake Reservoir from tiny, 60-acre Sophie Pond. Dams were also constructed on the South Branch of the Black River (South Lake) and

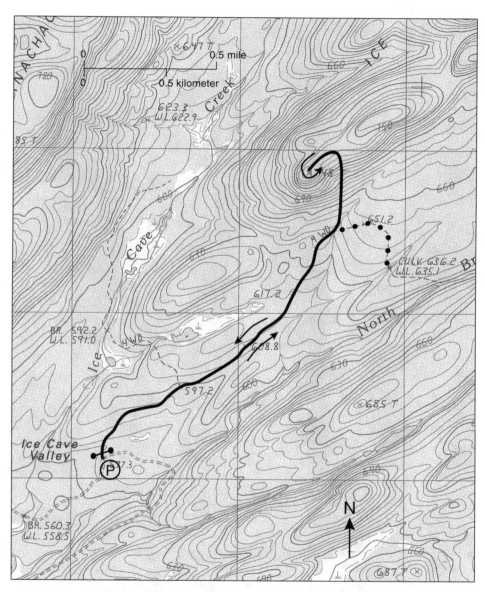

at Twin Lakes, where a marsh was flooded. Modern trails explore both of these areas.

The dam on North Lake was responsible for the worst flooding ever in the Black River basin. Snows were particularly heavy in the winter of 1869, and by April of that year the runoff was enormous. The gatekeeper, who lived in the State House, which stood not far from the dam, slept through a night of quickly rising water. The water behind the

Balancing Rock on Ice Cave Mountain

dam should have been lowered in anticipation of the floods, but it was not. The earth-and-timber dam gave way, flooding the valley below, just minutes after the residents of Forestport were warned of the impending disaster.

Sawmills, gristmills, tanneries, wagon factories, bridges, flumes, and dams were all swept away. The devastation was felt as far downstream as Watertown. The *Utica Weekly Herald* described "logs 30 feet long, catching in the drift [and] thrown end over end and snapped like pipe stems. The crashing and pounding together of the fallen monarchs of the forest drowned for a time the roar of the waters. An eyewitness said: 'The logs seemed to be fighting with each other, and when caught in the drift, would be almost instantly stripped of their bark, twisted, split and broken like straws.' This immense weight of driftwood and water was thrown against the dam at Forestport. Those who were at work upon the dam had barely time to make their retreat in safety, when the North wing gave way. Through this gap nearly all the lumber above the dam was carried. The current tore out a channel nearly 40 feet deep."

The dam was rebuilt, and the North Lake area continued to be a center of logging activity into the 20th century. The Gould Paper Company owned the land along the north end of North Lake. The Reverend Frank Reed visited the area and described in his book *Lumberjack Sky Pilot* the winter log hauls just before and just after World War I. In those days, logs were still being floated to mill by river. Even though the Black River was so close by, the Gould mill was on the Moose River, so the logs cut at North Lake had to be hauled across the wilderness to a landing on the Moose's South Branch. On his first visit, Reed described a camp near the summit of Ice Cave Mountain where the

more than one hundred teams of horses used for the haul were housed. When he returned again after the war, he found that the company had replaced the horses with Linn tractors, one of which could handle the load of twenty teams, hauling bundles of logs through the snow much like a train. This was the first time such tractors were used in an Adirondack logging operation.

Ice Cave Mountain came into the public domain when the state purchased a conservation easement on the tract in 1990. The forest is still being actively logged, but you can hike and camp here just as you would in the Forest Preserve. This innovative land-sharing strategy is being used more and more frequently in the park, since it preserves private ownership while permitting public access.

How to Get There

Turn off NY 28 in Forestport, immediately north of the bridge over the Black River, and head east toward Forestport Station. At 1.2 miles you reach a fork and the tracks of the Adirondack Railroad, and just beyond is the Buffalo Head Restaurant. Turn left at the fork, and drive for another 14.7 miles past the tracks to the foot of North Lake. The access road to the trailhead is the narrow gravel road to the left, immediately before the bridge over the spillway. However, you may want to continue straight for another 0.25 mile to see the current North Lake dam. The road crosses on top of it without the benefit of a guard rail.

Turning left onto the access road, you circle around the west side of the lake. There are numerous campsites along the shore that you can drive to. In 0.5 mile you come to a gate that is closed in the spring until mid-May.

After driving for 5 miles, you come to an unusually large parking area, where the continuing road is gated at all times to the public. Actually, there are two gates at the northwest corner of this clearing. The one to the left (north) is the start of the route to Ice Cave Mountain.

The Trail

Setting off on foot beyond the gate, you follow an old gravel logging road for the first 1.4 miles. The route is wide and clear, and you practically sail along it. You pass several clearings and skid trails, signs of the latest logging activities. The only major fork occurs within the first ten minutes, when a slightly narrower road branches off to the left to penetrate into the Ice Cave Valley. Take the right (straight ahead) fork for the mountain.

The road rises in gradual stages toward the foot of the mountain. In less than 30 minutes, at 1.4 miles, watch for where a small seasonal stream has washed out a portion of the road. To the left, beside the stream, you should see a few ribbons and the letters "ICM" painted on a rock. This is the start of the herd path up the mountain. The first few yards of the path are very muddy, for it is currently routed too close to the stream.

You quickly pull away from the stream and head northerly for the foot of the mountain. At times the route seems as clear as a trail, but at other times a missing ribbon could have you searching about for where to go next. The flagged path leads through a patch of jagged rocks that have broken off the side of the ridge to the left. The rocks are now covered with rich mosses and ferns, and one even supports a large spruce tree.

After a brief stretch of moderate climbing, you reach a level area with a large wet area. Beyond, the flagging leads you very steeply up the final climb to the summit of the ridge. Fortunately, this stretch is short. The path levels off gradually and swings southwest to follow along the ridge.

Just two minutes after reaching the summit, the path leads you directly to the edge of the largest fissure. From this spot you can hold on to a tree and peer over the edge. The bottom, with whatever winter ice may be left, is some 50 feet below you. The path continues around to the left. Within seconds you come to a natural ramp leading down to an inviting ledge inside the cave. The view from the ledge is spectacular, of course, but bear in mind that it is usually wet and slippery and that a single misstep would prove disastrous. The path loops around this opening to a safer view from the same angle, but without the walk into the cave.

Just a few feet away from that last view of the big cave, the path crosses a natural bridge over a narrower, darker fissure—one that you might not necessarily see at first, so watch your step. You need a flashlight to see inside this one. Just beyond, the path ends in a tiny opening in a spruce stand with a partial view over the S-shaped North Lake.

This is the end of the recommended hike, but there are other features on the mountain that bushwhackers may wish to seek out. Just 200 feet away from that opening at the end of the path is a tiny rock perch with a view across the Ice Cave Valley and North Lake to Starr Hill in Oneida County. To reach it, you have to struggle through a dense growth of young spruce and balsam along the side of the mountain just to the west of the caves. If you backtrack down the path to the point where it turns to descend off the mountain, you can turn left off it and bushwhack for 10 minutes to a huge balancing rock on the west side of the mountain. This 15-foot-tall erratic was deposited by the glacier on the very edge of a steep drop off; a corner of it even hangs over the edge. Much further back on the mountain, on its northwest arm, you will find the most dramatic of any lookout on Ice Cave Mountain, but that bushwhack is for the experts only.

If you are not a bushwhacker, return by the same route you walked up. Watch your step down the one steep slope.

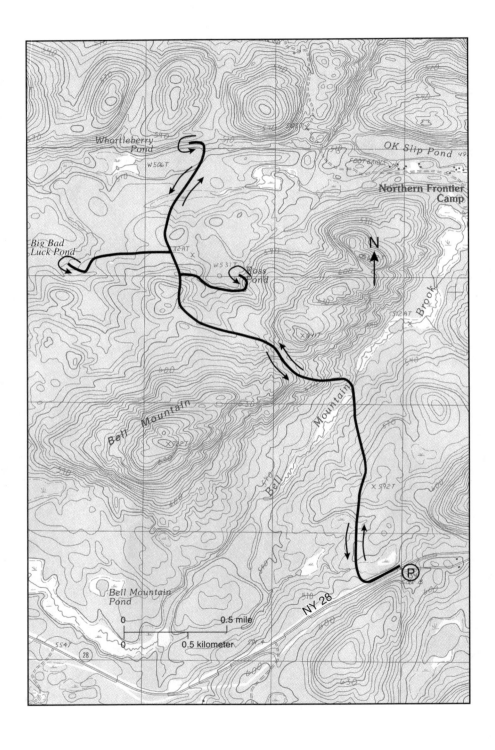

7

Ross, Whortleberry, and Big Bad Luck Ponds

Distance (round-trip): 8.1 miles

Vertical rise: 1,080 feet

Hiking time: 4–6 hours

Map: USGS Metric Dutton Mountain

From a single starting point on NY 28, a sensible trail network accesses these three beautiful, quiet ponds. Depending on your preferences, you can turn this outing into an interesting day trip or an overnight adventure. Despite the impressive figure at left, given for the vertical rise this is not a difficult trip. The grades are distributed throughout the hike, with the only substantial climbs being those leading into and out of the Bell Mountain Brook valley. You can walk the route in a minimum of four hours, but to enjoy the area you should allow for at least six.

How to Get There

From the intersection of NY 28 and 30 in the hamlet of Indian Lake, drive east on NY 28 for 7.8 miles to where an unnamed spur road forks to the right. Here, at the intersection, you will find the designated parking area. The trailhead itself is actually 0.25 mile west back along the highway. It is recommended that you park at the lot and walk the short distance to the trail, rather than parking on the narrow shoulder.

The Trail

Starting from the parking area, cross the highway and walk for 0.25 mile west alongside it to the trailhead sign and register. Trail signs here give the distances as 2.5 miles to Ross Pond, and 3 miles each to Whortleberry and Big Bad Luck Ponds. From the register, the red-marked trail plunges into the woods. Private land is very close on the left, and a wetland is not far off on the right. This leaves the trail with nowhere to go but straight through a balsam bog. The footing can be quite muddy at any time of the year.

Within two minutes, though, the trail turns right onto an overgrown old road, and its condition begins to improve. (If there are no signs at this intersection, take note of the spot so that you will not miss the turn on your walk back.) After a brief glimpse of an open beaver meadow on your right, the trail approaches the foot of a hill and climbs gradually over it, under the cover of a stand of white pine.

The descent on the other side of the hill, into the Bell Mountain Brook valley, is long and uneventful. Near the bottom you begin to see open wetlands along the brook to your left, and after 30 minutes of hiking, at about 1 mile from the highway, you reach the brook itself. There is no bridge, so you have to step on rocks. This is a shallow watercourse, and not very wide, so the crossing is usually easy.

Beyond the brook, the trail makes its longest and steepest climb. A 15-minute journey up this hardwood-covered hillside brings you to the height-of-land, a deep notch on the side of Bell Mountain. A painted rock to the side of the trail marks the point from which an abandoned path once led directly to Ross Pond.

You pass through the notch, gradually descending westward to the level of a series of swampy beaver ponds. Stop to view the reflections of the dead trees drowned by beaver dams. Expect to encounter a few short wet sections in the trail as you pass through.

At 2.2 miles from the highway, after walking for an hour, you reach an intersection with the yellow-marked, 0.3-mile trail to Ross Pond, the most scenic pond in the trio. Turning right onto this trail, you quickly come to the pond. The trail contours around its edge through a dark hemlock stand, with a small island not far off shore. The trail loops around the south end of the pond to a designated campsite on the east side. The site is large enough to hold several tents, and nearby there is a rocky point with an unsurpassed view over this little pond. Not surprisingly, this seems to be a popular camping area, with the litter to attest to the fact. The pond is stocked with trout, which helps to account for its popularity.

To continue the hike, return to the red trail and turn right. After a series of short ups and downs, you reach another intersection in 10 minutes, this time with the blue-marked trail to Big Bad Luck Pond. For now, continue straight on the red trail, which will lead in another 0.5 mile to Whortleberry Pond. The trail leads through an interesting stand of pines, spruces, and balsams, intermixed with birches and maples. The trail ends somewhat awkwardly in a large clearing, where only mosses and lichens have so far been able to re-cover the exposed bedrock. A fire ring suggests that people have camped here in the past, but who would want to pitch a tent on these undulating rocks? On the far left side of the clearing you will find a herd path leading down to the nearest spot on the shore of Whortleberry Pond.

A more interesting way to enjoy this pond is by proceeding another 0.25 mile around its east end along an informal, unmarked footpath, which continues straight across the clearing from where the DEC trail ends. It leads northeast to a fork, where you should bear left. You quickly come out in a hobblebush thicket beside a beaver meadow. Look for a blue paint blaze on a cedar tree to the left. The path turns sharp left there and leads across the outlet to an informal campsite on a rock bluff beside the pond. From this spot you can see all of the pond's pine-rimmed shoreline.

So far, you have walked 4.1 miles.

Big Bad Luck Pond

Retrace your steps to the red trail and follow it back for 0.5 mile to the Big Bad Luck trail. Turning right, you will follow the blue markers through the most beautiful softwood forest along this whole trail system. Ten minutes from the junction you encounter a boggy area bridged by short logs, and shortly afterwards you arrive at a scenic bend on the wide outlet of the pond. The trail loops inland to the left and ends a minute later at the east end of the pond.

Big Bad Luck Pond is the only one of the three ponds on this hike without a campsite readily available from its trail. It's likely that sites do exist further down the pond, but you would need a boat to reach them. Big Bad Luck is known for its warm-water fishery of bass and pike, and fishermen are sometimes enticed into carting boats to its shore. Without a canoe or inflatable craft, the best view of the pond is from a point to the right of the trail.

How Big Bad Luck Pond got its name is a mystery. Maybe a guide was trying to protect his favorite fishing hole from others and so gave it a forbidding name. Maybe a fisherman's boat overturned and he lost all his gear.

The final leg of the hike takes you back to the red trail, and then southeast along it for the last 2.5 miles back to the trailhead, concluding a very fulfilling day spent in the woods.

8

Falls on the West Branch of the Sacandaga

Distance (round-trip): 6 miles

Vertical rise: minimal

Hiking time: 6 hours

Maps: USGS Metric Three Ponds Mountain, USGS Metric Wells

Silver Lake Wilderness Area

The falls on the West Branch of the Sacandaga will leave you amazed that such a place can exist so close to the fringes of civilization. The access route is incredibly challenging, the falls themselves are little known, and much around them remains to be explored and discovered. The remote stretch of river by the falls has been favored for years by a few hunters and fishermen, but only in recent years have hikers begun to appreciate its beauties.

The West Branch of the Sacandaga uncoils within the Silver Lake Wilderness. The river is formed at the confluence of three south-flowing outlets from three separate ponds; their union flows west, then north, then east, and finally south again, enclosing one of the Adirondacks' most secret realms. The gem of that interior is certainly the series of falls on the West River, as natives have called this branch of the Sacandaga since the day when lumbermen and trappers first penetrated its wild recesses.

The trail, path, and bushwhack route described here will take you to the first pair of falls. They are almost 3 miles upstream from Whitehouse, the site of a lovely old lodge whose chimneys today stand forlornly guarding the spot where the Northville-Placid Trail crosses the river. If you are really adventurous and want a great challenge, you should extend the bushwhack through the deepest part of the West River's gorge to a second pair of falls, past a quiet flow, and to a final falls just below the flow formed where the out-

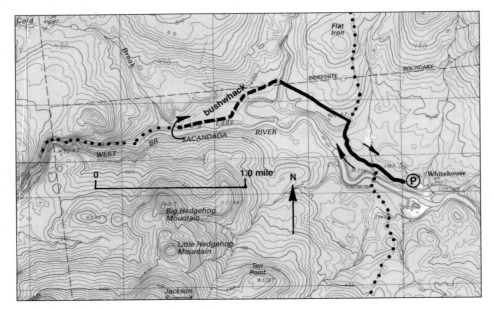

let of Piseco Lake joins the West Branch. (See my *Discover the Southern Adirondacks* for a description of that route.)

How to Get There

Turn west from NY 30 at the southern end of the hamlet of Wells onto Algonquin Drive. West River Road forks left 0.7 mile from NY 30 and continues 1.7 miles to Blackbridge. Over the next 1.7 miles west to Jimmy Creek, the road is close to the river and its wild rapids. Then West River Road pulls away from the river, continuing west for a total distance of 8.6 miles from Wells to the parking area in the fields that surrounded Whitehouse.

The Trail

A path from the west end of the parking area leads west along the abandoned road to the Whitehouse site. In 0.1 mile you reach the trail register for the Northville-Placid Trail. If you walk south along the trail, you reach the huge stone fireplace and chimney for the lodge. Just beyond is the bridge over the West Branch. You should turn right, north, at the register, and head northwest on that trail for 0.8 mile to a fork. The marked trail continues north, but you turn left to continue west. Although the route is now unmarked, it follows an abandoned roadway. After 0.6 mile you reach Hamilton Lake Stream in an area used for camping. Cross the stream by hopping rocks in low water, or wading if it is high. The washed-out bridge has not been replaced. Across the stream a faint path heads southwest toward the river. Because hikers have taken many different routes, you may have trouble finding an obvious path, the best of which roughly follows the hypotenuse of a triangle, the two legs of which are the stream and the river, so you cannot get lost. You will approach the West Branch just below the flow called Big Eddy, which will make you wish the entire route had been along the river. There is a camping spot here.

The footpath continues west along the north shore of the river, and you should follow it as far as you can. The majority of visitors here are fishermen whose destination is the pools in Big Eddy, so the foot tread rapidly disappears. A path of sorts exists beside Big Eddy as far as the crossing of Cold Brook, which empties into the West River with a small waterfall. Look out for poison ivy on the bank beside the confluence of Cold Brook and the river. West of Cold Brook the path really disappears, and you must follow the shore, or, in low water, hop along the rocky streambed. You pass one more deep pool with an overhanging ledge before reaching the boulder-strewn waterway that leads into the deep gorge.

So far the hike has been relatively mild. You will probably need only a bit more than 20 minutes to hike the section on the Northville-Placid Trail, an almost equal amount to reach Hamilton Lake Stream, and about 40 minutes to cover the 0.8-mile distance to Cold Brook. However, you will need more than 40 minutes to trek the next rugged 0.6-mile distance through the deepening gorge to the first falls.

By the time you reach the falls, the cliffs of the gorge walls are nearly 400 feet high. The growing mound of boulders and blocks leading up to the falls makes an increasingly difficult walking route.

The level of the water has a great impact on the difficulty of the walk and the beauties of the gorge. In high water, walking becomes difficult, and you may have to approach the falls by scaling the hill behind the cliffs. In low water you can find a route over the boulders within the narrowing gorge, but then the falls are less dramatic.

The second falls are scarcely 200 yards beyond the first, but because the ravine curves, you can't see them until you are nearly upon them. Even more peculiar than the visual separation of the falls is the

➤ Bushwhacks

Adirondack hiking routes are varied. Those with marked trailheads, trail markers, and maintenance by the DEC are referred to as trails *in this guide. Traditional unmarked routes of fishermen or hikers where foot tread shows the way are referred to as* paths *in this guide. For these a map and compass is a good idea, because following unmarked paths is not always easy.* Bushwhacks *are defined as routes where no path exists. You go cross-country on them with the help of map and compass and a lot of experience. As some of the best Adirondack destinations have no paths or trails, you should practice bushwhacking, initially accompanied by someone who has such experience.*

length of time it takes to walk between them. In high water you definitely must climb the hill behind the cliffs from the east. Even then you will have to be content with a view from above, for descending to the second falls is all but impossible. In low water I have spent at least 40 minutes clambering over boulders the size of buses, through openings in the pile of blocks, and leaping across crevices to reach the second falls. If you attempt this section, be careful.

As you climb along the ledge you will notice that the high-water mark is more than 20 feet above summer low point. Swirls of natural foam frost pools of tea-colored water. In dry times, the sprays that cascade from the narrow clefts are almost lost in the complex of boulders. In spring, or after periods of heavy rain, the water falling 240 feet through the mile-long gorge creates a roar that barely hints at the brutal force capable of tearing boulders from ravine walls and hurling them into the huge piles that are the West River's falls.

In any season, a trip to the falls is a rough experience. You will remember your day's trip to this dramatic spot as a truly great adventure.

Good Luck Cliffs

Distance (round-trip): 4.4 miles

Vertical rise: 700 feet

Hiking time: 3 hours

Maps: USGS Metric Morehouse Mountain; USGS 7.5' Canada Lake

The trek to Good Luck Cliffs is one of the best short hikes in the southern Adirondacks. The route combines a walk along a snowmobile trail with a climb through a small gorge on a footpath. A jumble of easily explored boulders and crevices line the gorge. The footpath circles behind the nearly 500-foot-high cliffs to emerge on a small overlook with a dramatic view across the foothills of the Adirondacks to the skyline of hills south of the Mohawk Valley.

The footpath is fairly well defined, but there are three points at which you may have difficulty, so take a map and compass and pay close attention to the landmarks along the route. The trek through the gorge is not marked by trail disks. The footpath was flagged in an experiment by the state to discover if hikers would create a defined path along marked routes where no trail cutting and grooming was to be done. Here the results are clear, for a footpath has developed and it is a delight to follow.

How to Get There

The trail starts on NY 10, opposite a parking turnout 100 yards north of a bridge over the Sacandaga River and 6 miles north of the intersection of NY 10 and NY 29A at Pine Lake.

The Trail

The trail is marked with a signboard designating the distances to Good Luck Lake, Dexter Lake, and Potters Homestead. Follow it west for just under 0.5 mile to an intersection. The route to Dexter Lake is straight

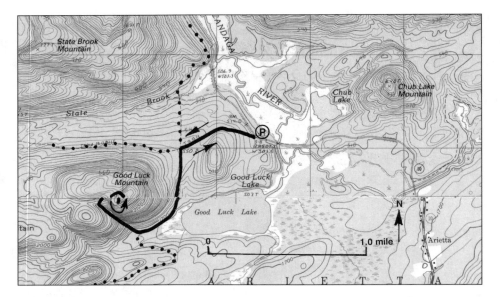

ahead, but you should turn left on the trail to Good Luck and Spectacle Lakes. Here the trail follows an old logging road down a gentle incline for 0.7 mile, and as it approaches the first low point you can see Good Luck Lake through the trees on your left. This is the easiest approach to the lake via this trail. With a short bushwhack (200 yards), you can quickly find informal footpaths connecting the good campsites on the lake's handsome and dry northern shore. If you do this, you really should stay above the marsh that edges the western shoreline.

Another, easier approach to the lake is a short, informal, and unmarked footpath that leaves the highway opposite the parking area and 50 yards southeast of the marked trailhead. It leads to Good Luck's northern shore in 0.5 mile.

Good Luck was named not for its good fishing, although fishermen visit it regularly, but because of an incident on its shores that ended well. As Jeptha R. Simms relates in *Trappers of New York,* the party surveying and laying out the roadway (now called the Nick Stoner Trail) through the Sacandaga Valley was working at Good Luck Lake to hollow out a canoe from the trunk of a tree. The son-in-law of chief surveyor Lawrence Vrooman spotted a loon on the lake and "discharged his gun at the loon, off on the water. The piece burst and scattered its fragments harmlessly in every direction. The accident terminated so fortunately, that the name the lake now bears was entered in the surveyor's field book."

To find the cliffs, continue on the snowmobile trail until it crosses a small stream within sight of the lake, about a 15-minute walk from the four-way intersection. There are currently some planks at this crossing. Continue 150 yards up a rise and down to a second stream. This one has a snowmobile bridge. Just beyond it, the trail, which has been on a southwesterly course, takes a curve to the south. You will leave the trail at this stream to follow the footpath on its eastern side. After 200 yards, you go straight where the stream swings west. The footpath and the stream meet again in about 300 yards and this time you cross

Good Luck Cliffs

the stream and continue to the northwest, close to the stream.

The footpath immediately begins to climb through the gorge. Rocks and cliffs are visible across it to your right. The first pitch is fairly steep; you attain 300 vertical feet in just 250 yards. The main cliffs become visible through the trees on your right, as do the boulders and slabs that have fallen from them to litter the floor of the draw. Do not follow any route that takes you more than 50 yards from the base of the cliffs, although the chasm below the cliffs is such an impenetrable mass of blocks and crevices that it is often difficult to get much closer.

After a climb of almost 500 feet, at a point where the path levels off somewhat, a smaller footpath heads 30 feet down a slide to the base of a huge mass of boulders. Stop and explore the area: Peer into the 12-foot-deep cave created by overhanging ledges; climb the boulders to observe the cliffs above and the valley below. The perch is overhung by a thin slab 40 feet tall.

The footpath continues northeast for 50 yards, crosses the tiny stream, and climbs steeply again below the cliffs in a more northerly direction. You walk beyond the cliffs to climb the summit from the west. The last 50-foot pitch to the summit ridge is quite steep and close to the beginning of the rock ledges. Make your way across the summit heading toward a break in the trees that indicates the lookout on the clifftop.

You emerge on a small rock crest exposed to the south and west, overlooking Spectacle Lake and the foothills of the Adirondacks as they fade into the Mohawk Valley.

You should follow the same route for the return. Remember, this is not a marked trail, so you should be prepared to search for the route as well as for the features created by the fallen boulders.

10

Pine Orchard

Distance (round-trip): 4.8 miles

Vertical rise: minimal

Hiking time: 2½ hours

Map: USGS Metric Harrisburg

Pine Orchard is a gem of a walk wrapped in the deep woods of the southern Adirondacks. Inside Pine Orchard you will discover a treasure that is rare anywhere in the park, yet here very easy to find.

Virgin pine once covered large sections of the Adirondacks. As lumbermen and settlers moved into the mountains after the Revolutionary War, these magnificent trees were the first to be felled. They not only made the tall masts for sailing vessels, but also their building quality was unsurpassed. The giant pine, some 15 feet in circumference, are the eastern equivalent of the Olympic rain forest's redwood; a walk among them is equally awe-inspiring.

A few virgin stands of pine remain, and one of them covers a small hill northeast of Wells. You will find larger stands on the Oswegatchie, but none so close to a trailhead. I have been impressed with Pine Orchard for years, but it was not until I had seen many of the other notable Adirondack pine forests that I could truly appreciate its significance.

Pine of 5 and 6 feet in diameter were common in the early 18th century. Adirondack logs were traditionally cut in 13½-foot lengths, and sometimes the butts, or first cuts, were too large to be moved by man or horse. Charges of black powder in a special splitting tool were used to break the huge ends in two so they could be carried to mills.

Core samples indicate that Pine Orchard's trees date back to 1815. It is likely that a hurricane about that year felled all the ex-

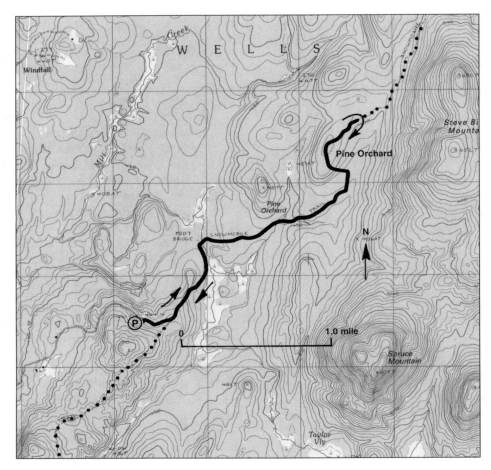

isting trees on the knoll. White pine quickly pioneered on the knoll, and they may have been too small to cut when the region was first logged. Whether this explains the origins of Pine Orchard or not, you will find the trek to Pine Orchard among the most delightful of nature walks, and it is certainly the easiest of hikes, following the relatively level stretch of an abandoned roadway once used by loggers.

How to Get There

To reach Pine Orchard, drive north on NY 30 through Wells and turn right on Griffin Road at the north end of the hamlet, just south of the bridge where NY 30 crosses the Sacandaga River. Follow Griffin Road north along the east side of the Sacandaga for 0.8 mile and turn right on Windfall Road, which parallels Mill Creek for a short distance. Follow Windfall Road for 1 mile, and turn right at the *first* road on your right (Dorr Road). Drive along Dorr Road for 1.9 miles, past stretches of forest preserve, to a private inholding. The owner has posted a VISITOR PARKING sign on a small turnout on the right. He permits hikers on their way to Pine Orchard to park here on his land.

The Trail

The trail begins along the continuing road, past the last house, and heads into the woods, very quickly reaching state land again. At that point a cable blocks the roadway. Please respect the private property, touching nothing as you walk through, so this much-appreciated permission to park and cross the private land will continue.

Walk east past the cable on the continuing roadway that is now marked as a snowmobile trail. It connects with the trail from Willis Lake, which comes in on the right, or south, just beyond the cable. See *Discover the Southeastern Adirondacks* for a description of this route, which passes the Fury Ponds. The direction you walk, now northeast, is labeled with a sign showing a destination of NY 8 at Georgia Brook, 8.2 miles to the north.

You start gently downhill, viewing the flow created by a new beaver dam on the right. In 20 minutes and 1 mile from the parking area, you cross a stream. A snowmobile bridge carries you over the tributary of Mill Creek. A gravel area just beyond has been used as a campsite. So far the spruce, hemlock, and birch are occasionally quite small and very dense. Ten minutes past the bridge you will see the first big pine.

Five minutes later, about 0.6 mile from the bridge, another bridge helps you across a small stream that feeds the flow. The trail continues with another little stream on the right and then heads north up a slight rise. More giants greet you as you climb the hill, and a few significant red spruce appear among the pine. The trail makes a sharp right turn and then circles toward the crest of the hill. Most of the giant pine are near the top, with the highest to the right of the trail. The trail continues north, and as soon as it leaves the crest it enters a grove of enormous hemlock. You reach the hemlock, marking the end of Pine Orchard, after a leisurely, hour-long walk of 2.4 miles.

You may want to try and find the largest tree in the pine stand. It appears that most of the pine of 15 feet in circumference are doubles, a phenomenon that occurs when blight strikes. The largest single trunk I found was just over 13 feet in circumference, or more than 4 feet in diameter. Try some elementary trigonometry to estimate the height of the larger trees. Unfortunately, the giants in the orchard crowd so densely together that it is difficult to see their tops, and measuring the base of a right triangle to an established sighting angle is equally difficult. I calculated a few that approached 150 feet in height. Even without trying to measure the trees, you will enjoy strolling in the parklike, open understory beneath these Adirondack giants.

➤ Why Pine?

Fire plays an unusual role in the development of the Adirondack forests. Stands of giant hemlock occur only in areas where there have been no fires, but groves of pine spring up only after a fire or blowdown. A pine forest is not a climax forest. Pine seedlings do not sprout beneath their elders. Spruce, balsam, and birch can pioneer below a tall pine stand, and here at Pine Orchard, the pine are so old that maturing yellow birch and maple are filling the niches beneath the remaining giants.

The view across Piseco and Spy Lakes from Echo Cliffs

11

Echo Cliffs on Panther Mountain

Distance (round-trip): 1.4 miles

Vertical rise: 600 feet

Hiking time: 1⅓ hours

Map: USGS Metric Piseco Lake

Echo Cliffs curve around the western slopes of a shoulder of Panther Mountain overlooking Piseco Lake, and the view from the clifftops is more than ample reward for this short and easy climb. The mountain is a good destination for a first hike into the southern Adirondacks region.

Piseco lies in the middle of a region of hills and mountains where every valley seems to contain a small and often remote and uninhabited lake. Nearly 100 hiking destinations in the country of the West Branch of the Sacandaga River, the area just south of Piseco, are described in another of my guides, *Discover the Southern Adirondacks.* A day hike to Echo Cliffs, which offer a sweeping overview of that area, is an excellent introduction to some of those adventures.

How to Get There

From the intersection of NY 8 and NY 10 by the southeast shore of Piseco, head west on NY 8 for 2.8 miles to West Shore Road. Follow that road north for 3.6 miles to the trailhead on the west side of the road, and park along the road's shoulder. The spot is 0.5 mile south of the entrance to Little Sand Point Campground, the middle of three handsome state campgrounds on the west shore of Piseco Lake that offer good camping, boating, fishing, and access to hiking trails.

The Trail

The trail is well used, as the initials carved on the smooth bark of every beech tree

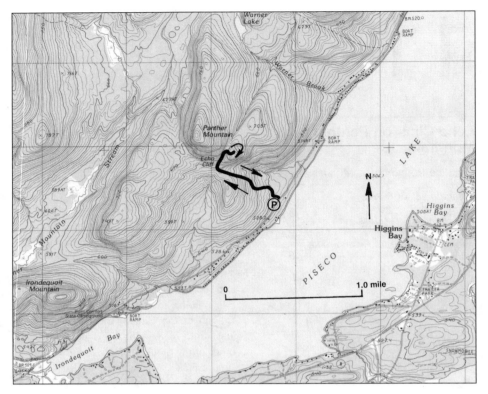

along the way indicate. You could almost conclude that the beech dieback was a protest at such desecration, but the real reason so many beech are dying is the preponderance of mature beech. Those trees were not harvested when local forests were either stripped of their softwoods or culled for their valuable hardwoods. The dieback, which you will observe on this climb, is nature's way of restoring balance, while erasing the tempting slates on which those hikers with no reverence for the woods have left their feeble marks.

Rocky and washed-out stretches also indicate that the trail is fairly popular. Many flowers of the deep woods bloom here in their seasons: violets, trillium, jack-in-the-pulpit, dwarf ginseng, and trout lilies. As you start to climb, magnificent maple line the

trail. Then, continuing generally west, you pass through a hemlock glen.

As the trail makes a distinct curve to the right, in the vicinity of one of the few trail markers, look right, northwest, through the trees and you may catch a glimpse of the cliffs. In early spring or late fall their 200-foot vertical rise is easy to spot; in summer you may miss them entirely.

The climb steepens, and boulders line the route where you approach a ledge and turn right below it. You pass a small intermittent stream with hardly enough flow for a drink in wet weather, and then begin a short, steep climb below tall spruce whose roots provide stairs on the sharp incline. Your route is now behind the cliffs. Shortly you have a glimpse of the lake through the trees. Cross the spruce- and hemlock-covered promontory to emerge on the narrow ledge. This ledge, at 2,420 feet in elevation, is well below Panther's 2,716-foot summit.

The evergreens open to a panorama of the Silver Lake Wilderness across Piseco and Spy Lakes. Few tall mountains are visible in the distance, and the dense forest cover is broken only by streams and ponds. Hawks soar in the updrafts above the cliffs. The water of Piseco Lake mirrors cloud patterns.

Summer homes dot the shores of Higgins Bay opposite Echo Cliffs. The narrow strip of land between the bay and Spy Lake is the site of the area's first settlement, which began in the 1820s and was called Rude-ston after one Eli Rudes. Several sawmills and a tannery were built in the vicinity.

In 1838 a village was designed for the north shore of Piseco by Andrew K. Morehouse, who envisioned a thriving community with a "gristmill, sawmill, machine shop, a large hotel and boarding house and some half-dozen dwellings." Strong inducements were offered to settlers, but fewer than 200 of them stayed more than a week.

This saga of disappointment in the wilderness is typical of most early-19th-century settlers' adventures. Details of many such failures are chronicled in the *Hamilton County History,* by Aber and King. Read the chapter on the Town of Arietta to gain insight into the land you survey from Echo Cliffs. Its abandonment explains why so much of the southern Adirondacks was incorporated into the Forest Preserve, creating the largest chunk of state land in the Adirondack Park.

12

Goldmine Stream Waterfall

Distance (round-trip): 2.6 miles

Elevation change: minimal

Hiking time: 2 hours

Map: USGS Metric Morehouse Mountain

This is an adventure in discovering one of the Adirondacks' more secret places.

How to Get There

There is no marked trailhead. This route is an unmarked path and finding the beginning of it can be difficult. The Powley-Piseco Road heads north from NY 29A in Stratford and bends northeast to intersect NY 10 south of Piseco. The northern half of this 19-mile road is unpaved—a marvelous drive through wilderness. The beginning of the path is 12.5 miles north of Stratford and 6.6 miles south of NY 10. Park at the edge of the road.

Approaching the beginning from the south, notice a camping turnout at 12.3 miles. Down a slight grade at 12.5 miles there is a very small open meadow on your right. On your left, just before the meadow, look for a tree with three blazes. The narrow footpath begins here.

The Trail

Sportsmen and hikers have made this one of the best unmarked paths in the Adirondacks. An anonymous visitor and his sons have cleared the deadfalls from the path. A five-minute walk from the beginning takes you across a half-log bridge. Beyond it the caretakers have placed sawed rounds of downed hemlock in the muddy spots. (Watch out—they can be slippery when wet!)

The route is southwest on high ground through a spectacular forest. After another 10 minutes of easy walking, the path curves to the northwest and descends to cross an

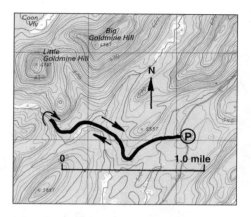

intermittent stream. A slight rise follows, then the path descends more steeply, to cross a stream that is not shown on the new metric map. Watch your footing as you hop rocks for the crossing. On the descent to this stream, you can glimpse through the trees the tops of Big and Little Goldmine Hills and the draw between them. Beyond this stream, which marks the halfway point in both distance and time, the continuing path is relatively level through spruce flats with the marsh opening vistas through the trees to the south.

You reach the outlet of Christian Lake in a marshy area, which can be flooded. On more than one occasion I have had to turn back to wait for lower water, for the marsh extends both up- and downstream. In low water, you can cross the stream on a slippery log. A short level follows, then the path begins to rise at about the time you hear the waterfall in the distance. After climbing at least 30 feet in elevation, head left toward the sound of water. You arrive just below the waterfall, which is a series of chutes plunging into a walled trough. You can picnic on the rock ledges beside the water. Above the falls, water slides over a smooth, golden granite outcrop into a deep pool.

➤ Old-Growth Spruce

Adirondack lumbermen sought softwood stands because only pine, hemlock, and red spruce could be floated to downstream mills on the region's rock-based, steeply dropping rivers and streams. Spruce was the most sought-after of the softwoods. It was more abundant in the northern Adirondacks. Southern Adirondack stands of spruce were often isolated and hard to reach; as a result, a few never-cut stands of spruce can still be found. Red spruce rarely exceed 30 inches in diameter. It is not an especially handsome tree but the long, straight trunks, rising to a small growing tip, made the species economically desirable. Hence, finding an uncut spruce stand is a rare experience, one that is almost never duplicated in other parts of the eastern United States. These old-growth stands are distinguished by the varied ages of the trees, the deep rich mosses covering the forest floor, and the amount of dead and downed wood.

The path continues northwest for about 0.25 mile, gradually petering out near the stillwater above the falls. To the north, at the point at which you headed toward the falls, you may spot an old foundation, a dug well, and other signs of an old settlement. I have been told that the dug well was actually the entrance to a gold mine, but if it is like the numerous other such "gold mines" in the southern Adirondacks, it was someone's scheme in the 1890s to attract incautious investors. Gold has never been found in this region.

Return along the same path. The only place that may confuse you is just east of the second stream on the return, the one not shown on the USGS map. It appears as if a

Goldmine Stream Waterfall

path leads right here along a stream that flows into the outlet. Your route here is slightly left and uphill.

There are several other points of interest along the Powley-Piseco Road. At 8.2 miles north of Stratford, a path leads beside Brayhouse Brook to the confluence with East Canada Creek and then on about 200 yards to a lovely waterfall that my family calls the "Potholers," for the potholes carved in the rocks above the falls. At 11.75 miles north of Stratford, the road goes through a stand of virgin red spruce that straddles the road. At that point, on the west side of the road, is the largest red spruce tree in the Adirondacks, 33 inches in diameter. Walk into the woods on the east side of the road to view more giants.

13

Peaked Mountain

Distance (round-trip): 8.2 miles (6.4 miles if you approach the trailhead by canoe)

Vertical rise: 1,245 feet

Hiking time: 5 hours

Map: USGS Metric Thirteenth Lake

Siamese Ponds Wilderness Area

Peaked Mountain and its eponymous pond lie in the northeastern corner of the Siamese Ponds Wilderness Area, just west of the shores of Thirteenth Lake. Thirteenth Lake, more than 2 miles long and very thin (less than a third of a mile wide), occupies a fault valley that extends south beyond the lake, along the headwaters of the East Branch of the Sacandaga River to NY 8. Gore, Harvey, Balm of Gilead, and Durant Mountains—the Garnet Hills—rise to the east of the fault. Ruby Mountain and a cluster of little cones rise to the west of the fault. The cluster includes Big and Little Thirteenth, Hour Pond, Slide, and Peaked Mountains. The sharpest of the cones are Slide and Peaked; both have rock outcrops, cliffs, ledges, and narrow views. Peaked Mountain has a newly flagged trail.

The garnet history of the region is told in *Discover the South Central Adirondacks,* which describes trips to many of the Garnet Hills. The Siamese Ponds Wilderness Area Unit Management Plan sets aside areas that will remain trailless, identifies areas and accesses that the state should purchase, closes certain roads that penetrated the Wilderness, and recommends the marking of a new trail. Peaked Mountain is the locus of that trail. The justifications for it are many—there are few trails to mountains with views in the region; there existed a marked DEC trail to Peaked Mountain Pond at the foot of the mountain; and the climb up the mountain has long been a favorite bushwhack route, along which many hikers have managed to get lost. It is a short, steep, but

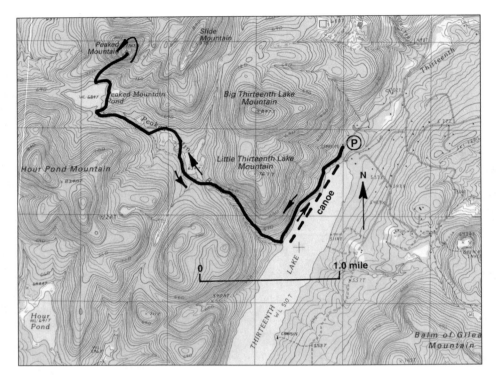

confusing little cone, so the new trail is most welcome. However, in the manner suited to Wilderness Trails, this route will be marked sparingly, preserving the region's wilderness character. Even the route to the pond will remain difficult, since the trail builders are losing the ongoing competition with beaver, which manage to discombobulate the trail regularly.

How to Get There
From North Creek, head west on NY 28 along the Hudson River to North River and turn south on Thirteenth Lake Road. That road climbs steeply away from the Hudson. At 3.5 miles, bear right. The way left leads to Garnet Hill Lodge (a good place to stay for hiking and cross-country skiing in the region) and to the major trailhead for interior trails in the Siamese Ponds Wilderness Area. The way right leads less than 0.5 mile

to a parking area for Thirteenth Lake, where you will find fireplaces, a swimming beach, and a place to launch canoes. You can canoe or walk to the trailhead, which is 0.9 mile south along the west shore of the lake.

The Trail
By canoe, head to the first cleft in the steep mountains on the west side. Here a slanted rock provides a landing and a footpath leads south for 100 yards to the trail. The spot is just south of the last rock ledge in a low area not far from Peaked Mountain Brook.

If you are walking, the trail from the parking area stays close to the shoreline, generally a few feet above it. There are outcrops and views and few markers as you walk south. Note that the trail turns west just to the north of Peaked Mountain Brook, the first real stream you meet, so if you reach it, look about for the beginning of the trail.

The trail, sparsely marked with red disks, begins by following the stream uphill. (Mileages begin at the lakeshore.) The trail starts off moderately steeply beside the brook's boulders, cascades, and numerous little waterfalls for 0.6 mile, a 15-minute walk that climbs 325 feet. Then it is more gentle, until at 0.8 mile you cross the brook by hopping rocks. You stay in the valley all the way to Peaked Mountain Pond, winding from side to side across the flooded brook because of beaver. A little more climbing brings you at 1 mile, in 30 minutes, to views of the first flow along the brook and of the mountain beyond it. You stay south along this first flow.

About 100 yards past the first flow, red DEC markers and new flags—a multitude of markings at present—direct you across the stream and slightly uphill to the north of the second flow. This route has minimal foot tread, so the marks are temporarily needed. It takes you over a little ridge and through deep forest and out again to a beaver meadow, this one currently flooded and full of water. There is even a sign and arrow indicating the direction of this rerouting, so you can easily follow this new way. You can see Hour Pond Mountain to the south across this flow.

The trail crosses the stream again, heading to the south side of the next flow. Note that the entire time you are making these S-curves, you are near the bottom of the very narrow valley. The third meadow, at 1.6 miles, is a wonderful little place with views of Peaked Mountain across it. Flooding in this meadow has forced hikers to veer more and more to the south, away from the prescribed route. You wind around several large boulders, then just short of 2 miles (a good hour's walk) you continue briefly west through the woods. As you cross a little stream, watch closely for the red marker that directs you up over a ridge to a rock ledge on the south side of the outlet of the pond at 2.2 miles, a 70-minute climb of 425 feet from Thirteenth Lake.

Peaked Mountain looms above you. There are paths along the south shore, but to find the trail up the mountain, you head along the north shore. First you must cross the outlet brook—just one good jump if you do it right at the outlet of the pond—and you will find a narrow footpath along the north shore. New red trail markers now mark the route all the way to Peaked's summit. The trail goes up and over a knoll and down to a campsite at water level. It continues along the north shore of the pond, around a bay, and, with more than adequate red disks, leaves the shore at 2.6 miles. The 660-foot climb from here to the summit is under 0.6 mile long and takes about a half hour.

The trail leaves water level of the pond by making two very steep zigzags before attaining the narrow ridge and settling down into a sharp climb to the north. The trail is back from the edge of the cliffs and away from danger, but it is so precipitous in places that it is already becoming eroded. The route up the cone is well flagged, but you should pay careful attention to it. At one point you climb up below a rock ledge and really have to scramble to round it. Above the scramble, you go through a narrow passage walled by spruce and balsam and emerge on a flat rock with your first view.

At this point, the trail heads left, away from the cliffs, then zigzags back toward them for the final approach to the tiny top of the 2,919-foot mountain. From it there are views down into the pond, west all the way to the mountains west of Indian Lake, and, from a tiny vantage at the top of the cliffs on Peaked's northeastern face,

Peaked Mountain

directly over to Slide Mountain. From this point, you can trace your route along the brook past the flows.

There are still problems to surmount on the return. The first is near the summit—watch closely for the flags. You must make a sharp zigzag to the left and then right onto open rock to stay on the marked route. Do not be tempted to head off west onto open rock there. Your route is only temporarily a steeper way. The red disks should keep you from making the mistakes bushwhackers have made in the past. As you descend along the ridge, remember the last zigzag that will take you to water level. Here you turn left from the ridge, again following a steeper course for 100 feet or so.

There are sufficient new markers to take you around the pond, but stay close to its shore until you are across the outlet. Then plunge into the woods and pick up the old route again. It is possible to stray even on the return, especially where a number of footpaths have been worn to circumvent the beaver flooding. Remember to stay low in the valley, so if you do wander from the trail, you will quickly return to it. The places the trail changes direction to cross the brook are and should remain well marked. If you do not stray from the route, it should take less than two hours for the return from the peak to the shore of Thirteenth Lake.

Managing the Adirondacks

In the 1960s there were many threats to the Adirondacks. Modern vacationers with their leisure time and mobility flocked to the mountains in record numbers. (Think about how recently the automobile affected accessibility to the mountain recesses—automobiles were not widely used until after World War II.) There were suddenly proposals for huge developments of second homes in an area where there was almost no land-use planning. Snowmobiles and other motorized vehicles began to penetrate every corner of the wild public lands. The concerns of those interested in preserving the Adirondacks in their natural state became focused after a brief and abortive attempt to make a part of the Adirondacks into a federal park. As a result, then-Governor Rockefeller appointed a Temporary Study Commission, which was chaired by Harold K. Hochschild. From the work of a professional staff, the commission produced a report in 1970, *The Future of the Adirondack Park,* with 181 recommendations, and documents describing the natural resources of the park that substantiated the recommendations.

One of the recommendations was that the Adirondack Park Agency (APA) be created. The Adirondack Park Agency Act, passed by the state legislature in 1972, detailed how the agency was to regulate development on private lands. It also stated that the agency should prepare a State Land Master Plan (SLMP) outlining how the public lands, the Forest Preserve, were to be managed by the Department of Environmental Conservation (DEC). The SLMP divides public lands into categories: Intensive Use Areas, which are the campgrounds managed by the DEC; Canoe and Wilderness Areas, in which no motorized access is permitted; and Wild Forest Areas, the principal recreation areas of the park. The SLMP defines Wilderness in a manner that is similar to the federal definition.

Fifteen Wilderness Areas were delineated and their characteristics described in the SLMP. Guidelines for Wilderness management were detailed. But the SLMP left to the DEC the responsibility for creating detailed management plans for each Wilderness Area that would interpret the

SLMP. For a decade, efforts to establish Unit Management Plans floundered. Finally, the process began. The Siamese Ponds Wilderness Area was the first for which a Unit Management Plan was begun and completed.

Writing the plan was a difficult and prolonged process. Many individuals—local residents, preservationists, sportsmen, and hikers—met regularly to hammer out the details. Their recommendations were further modified by the APA and finally, in 1987, the plan, with some of the advisory group's recommendations, was approved by the governor. In a way, the plan they produced is a prototype of those that have followed. It exemplifies the way Adirondack Wilderness is to be protected—and used.

14

Moose River Plains

Distance (total trip): 5.4 miles

Vertical rise: minimal

Hiking time: 3½ hours

Maps: USGS Metric Wakely Mountain; USGS Metric Old Forge

The Moose River Recreational Area has long been a sportsmen's paradise. In 1963 the state acquired 50,000 acres from Gould Paper Company, the heart of the region surrounding the South Branch of the Moose River in western Hamilton County. The area is now open to sportsmen, campers, and hikers. You will find that there are many exciting destinations in the Recreational Area and the adjacent wilderness area besides those outlined in this hike and in Hike 15 (Brooktrout Lake and Falls Pond). All of them are described in *Discover the West Central Adirondacks.*

A good dirt road runs almost 24 miles through the Recreational Area, starting on the east at the Headquarters Gate by the Cedar River Flow south of Indian Lake and ending on the west by Lake Limekiln Gate south of Inlet. More than 150 campsites have been designated along the roadway, so if you prefer camping from your car to carrying a backpack, the Moose River Plains area is for you. The campsites are dispersed along various access roads, well separated from each other. Signs indicate safe springs beside the road. A few campsites are near lovely streams, some are near accesses to ponds, and a few are in deep woods. Tent camping is allowed on all of the sites and at any undeveloped site in the interior as long as it is 150 feet from water and trails.

If you are spending the night or just driving through, you must register at the booths at either end of the access road. You will need a camping permit if you stay

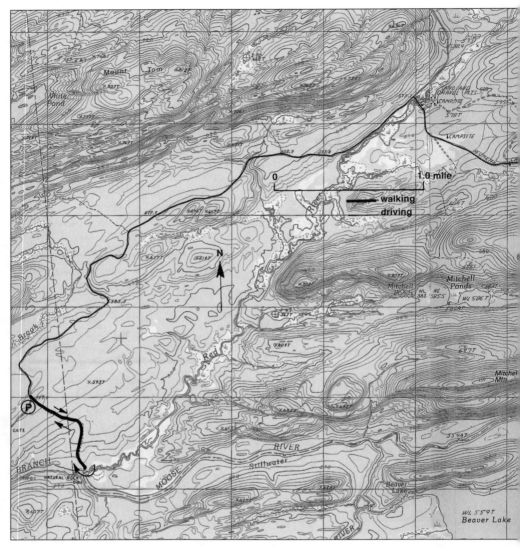

more than three nights. The area opens to the public about Memorial Day, or after the dirt road has dried out. Consult the DEC's Moose River brochure for complete details (see Introduction). You will most probably want to visit here later in summer, when the number of blackflies has dwindled. But you should go before hunting season begins, when access is limited to cars with chains or four-wheel drive. And you certainly will want to bring a fishing pole and canoe. The Moose River's ponds are quite accessible.

One 3-mile-long stretch along the Moose River is natural meadow and open field. These plains are as intriguing to Adirondackers used to unbroken forests as a water hole is to visitors in the desert.

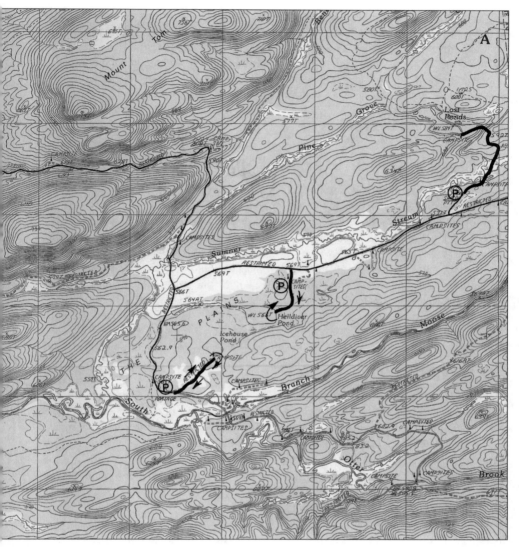

The scrub growth infrequently dotted with trees is a natural phenomenon explained by the poor sandy soil remaining from a glacial lake that once covered the area. The vast expanse is so unusual in the Adirondacks that early visitors were convinced the plains were man-made, specifically the work of Native Americans. They were reputed to have regularly burned the plains to provide a habitat for deer and other game. The berries and low browse are natural and attract deer especially. In winter the plains becomes a huge deer yard.

Because it has been fewer than 35 years since the last logs were taken from parts of the area, scrub forests, thick with small new growth, cover much of the remainder of the Recreational Area. Edging the road are significant stands of large pine, spruce, and balsam and magnificent tamarack. A network of logging roads covered the area, and those not open to vehicles are now the area's foot trails. All are easy for walking. This "hike" actually takes you on four separate short trails, to give you a general introduction to the Moose River Recreational Area.

How to Get There

Start at the eastern end of the road through the Recreational Area. To reach that entrance from Indian Lake, drive west on NY 28/NY 30 for 2 miles and turn west, then south on Cedar River Road. It is almost 12 miles to the Headquarters Gate near the Cedar River Flow. You pass the trailhead to Wakely Mountain (Hike 34) just before you reach the gate.

The Trail

From the eastern gate, 0.0 mile, near Wakely Dam head west. The Northville-Placid Trail forks left 1.2 miles from the gate, leading to lean-tos by the Cedar River Flow and in the interior of the West Canada Lakes Wilderness. At 1.7 miles you reach a section of land sold to the state by International Paper Company. Currently, the marked campsites begin at 3.3 miles.

South of the road you begin to see Little Moose and Manbury Mountains, which rise more than 1,200 feet above the plains. You will cross several small streams, including Cedar and Bradley Brooks, all flowing into the South Branch of the Moose River, which is south of the road. Just beyond, where you cross Silver Run, interesting cliffs overhang a lovely flow north of the road.

At 9.3 miles, turn left for a quick look at the Moose River. Several of the nearby camping spots are nicer than most. As you start west again, you begin to see in the

distance Mitchell Ponds Mountain, with its cliffs guarding the west end of the plains.

The preponderance of low cherry, elderberry, birch, and mountain ash explains the area's wildlife, but now a few of the truly giant pine appear. At 10.8 miles you reach a side road that leads north toward Lost Ponds, the first of your destinations on foot. Drive 0.4 mile from the main dirt road and park. You'll want to pick a few blueberries before you start walking north on the dirt roadway, following the yellow trail markers. The trail is so smooth and easy that fishermen use wheeled carrying devices to transport canoes to Lost Ponds. At an unmarked intersection by a campsite, just before the roadway bridges the outlet of the eastern pond, turn right, or east, onto a very narrow footpath. It leads 100 yards to the eastern Lost Pond, which is a dammed tributary of Sumner Stream. Its shores are fairly swampy, and the lake is more suitable for exploration by boat than by foot.

Continue on the yellow-marked roadway beyond the bridge and then fork left. (The sign says only TRAIL to differentiate this route from the myriad interconnected logging roads.) This path leads to the south side of the western pond, where there are signs that deer have heavily browsed the banks. A rock ledge topped with enormous pine faces the north shore of this very handsome pond. This is brook trout water—no bait is allowed. I am not sure about the fish, but the plants are varied and interesting, with trillium and trailing arbutus, lots of woody bog plants, and, of course, blueberries. If you are just exploring, the 1.2-mile round-trip walk to visit both ponds should take under an hour.

Returning to the main dirt road, continue west for another 1.5 miles to a turnout on the left, or south, for Helldiver Pond. You can drive this side road for 0.2 mile, leaving but 0.3 mile to walk to the pond. It is named for the hell divers, or grebes, that have nested here. From the parking area beneath notably tall pine, you plunge into a dense, dark, and relatively rare white spruce stand on a yellow-marked trail. The path veers right and emerges in a wet field on a corduroy walkway across the sphagnum mats that ring this boggy pond. You will want a camera. This is one of the great quaking bogs, with bog rosemary, pale rhododendron, leatherleaf, Labrador tea, mats thick with cranberries and sheep laurel, and painted trillium, creeping white winterberry, and goldthread along the borders. The pond delights naturalists as well as fishermen.

To find your third destination, return to the main road and continue west another 0.8 mile through the most open part of the plains to a major intersection. Bear south for 0.5 mile to a sign for the trail to Icehouse Pond. Park at the roadside, below one of the region's giant pine, which serves as the best signpost for the trail. Head east through fields typical of the plains: Small cherry, aspen, shadblow, willow, and birch are dotted with clumps of larger spruce, balsam, or tamarack. A fence keeps deer out of a small area where trees really thrive, demonstrating how the forest can grow when not browsed by deer. Another feast of blueberries awaits summer hikers. This short trail quickly leads to beautiful deep woods surrounding the pond. Clumps of oversized painted trillium fill the banks beneath tall spruce.

Returning again to your car, head back north toward the intersection, then head north and then west, following the road past many lovely vistas of bogs, brooks,

and ledges for 3.5 miles to an intersection beside the Red River. For your last destination on this day in the plains, turn left, or south, on a road that takes you to the western boundary of the Recreation Area, to the edge of the private lands of the Adirondack League Club.

The road follows the meandering Red River for 3.9 miles to a trailhead on the left, or east, side of the road. Here a sign indicates where a very narrow, yellow-marked trail heads downhill into the woods, descending to the level of a sphagnum bog. A footbridge carries you dryly across. Notice how much larger the stumps of harvested trees are than anything else growing here.

You reach an intersection with an old logging road and turn right. More bogs and wet places fill the level route. You do need the trail markers, for the foot tread of other hikers is barely visible. There is one exceptional patch where the bright, light greens of sorrel are massed beneath a deep, dark spruce stand. You begin to hear water after only a half hour, so the trail seems shorter than the 1.8 miles stated on the trailhead sign.

You have reached the confluence of the Red and Moose Rivers. Both are blocked by a smooth, natural rock dam, with quiet flows above and rapids below. This is a spot for summer swimming after a day of exploring and hiking. There is a campsite on a spruce knoll beside the dam. You have had a good woods walk to a special place, a suitable finish to a day of discovering the Moose River Plains.

If you wish to follow the main road out to the western gate, return to the intersection by the Red River and bear left, or north, toward Limekiln Lake and NY 28 at Inlet.

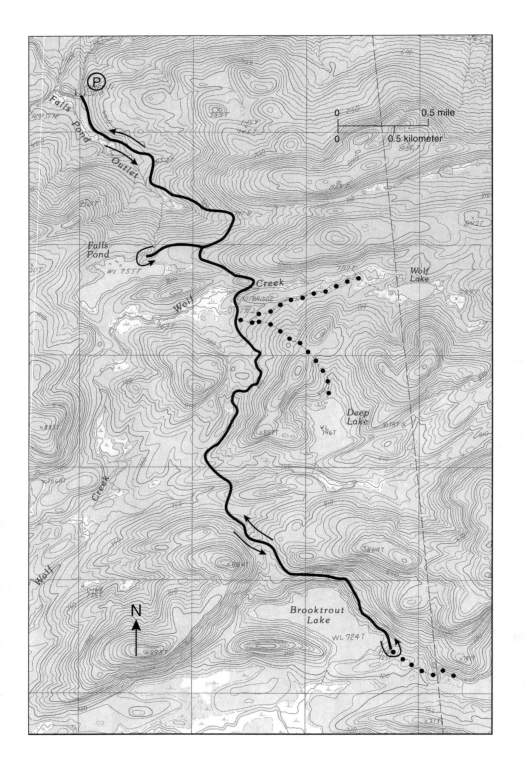

15

Brooktrout Lake and Falls Pond

Distance (round-trip): 10 miles

Vertical rise: 2,244 feet

Hiking time: 6 hours

*Maps: USGS Metric Wakely Mountain;
USGS Metric West Canada Lakes*

West Canada Lakes Wilderness Area

To the south of the Moose River Plains lies the 156,000-acre West Canada Lakes Wilderness Area. This is one of the most remote regions in the park, known mostly to backpackers. At the core of this tract lies the West Canada Lakes themselves. Their outlets combine to form the West Canada Creek, while neighboring Brooktrout Lake sends its waters to the South Branch of the Moose River. The trail described here is actually the shortest route into the region, at just over 5 miles. It is short enough to be suitable for a lengthy day trip, but it is more commonly used as part of a backpacking trip through the heart of the West Canadas.

French Louie, the famous French Canadian hermit and guide, probably knew these woods better than anybody who came before or after. He made his home in a cabin at the east end of West Lake, where he lived year-round for thirty-five years. In the winters he would walk his trap lines, moving from pond to frozen pond, where he had set traps for marten, mink, fisher, and otter. His winter treks frequently took him through the same woods you are about to walk through. In those days, the wilderness was even more inaccessible in the winter than it is today. He would pack the furs out to Speculator in the spring to sell them.

Louie maintained several other small camps and lean-tos all over these woods to accommodate him on his travels. Near the start of this hike, he tapped a stand of tall maples to make his own sugar and syrup. He boiled the sap himself in a little cabin he built on-site.

Brooktrout Lake

Several profound changes have occurred to these woods since those days, however. Louie's sugarbush no longer stands—the Gould Paper Company harvested the timber there decades ago, along with much of the surrounding forest. Even more disturbing is the loss of one of Louie's prime fishing spots. Brooktrout Lake was one of the first Adirondack lakes to be rendered lifeless by the effects of acid rain.

Even so, much of the natural beauty of this region remains, and a hike to Brooktrout Lake will not disappoint you. In addition, a short, 0.3-mile spur from the main trail leads to Falls Pond. If you intend to camp, you will find a lean-to at Brooktrout Lake, a tent site at Falls Pond, and several roadside campsites near the trailhead.

How to Get There

The trailhead is located deep within the Moose River Recreation Area. See Hike 14 for background information on the area. If you enter the Moose River Plains from the Limekiln Gate, drive down the main road for 10.6 miles to a major intersection. If you enter from the gate at Cedar River Flow, drive west for 13 miles. The distances do not sound great, but even when the dirt roads are in good condition travel is slow.

Bear south at the intersection. Within 1.5 miles you cross the South Branch of the Moose River. At 3.4 miles you cross Otter Brook. Turn right at the intersection just beyond. The trailhead is to the left of the road at 4.5 miles. There is room for about 10 cars to park.

The Trail

Beyond the trailhead register and gate, the yellow-marked trail follows an old gravel road past a string of beaver meadows. A piece of the road has washed out at 0.5 mile, and you may need to cross the stream

50 Hikes in the Adirondacks

on a beaver dam to the left. The trail is quite rocky and wide as you climb up through the valley of Falls Pond Outlet. The surrounding forest is young, but it does manage to shade the trail from the summer sun.

At 1.4 miles, look for a trail sign to the right of the trail. This marks the start of the short side trail to Falls Pond. Turn right here, and follow the trail away from the road toward the open meadow on the outlet of Falls Pond. Just as you approach the meadow, you may hear cascading water downstream to the right. Indeed, there is a small waterfall at the foot of the meadow, about five feet high and out of sight of the trail. Presumably, this is what gave Falls Pond its name, and it is worth a brief detour.

The trail skirts the edge of the meadow, heading upstream to cross the outlet on a natural rock barrier. The trail officially ends at a rocky promontory beside the pond, but a herd path leads right to the well-used campsite near the shore. The balsam forest extends all the way around the pond, and in the water sit a number of small rocky islets. Pink lady's slipper grows nearby. The walk to the pond takes but 50 minutes and is 1.7 miles long.

Backtrack down the foot trail to the old road, and then turn right to resume the journey to Brooktrout Lake. After a slight rise, the road continues on the level. Just 0.5 mile after the Falls Pond intersection you reach an area where two streams flow from left to right. The metric USGS map labels the first as Wolf Creek, but clearly the second is the more substantial stream of the two. There should be a footbridge here, but as of late 2002 it was decrepit and unusable. The footbridge may not be replaced, but you can cross the stream easily on rocks. There is a handsome gorge just downstream.

Clearings on either side of Wolf Creek hold the hardware and paraphernalia of an old logging camp. About 100 yards beyond the bridge a second road branches off to the left. Trail signs still indicate a DEC side trail leading east along that road to Wolf and Deep Lakes, but these routes have effectively been abandoned. The route to Wolf Lake in particular is quite rough and wet. Severe beaver flooding has plagued this former trail for years, and the balsams and spruces have concealed much of the rest. Today, Wolf Lake is a haven for not only the beaver, but for deer, coyotes, and even moose as well.

For the purposes of this hike, continue straight on the main trail for Brooktrout Lake. The next segment rises up a slight grade on exposed bedrock, like a paved sidewalk. You bear right through a meadow and cross the first of several boardwalks. Roughly 0.4 mile from Wolf Creek, the trail bears left around a boggy meadow. You then descend through the woods to reach a second meadow, this one flooded by the beavers. An old, overgrown S-shaped dam bisects the pond. The reflections in the water are quite pretty.

The old road becomes increasingly wet and rugged until it ends 1.2 miles from Wolf Creek. The trail continues on as a narrow track through a stately forest. Tall spruce line the trail as you descend to the banks of Deep Lake's outlet stream. This is a wonderful place to stop and rest. You have to step across the stream on rocks, and shortly beyond you cross a second, smaller stream.

The trail angles southeast and begins to climb toward a pass in the ridge north of Brooktrout Lake. Along the way are several muddy stretches. You reach the height-of-land 1.9 miles from Wolf Creek, and what follows is a long and sometimes steep descent around the north side of the lake. Only occasionally can you catch glimpses of the lake through the trees. The descent lasts 20 minutes, and finally, 2.8 miles beyond Wolf Creek, you reach the lean-to near the east shore of the lake.

The lean-to does not face the lake, but a well-worn trail leads to a scenic spot on the shore. You can hop on rocks down the length of the shoreline to extend the view of this lovely place. Although the lake contains no fish, loons have returned in recent years. It is not clear what they are feeding on. The foot trail continues on for another 0.7 mile to the west end of West Lake, and then continues on around its north shore to intersect with the Northville-Placid Trail near the site of French Louie's cabin. Those destinations are certainly beyond the reach of day hikers. But if you choose to camp at Brooktrout and want to explore the area further, consult *Discover the West Central Adirondacks.*

16

John Brown's Tract

Distance (around loop): 9.6 miles

Vertical rise: minimal

Hiking time: 8 hours

Map: USGS Metric Thendara

Ha-de-ron-dah Wilderness Area

A hike in John Brown's Tract takes you west beyond the mountain region that generally distinguishes the Adirondack Park. You will visit the rolling country that tempted early settlers. Their story is as fascinating as the walk through the deep, quiet woods that now conceal almost all evidence of their presence.

The story of John Brown's Tract is a tragedy of greater proportion than any of the other failures that marked early attempts at Adirondack settlement, and it is one of the oldest tales in the mountains. It began in Rhode Island with the family and fortunes of John Brown, a businessman whose generosity to Rhode Island College caused that institution to be renamed Brown University. In 1796, one of his sons-in-law misspent a $210,000 fortune on the disputed title to 210,000 acres in Herkimer County. John Brown spent another $250,000 straightening out his son-in-law's folly and clearing title to the parcel, which was part of the Macomb purchase. Brown then divided the purchase into townships with the names of virtues he espoused: Industry, Enterprise, Perseverance, Unanimity, Frugality, Sobriety, Economy, and Regularity.

John Brown visited the area only once, but he had a 25-mile-long road built from Remsen, north of Utica, for the settlers he enticed to his community of Middle Settlement in Township 1, Industry. No sign remains of Industry's log houses, barns, and clearings, but the hike outlined visits Middle Settlement Lake and follows in part a trail along John Brown's Road.

The tragedies that befell a second son-in-law, Charles Frederick Herreshoff, were even more devastating. But from the failures of Herreshoff's attempts to bring settlers to Township 7 sprang some of the Adirondacks' most notable events. The community he founded later grew into the lovely resort of Old Forge. Otis Arnold acquired Herreshoff's mansion and turned it into the Adirondacks' first hotel. And that hotel was visited in 1856 by the first woman to make a camping trip across the Adirondacks. The isolation of that Adirondack wilderness is graphically illustrated by the story that one of the first female travelers, Lady Amelia M. Murray, lady-in-waiting to Queen Victoria, was said to have been the only woman other than their mother that 6 of Arnold's 12 daughters had ever seen.

You will want to read more of the history of the ill-fated settlements; the story of the failure of Herreshoff's iron mine, one of the first in the Adirondacks; and the adventures of the wild days when trapper Nat Foster occupied Herreshoff's mansion and murdered a Native American. Either Alfred L. Donaldson's *The History of the Adirondacks* or Joseph F. Grady's *The Adirondacks, Fulton Chain–Big Moose Region,* would be a good introduction.

Your hiking introduction to John Brown's Tract is a long, level loop generally following the valleys between long ridge hills. The hike takes you past several lakes in the Ha-de-ron-dah Wilderness, each desirable as a camping or fishing destination. The route is designed to give you a feel for the wilderness that greeted those first settlers.

The surrounding forests were burned in one of the worst of the 1903 forest fires, ignited by a spark from a wood-fired locomotive on the rail line near Thendara. In spite of that fire, the forest through which you walk has almost regained wilderness stature.

How to Get There

Park at the Scusa access, a large turnout on the south side of NY 28, 3 miles south of the railroad overpass near Thendara. The trailhead is north across the highway.

The Trail

The trail, marked in red, heads up a ridge through state land. You can walk the 0.6-mile distance to Brown's Tract Road in 15 minutes. You will return to this junction on the right-hand fork from Grass and Cedar Ponds. For now, turn left on the yellow-marked Brown's Tract Road. It is a lovely, smooth path, leading south-southwest around Bare Mountain. Only a few glacial erratics lie beneath the forest of enormous beech, birch, and maple. In 20 minutes, 0.9 mile from the junction, you should reach a second intersection. Here you will fork right on the blue trail, heading 1.7 miles to Middle Settlement Lake.

Narrower and showing much less use, this trail is a good stretch-your-legs, wilderness route. As you wind west along a ridge only slightly elevated from the surroundings, you can see swamps opening on both sides of the trail. There is a particularly beautiful vista across a ferny meadow on your right as you cross a double-log bridge. Where the trail angles northwest across a plateau, I was most impressed with the openness of this forest's understory, and I stopped at least a half-dozen times to watch for black-throated blue warblers, vireos, and thrushes. You know you are nearing Middle Settlement Lake when suddenly, in the midst of the unbroken forest, one of the Adirondacks' great big boulders appears. It is a part of

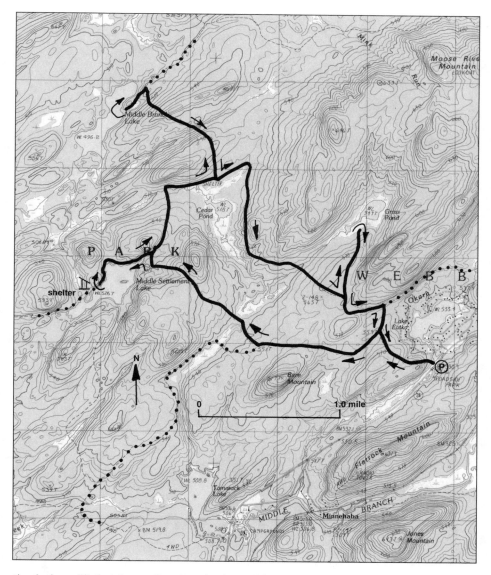

the facing cliff that has split away. At the trail junction below the cliff, you turn left on the yellow-marked route to walk the short distance to Middle Settlement Lake.

The trail winds across a wet inlet area between boulders and starts along the northern shore of this swampy little lake, whose shores are made muddier by the flooding of recent beaver work. No matter, for it makes a better home for the nesting loons that you are sure to find. Within 260 yards of the inlet, a red-marked trail forks right for a short detour up a steep pitch and around to the top of the cliff. The view is crowded by maples, but you do look out across the pond. Return to water level. The

---

John Brown's Tract

Middle Settlement Lake Lean-to

yellow trail continues west, passing Middle Settlement Lake Lean-to in less than 0.5 mile. Sited on rocky slabs that slope down to the water's edge, the lean-to is a perfect destination for a first backpacking trip or a hike with children.

To continue the loop, head back to the intersection below the cliff to take the yellow trail east. One overhanging section of cliff forms a small cave that appears to have sheltered hikers. You wonder if early settlers also found shelter here.

The yellow trail starts out along the left side of the draw, behind the huge split boulder and beneath the cliff. By this route it is just over 0.9 mile to the Cedar Pond intersection. After a 20-minute walk, the trail crosses the end of the ridge and heads down and crosses Cedar Pond Outlet. Where you can see a marsh through the trees is about the closest you will get to Cedar Pond on a trail. Cedar Pond is small and surrounded by a beautiful long meadow full of big, twisted stumps.

Ten more minutes should suffice to get you to the next intersection. You could shortcut your circuit of John Brown's Tract at this point and head back south on the red trail, but if you are still game for adventure, head left, north, for 1.3 miles to Middle Branch Lake. The trail starts up a series of short ledges, goes over a height-of-land and down into a swale, and then cuts down more steeply and crosses a stream on the predictable split-log bridge. Only a thin layer of sand covers the valley bottom, revealing the glacial wash that is typical of the tract's long valleys.

Beyond the stream you head up beside big ledges and around a cliff on your left. Across the second height-of-land you start to descend, and before long you reach still another intersection, where you can see Middle Branch Lake through the trees. The right fork, still marked with yellow, leads back to Thendara. The left fork leads along a red-marked trail to a lean-to, where you should stop for lunch. This is certainly the prettiest of the lakes you visit; its loons may swim by quite close and its shores are lined with Labrador tea.

The return from Middle Branch Lake to the junction near Cedar Pond takes about 45 minutes. South and east of this point, the trail shows much heavier use. The first stretch is very handsome, through a dense spruce bog with a beautiful ground cover of sorrel, bunchberry, creeping white winterberry, and beech fern. You keep to the long winding ridge of an esker with deep bogs on both sides.

The next unbroken chain of wilderness is measured by a series of minor events: two stream crossings; a stand of tall, straight trees towering over a parklike setting where a variety of ferns carpet the forest floor in a mottled rich green; a ledge covered with huge black cherry trees; more impressive fern-crested ledges; another small stream crossing; and finally, after nearly an hour of walking, the crossing of Middle Branch Creek, which is the outlet of Grass Pond. Beyond, the trail makes a 90-degree turn left, and the tree cover becomes lower. The long, level walk begins to lose its excitement just about the time you reach the Grass Pond Trail junction, 70 minutes and 1.7 miles from Cedar Pond.

To visit Grass Pond, turn left and walk for 0.5 mile (15 minutes). A very old beaver dam holds almost no water. However, the pond is not merely grassy, for you can find sundew, lady's slippers, and the hoofprints of many deer along the shore.

When you return from the side trip to Grass Pond, you have 0.5 mile to walk to Brown's Tract Road. Head south and then east along the red-marked trail to a newly marked intersection. The way left leads to Okara Lakes. You go straight, across the trail makes a sharp right turn to avoid private land, then reaches Brown's Tract Road. You are now heading briefly west but shortly make a left turn to head south for the final 0.6 mile to the highway and your car. It takes about 30 minutes to walk from the planking to the trailhead.

17

Vista Trail and Bald Mountain

Distance (total trip): 8.1 miles

Vertical rise: 1,300 feet

Hiking time: 7 hours

Maps: USGS Metric Old Forge; USGS Metric Eagle Bay

Fire tower

The western foothills of the Adirondacks diminish to a series of long ridges whose major axes point slightly north of east. Few rise more than 500 or 600 feet above the surrounding countryside, but glacial scraping has left many with steep cliffs flanking their long sides. The most visible and dramatic ridge is the row of hills along the north shore of the Fulton Chain, stretching from First through Fourth Lakes.

Two trails on that escarpment connect a row of extraordinary vantages that stud the ridgeline like gems on a necklace. For the best walk in the Old Forge area, you should combine both trails into one long day's outing. The combination is possible because the Vista Trail ends at the trailhead for the Bald Mountain route.

If you have only a little time, you should climb just Bald Mountain on the western end of the chain. Walter O'Kane's description of this trail in his 1928 classic, *Trails and Summits of the Adirondacks,* as ranking "first or nearly so in the amount of reward that it offers for a minimum of climbing" is still accurate. But if you want a full day's adventure and a long hike, you will want to combine the Vista Trail with the hike up Bald Mountain. For this trail, and for the combined outing, it is best to have two cars, one at each trailhead.

The Vista Trail winds along the eastern slopes of the chain north of Fourth Lake. The mountain range is sometimes known as Onondaga Mountain, while a peak above Mountain Pond is called Scenic Mountain.

The Fulton Chain, best known for its canoeing opportunities, dominates most of the views on this hike. Old Forge, at the west end of the Fulton Chain, was the major settlement in John Brown's Tract (see Hike 16), but unlike most of the tract, it failed to fade into the wilderness. In fact, it grew into a thriving resort community and now has many vacation possibilities. See David H. Beetle's *Up Old Forge Way* for a delightful series of stories about this community. Several state and private campgrounds are nearby, and a visit to the Northeastern Forest Industries Exhibit Hall, 0.6 mile east of town, is most informative. In addition, you should not miss a lake cruise on the *Clearwater,* which makes a 28-mile tour of the Fulton Chain starting at Old Forge.

How to Get There

The official Bald Mountain trailhead, which is also the trailhead for the western end of the Vista Trail, is on Rondaxe Road just north of its intersection with NY 28, 4.6 miles east of Old Forge. If you are hiking the complete route, leave one car here and continue east another 3.1 miles to the Country Lane Gift Store. The store is 1.5 miles west of Big Moose Road at Eagle Bay. The eastern trailhead is on the north side of the road 100 yards east of the store.

The Trail

Beginning at the eastern trailhead, the yellow-marked trail immediately heads northwest up the ridge. As you near the height-of-land, you will see a narrow footpath angling west up the ridge to the left. The more obvious trail, which you may want to take, continues straight. It leads to Bubb and Sis Lakes, two pretty, shallow ponds. Bubb is a mere 15-minute walk from the highway. One of the area's typical long ridges frames its northern shore. The trail skirts its south shore and then forks. The

way right heads north around Bubb Lake to Moss Lake; the left fork leads 100 yards through a spruce thicket to Sis Lake. It takes no more than 50 minutes to visit both and return to the junction near the height-of-land.

For the Vista Trail on Scenic Mountain, head uphill at the intersection following blue markers. You begin climbing directly up ledges. In five minutes you reach a level perch where an over-the-shoulder glance through the trees reveals the distinct profile of Blue Mountain to the northeast. This is Becker's Outlook and in earlier days its then open views attracted many vacationers. After another five minutes of climbing, you reach a junction where a sign points right to a lookout. Follow the red markers up a steep pitch to an outcrop with a view out over Bubb Lake to the mountains in the northeast. Now heading south of west along the razorback ridge, you continue climbing, but at a more gradual rate. The water of Fourth Lake is visible through the trees.

After walking 40 minutes on the razorback ridge, you reach a rock overlooking Fourth Lake and the rolling hills stretching away to its south. Within 10 minutes a second overlook with small views follows, just before the trail starts a short descent. Head down into the col between the ridge and the higher hill on your right. Angle right, crossing the valley floor, then up the higher ridge that follows. Another opening appears, this one with a fireplace. You will then find the trail confusing as it goes from one open patch to another, but it always stays close to the ridgeline.

After 80 minutes on the ridge, you reach open rock edged with deep moss and spruce trees. If you have made the trip to Bubb and Sis Lakes, this is 2 hours and 20 minutes from the start. You may want to stop here or at the next overlook for lunch. The through-the-trees view is east along

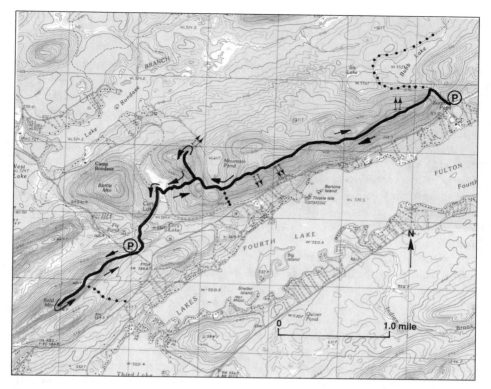

Fourth Lake, past Gull Rock Point and several islands, to the right of which you can spot a broad mountain with a fire tower. That is Wakely, 18 miles away.

Two overgrown overlooks follow, separated by a minor dip. When leaves are off the trees, you can look east from the first toward Black Bear Mountain and Estelle Mountain, which is southeast of Raquette Lake, now visible. Best of all is the shot straight down, south, to Fourth Lake, which seems almost tucked below the intervening cliffs.

From the second overlook, you seem to hang directly over the lake. You are on the narrowest part of the razorback ridge at the top of a nearly vertical cliff. The crescendo of improving vistas continues, for not only is this perch placed dramatically and precariously on top of a nearly 400-foot vertical drop, but it also permits points to the west

to come into view. This spot marks the end of the long stretch of unbroken ridgeline. If you pause often, as the changing perspective encourages you to do, your walk on just this section of ridge should take more than an hour.

The trail now ducks back into the woods and descends into a small valley. As you climb the next knob, stay left, on the Fulton Chain side of the ridge, going around and below ledges that form a 12-foot-high cliff near the top. This is a very difficult spot to navigate since you go around and below the knob and then up to it.

As you continue descending the ridgeline, the forest suddenly becomes more handsome and much taller, but openings allow you some glimpses of Second and Third Lakes. At the bottom of the next steep descent, you reach an intersection only 0.1

mile from NY 28. To continue the Vista walk, turn right, away from the Fulton Chain Lakes on the blue route. Mountain Pond greets you almost as soon as you turn north. Beaver have recently raised the level of the water in that pond, so dead spruce trees edge it and the walking can be muddy and terrible.

Beyond the south end of the pond, the trail heads up a ridge, climbing 100 feet into the saddle between two knolls. An extraordinarily tall and handsome spruce and hemlock grove awaits you as you mount the ridge. Just as you cross the ridgeline, a red-marked trail forks right up the knoll by a sign indicating SCENIC OVERLOOK. Of course you cannot resist another detour, so head up, staying right as footpaths branch off near the summit. You soon come to an overlook of Mountain Pond.

From here, its deep emerald water looks infinitely more inviting than from the shore. Cross the wooded summit of Scenic Mountain to an overlook to the north from which you see Lake Rondaxe and the meadows that stretch east from it, with the cliffs of Slide Off Mountain facing the ridge behind. Slide Off is a copy of the ridgeline you have been following. On clear days you can identify West Mountain and, to its right, the Santanoni Range, Mount Colden, and Mount Marcy. The scar of the slide on Santanoni helps identify that mountain, which is 43 miles away.

Returning to the main blue-marked trail, you drop precipitously along slippery, needle-covered slopes in a hemlock grove, then zigzag right along a contour before dropping again, this time swinging left around the northern marshes of Carry Lake. High water here almost floods the trail just before it emerges on the roadway, where you turn right, back north, crossing the marsh on a causeway. On the far side of the causeway, a state historical marker tells you

that you are walking along the route of a standard-gauge railroad that was constructed in 1899. Until 1933 the line carried passengers between Raquette Lake and Carter Station. The railroad had the first oil-burning locomotive in the Adirondacks, thus preventing the forest fires that were regularly ignited by the wood-burning monsters.

That sign at the end of the causeway is the only indication that here the blue trail turns left. It is 0.7 mile to the trailhead. The railroad continues north to Lake Rondaxe, but you walk south along the shore of Carry Lake. (The USGS map spells it *Cary,* but local signs and logic favor *Carry.*) This is a lovely stretch of trail with a needle-covered tread and views back to the mountain you just descended.

You cross an inlet on a log bridge and then climb another small rise, beyond which you can see Fly Pond. The trail heads south and up another ridge for 0.3 mile before reaching Rondaxe Road opposite the trailhead. The sign indicates it is 1.7 miles back to Mountain Pond, and with the additional detour to the overlook, you probably need 75 minutes for that segment of the hike.

For the second part of this trek, where the view is equal to the sum of those along the Vista Trail, you simply climb Bald Mountain. From the parking area, the ascent is only 400 feet in less than 1 mile. If the climb were not too short to call a hike, or if you were not apt to meet hordes of other hikers, it could be one of the most satisfying treks in the Adirondacks. But since you have certainly enjoyed a measure of solitude on the Vista Trail, you should complete the day with this trip.

You do not really need directions for the trail. After a short level stretch, it begins to climb along the razorback ridge, angling up and over it and reaching the first outcrop with a view in 10 minutes. Gentle

Looking North from the Vista Trail

LEE M. BRENNING

switchbacks bring you to the north side of the ridge, where you make a sharp left turn to cross a boggy swale on a bridge. Just beyond, the grade levels out. This is where the old trail from NY 28 up the south flanks of the ridge used to join the new route. The intersection is all but invisible now. Turn right to follow the ridge. The vista opens to include First and Second Lakes and Moose Mountain. Stop and enjoy the amazingly narrow spine, the magnificent view of Fourth Lake, and the incredible drop of the cliffs below to the south. Hollow footsteps on the exfoliated sheaves tell of ice-loosened slabs that may one day fall away, like the ones you see against the forest below.

The serpentine ridge continues west to the fire tower, to which the state has assigned the name Rondaxe Mountain Tower. It is open to the public, but you scarcely need to climb it for the view. The only significant improvement the short tower affords is a clearer look at two peaks in the distant northeastern horizon. The one on the right is Marcy, 56 miles away, and the one on the left is Colden. You can be certain of their identity if you are looking to the left of Blue Mountain, which, only 25 miles away, has an identifiable stubby profile. The best part of the view from the 2,350-foot summit is unquestionably the panorama of the Fulton Chain spread out parallel to the knife edge of cliffs that constitute Bald Mountain.

Vista Trail and Bald Mountain

18

Cascade and Queer Lakes

Distance (one-way): 9.7 miles

Vertical rise: minimal

Hiking time: 6½ hours

Map: USGS Metric Eagle Bay

Pigeon Lake Wilderness Area

Unusual names are not uncommon in the Adirondacks, but why would anyone name a place Queer Lake? No deep mystery surrounds this strange name; it probably only reflects the lake's eccentric shoreline. But to appreciate just how queer the lake's shape is, you have to walk there, and the best way is on a route that also touches Cascade Lake and Chain and Windfall Ponds.

These lakes lie north of Fourth Lake in the Fulton Chain and south of Big Moose Lake. Natives in the nearby hamlets of Eagle Bay and Inlet will tell you how the latter lake, Big Moose, and the surrounding country figured in the murder that Theodore Dreiser immortalized in *An American Tragedy*.

How to Get There

You will want to make this walk with friends so you can leave a car at each end of the loop. To reach the southern trailhead, drive to Eagle Bay on NY 28, 9.1 miles east of the information center in Old Forge, and turn north onto Big Moose Road for 1.4 miles to the new Cascade Lake trailhead. Arrange to leave a second car 2.3 miles farther north at a new trailhead marked Windfall Pond, where the yellow-marked trail comes out from Queer Lake.

The Trail

The sign at the Cascade Lake trailhead clearly indicates that the first road heading east is the beginning of the 5.5-mile-long Cascade Lake Cross-Country Ski Loop, which is also designated as a hiking and horse trail. Your trip follows that road-

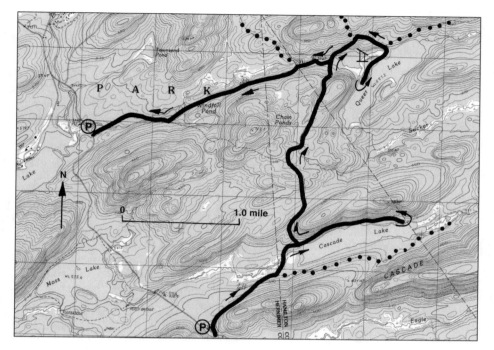

way to the lake and then north along it a short distance, before continuing on to the other lakes.

The dirt road used to be the principal access to an old estate that later became a girls camp. It is wide and improved with gravel, so you certainly do not need what few red trail markers there are to guide you. Trees along the roadside have been cut back for such a distance that the forest cover of tall, mature trees hardly forms a closed canopy. The road is so wide and straight that you can see quite far ahead, sometimes as much as 0.2 mile, a most unusual phenomenon on Adirondack trails. The route takes you up a short hill and then down a long, gradual incline. An old road forks right as you cross a corduroyed section. Continue straight, through a spruce glen with marvelous bunchberry beneath, to a large field. Your trail is along its left border, which is edged in pine with a carpet of sarsaparilla and Canada mayflower. Several good campsites can be found not far from the trail.

After crossing the outlet of Cascade Lake on a small bridge, the trail turns east for 100 yards to a junction that is 1.1 miles from Big Moose Road. A sign points left, north, to a narrow footpath with red markers. Routes connected to it lead in 1.6 miles to Chain Ponds, in 3.2 miles to Queer Lake Lean-to, and in 2.3 miles to Windfall Pond.

Unless you made a late start, continue straight for a trip along the north shore of Cascade Lake, a thin, mile-long body of water that is ideal for camping and canoeing. The only drawback is its proximity to the trailhead; the lake is so popular that it is sometimes crowded. The roadway is smooth enough for transporting a canoe the easy way, with a wheeled cart.

Many campsites are secreted along the several evergreen-covered promontories that edge the lake's shore. From the lake or its east shore, you can see the 200-foot-high cliffs that face the mountain to its north, but if you are going to finish the loop you will not have time for more than a 1-mile return trek down to the lake.

Back at the trail intersection, the narrow footpath climbs almost 200 feet to a spruce bog filled with lady's slippers, blueberries, and clintonia. Red trail markers define the route, which crosses the wet area and then rises gently to a mature forest with many yellow birch. Within 20 minutes you reach a height-of-land in a sort of natural rock garden where ferns seem to have found perfect niches among the boulders and tall, straight trees.

Huge yellow birch, the first of the giants you see on this hike, appear beside the trail. The trail winds through the mature hardwood forests and then angles left in a sphagnum bog covered with tall spruce. Beyond the bog, you climb a small rise and then reach a trail junction, 1 mile from Cascade Lake. Both continuing trails are marked with blue disks; the left leads 1.3 miles to Windfall Pond and then out to Big Moose Road, and the right, the one you follow, continues 0.6 mile to Chain Ponds and 1.4 miles to your first approach to Queer Lake. As you turn right, you enter a small valley with an unusual ledge off to your left and an enormous birch growing from a boulder on your right.

The short walk to Chain Ponds is through a beautiful and majestic forest of hemlock and spruce, one of those deep evergreen pockets all too rarely encountered. A bog appears through an opening on your right just before you reach the outlet of Chain Ponds. Cross the outlet on a natural bridge of well-placed stones and stop for a moment to look up the lake and examine the old beaver dam that raised the water level, cre-

ating a typical Adirondack stump forest around the shores.

The trail climbs a ridge on a carpet of sorrel and interrupted fern. Ledges 20 to 30 feet tall face the hillside on your right. Look for a balancing rock on one clifftop. The walk along the shore is one of the day's high points. You pass a spruce-covered peninsula formed by the continuation of a rock shoulder that edges the left side of the draw that the trail now enters. The deep, dark valley formed by the beautiful cleft in the rocks is overhung on the right by moss-covered ledges. Caves and crevices are sources of cool air. Mystery and a feeling of suspense accompany you. As the draw narrows, the trail is squeezed between boulders and huge slabs that have fallen from the cliffs.

The draw is all too short, and within 15 minutes the trail emerges and starts to drop sharply. Here the trail is narrow and rooted, and again you will be awed by the size of some yellow birch. In 10 more minutes you reach a trail junction within sight of Queer Lake. An informal path angles back right along its shore. A yellow-marked trail heads left, west, 2.6 miles to Big Moose Road. This is the route you will follow after you have explored Queer Lake. For now, bear right, where a sign points to the Queer Lake Lean-to, Mays Pond, and the West Mountain Trail.

You glimpse a small portion of Queer Lake as you cross the marsh at its western end on a slippery log bridge. You might notice an informal path that continues along the northern shore, but the trail, with its yellow markers, makes a sharp left turn uphill behind the lake. After a five-minute climb, you turn east and walk along the ridge, reaching another three-way junction within 15 minutes, at 3.8 miles. Here all the trails have yellow markers. The way left goes to Mays Pond and the route straight ahead leads to the lean-to in 0.5 mile. Continue right on the narrow trail that winds along the flat-topped ridge high above the lake and then turns to descend, meeting on the way down still another trail. The yellow-marked route turns north, left, in 2.3 miles to Chub Lake, and the red-marked trail drops down to Queer Lake.

Your first approach to Queer Lake is at the beginning of a boggy isthmus linking the shore with the long, narrow peninsula that almost divides the lake in two. Using a split-log bridge to cross the bog, you will walk along the north side of the peninsula under big spruce for 200 yards and then cross to a windswept promontory overlooking the larger portion of the lake. Here a lean-to has been placed to enjoy the best of both views and breezes.

An informal path from the lean-to continues to the end of the peninsula, heading toward ledges from which there is good swimming in deep, clear water. This peninsula almost reaches the western shore of Queer Lake. When you are in one portion of the lake, the separation is so complete that you have no hint of a lake on the opposite side. The shape is certainly peculiar!

When you start back, walk slowly along the boggy spit that takes you to the "mainland." Tall spruce protect an eerie shoreline edged with the naked spires of dead spruce, swamp laurel, and Labrador tea.

Return to the principal trail junction at the lake's western end and head right, west. Now is the time to enjoy the huge yellow birch. In the next hour of walking, you should spot dozens of these magnificent giants, some with diameters approaching 4 feet.

The trail begins through a valley, with low ground on your right and a steep hill on your left. Wet places make walking less than perfect, and roots poke out occasionally. A series of split-log bridges takes you across a wet meadow filled with lush clumps of *Gymnocarpium,* or oak fern. An arrow directs you left. The turn is poorly marked, but if you miss it you will quickly see the buildings of a private inholding. The trail heads up the hill and across its face before continuing in the valley in order to avoid this private land.

Past the detour, you reach another intersection where a sign indicates that you have traveled 0.7 mile from Queer Lake. There is no indication of the distance to Big Moose Road, but it is about 2 miles; the walk out takes just over an hour.

Stay straight ahead on the yellow trail to Windfall Pond, walking generally up the side of a hill for a half hour on a ledge below long, thin ridges. The footpath is narrow and appears infrequently used.

A spruce-covered plateau for camping lies between Windfall Pond and the trail. The lake is deep, its dark green waters reflecting the high hills that rim it. Its rock-edged shoreline invites swimming. The trail skirts the lake on the north as far as the outlet, staying most of the time 100 feet back from the water.

From the outlet it is 1 mile to Big Moose Road. You ford the outlet stream three times within a few hundred yards of the pond, but in the summer there is not likely to be much water to contend with. The trail continues downstream after the third crossing with the stream to your right, eventually approaching the side of a small meadow. A long section leading up to a footbridge over the stream is likely to be muddy. From the bridge you can stop to watch the stream flowing below over smooth bedrock into a miniature chasm, complete with diminutive cliffs and a dark evergreen canopy. The trail pulls away from the stream up the valley's right side, following the stream for a short distance on a ledge and then dropping down to recross it on a second footbridge.

Instantly the trail is wider. You have reached the point where "inbound" hikers stop, five minutes from the road. You turn away from the stream and a campsite that must seem attractive to those who haven't seen the beauty of the more remote spots you reached on this walk. In no time at all you reach the trailhead and waiting car.

19

Gleasmans Falls

Distance (round-trip): 6 miles

Hiking time: 4 hours

Maps: USGS Metric Number Four; USGS 7.5' Crystal Dale

The western Adirondacks slope off to small hills and sandy plains laced with wonderful, wild rivers that occasionally plunge over rock ledges in tumbling waterfalls. The waterfalls are the region's special places and the most wondrous of these is Gleasmans Falls, a series of small cascades on the Independence River. The falls seem especially vigorous and the water exceptionally turbulent because the river is confined to a narrow gorge lined with steep walls. The water drops 70 feet over boulders and ledges in a quarter of a mile. Lovely picnic spots, just off the trail on the northern rim of the gorge, overlook the swirling brown water, the sparkling falls, and the mounds of foam and froth whipped up by the rushing water.

The Independence River gives its name to the surrounding Wild Forest, which has been developed into a varied recreation area. The flat, sandy plains lend themselves to horse trails, and a new network of horse trails fans out from the Otter Creek Trailhead. Some of the old roads are designated snowmobile trails. These routes make excellent cross-country skiing routes. But the best parts of the Wild Forest are the hiking trails that thrust east toward the headwaters of the Independence River and Otter Creek, and the best of these trails is the route that passes Gleasmans Falls. The trip to the falls makes a lovely short day hike, and the trail continues on along the river and connects with routes to other streams and lakes in long, flat circuits that can be extended to backpacking routes. (All are described in *Discover the Southwestern Adirondacks.*)

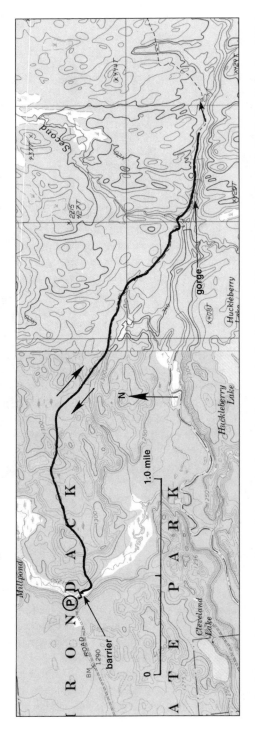

How to Get There

To find the trailhead, you have to make your way through a maze of often unmarked back roads. Leave NY 12 heading toward Glenfield. Signs to the Otter Creek Horse Trails are your best guide. After a series of turns, those signs put you on Erie Canal Road, at 5.9 miles. The Otter Creek Horse Trailhead forks right at 6.2 miles. Measuring now from that trailhead, continue on Erie Canal Road for 2.25 miles to turn right on Beach Mill Road. Cleveland Road forks right at 4.1 miles; stay on Beach Mill, which is the much narrower, one-lane, dirt road. The trailhead is at the end of the road at 6.35 miles.

The Trail

The yellow-marked Gleasmans Falls Trail itself is smooth, hard-packed sand, with almost no wet places. The forest is second growth, but with tall, straight trees for a high, closed canopy that makes you feel as if you are walking through a green cathedral. The understory is a carpet of ferns, mostly the lacy hay-scented fern, which is thought to produce a substance that inhibits the germination of trees. The relative absence of new young trees in the forest adds credence to this idea.

To walk the trail you need almost no instructions. You cross three streams; the first, Burnt Creek, is just east of the trailhead. At 0.4 mile you see the southern part of Beach Millpond through the trees. At 1.2 miles you cross Nickel Creek. A long, level stretch ends in a descent toward the Independence River. The first 2.5 miles of trail go quickly. You hear the roar of the river, then drop to river level by a rocky wash formed by the mouth of Second Creek, the third small stream. The trail turns east to follow the river, which is still out of sight. You climb to the rim partway along the gorge.

Gleasmans Falls Gorge

Gleasmans Falls is a series of falls in the deep gorge separated by pools and a narrow flume. The river drops 70 feet in the quarter-mile gorge. Walk at least as far upriver as the head of the upper falls before retracing your steps. Even though you cannot see the entire sweep of falls from any one point on the trail beside the gorge, stay on the trail unless it has been dry and the water is very low. Only then should you venture down to one of the vantages on the side of the gorge. Even under the best of conditions, be very careful.

20

Grass River Waterfalls

Distance (cumulative round-trip): 6 miles

Vertical rise: minimal

Hiking time: 6 hours

Maps: USGS 7.5' West Pierrepont; USGS 7.5' Degrasse; USGS 7.5' Brother Ponds

In one quiet, little-known corner of the Adirondack Park, the South Branch of the Grass River makes a dramatic exit by spilling over six large waterfalls just before crossing the Blue Line near Degrasse. After merging with the middle branch of the river, it crosses back into the park and drops over one more rock ledge at Lampsons Falls.

There is very little Forest Preserve land in this region, but fortunately the most scenic of the riparian corridors have been protected by state purchases in recent years. The Lampsons Falls tract was the first to be acquired in 1979. Then, in 1999, Champion International sold to the state the 16-mile stretch of land along the South Branch where it parallels Tooley Pond Road. This tract opened up public access to sites like Twin Falls and Rainbow Falls where previously hunting clubs had held exclusive leases.

Nowhere else in the Adirondacks is there such easy access to so many waterfalls on a single major river. Two of the seven cascades, Twin and Sinclair, are visible from roadside parking areas and require no walking to be able to enjoy them. The rest are only modest distances from the nearest road. All are fairly easy to find, although only Lampsons Falls is reached by a marked DEC trail. Hopefully more trails can be marked in this area in the near future. In the meantime, to find each of the other waterfalls you have to pay close attention to your odometer as you drive along the local roads to find the start of each of the well-worn herd paths.

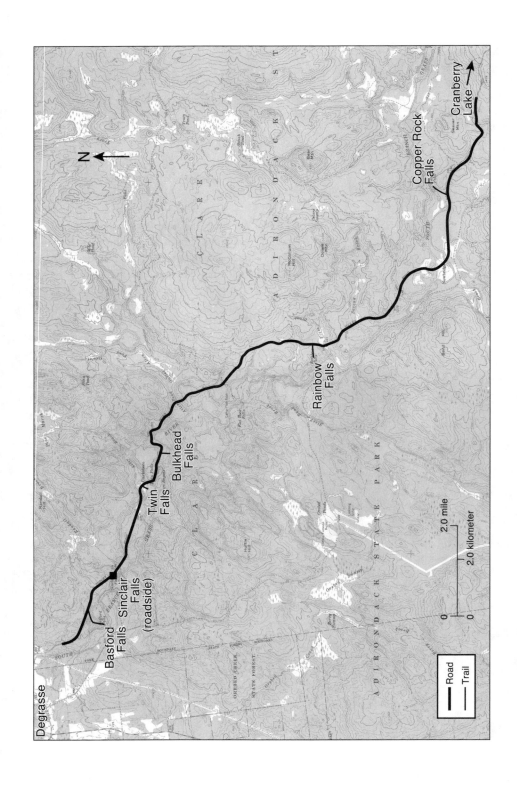

The Grass River Wild Forest is distant from all major population centers, so you will likely spend more time driving than hiking on this outing. The southeast end of Tooley Pond Road, the main entry point to the area, is not far from the state campground at Cranberry Lake, and this would be an excellent way to spend a day if you are staying at that facility. Although none of the seven walks described below are very long, the magnificent beauty of the falls and the sheer number of them will lead you to spend the better part of a day here.

How to Get There

This driving tour of the Grass River Wild Forest will take you down the entire length of Tooley Pond Road, then north on Clare Road to reach the final site, Lampsons Falls. The southeastern end of Tooley Pond Road is on the north side of NY 3, just east of the highway bridge over the Oswegatchie River at the foot of Cranberry Lake. Set your trip odometer to 0.0 at the intersection.

The Trail

For the first 5.8 miles Tooley Pond Road is an unassuming rural road passing a number of summer homes and hunting camps. Most of the road is paved, but one middle section leading up to Tooley Pond is not. At 5.8 miles you enter the Forest Preserve, and immediately on the left is Tooley Pond. There is a picnic area at the edge of the pond, and to the right is a parking area with a privy. Just a short distance beyond is the start of a marked loop trail to the summit of Tooley Pond Mountain. You pass the other end of the loop at 6.3 miles. The total length of the loop, including a 0.4-mile walk along the road between trailheads, is only 1.8 miles, but the view from the summit is subtle and is best enjoyed at the height of the fall leaf-viewing season.

The road begins a gentle descent, reaching the bottom at 8.1 miles. Look for a Forest Preserve marker, a sign explaining fishing regulations, and a red paint daub all in one place to the right of the road. This is the start of your first walk of the day: the herd path to Copper Rock Falls.

The path, marked with additional paint blazes, is narrow, a tad wet, and only 750 feet long. It leads directly to the base of the falls, where the river slips over gently sloping bedrock. The path quickly fades away, but you can easily walk up beside the rapids to the top. In times of low water, you can go out on the rocks.

There is a steeper waterfall at the top, on the other side of a small island in the river and partially hidden from the path. In high water, when you cannot step out onto the river rocks, you might only be able to catch a glimpse of that cascade.

Return back to your car and continue driving northwest along the road. Just 0.8 mile beyond Copper Rock Falls you cross the bridge over the South Branch. Maps still refer to this area as the settlement of Newbridge, even though not one building remains. In 1906 the Higbie Lumber Company, which owned this land at the time, established their company town here. The only modern facilities are the bridge and a small parking area.

At 10.6 miles you pass a marked canoe carry to the left, leading back to the river. This is the takeout point for canoeists paddling down the river. Just 0.2 mile beyond, also on the left side of the road, look for a large clearing barricaded with rocks. This site is the start of the path to Rainbow Falls, the most thunderous cascade on the South Branch.

Cross the clearing and look for the orange paint blazes marking the path. It follows an old logging road through an open forest to a smaller clearing near the river. At the far side, the path plunges into denser woods where there is a good footbridge over a side channel of the river. A moment later you emerge on a wet precipice near the top of the falls.

Rainbow Falls sends large amounts of spray into the air, coating the precipice and the walls of the gorge with moisture. There is a ledge about 80 feet downstream that makes a great place for a picnic, although even there the spray may reach you. No doubt it is the spray that gives Rainbow Falls its name: on a sunny day, a rainbow will most likely appear as the light strikes the airborne moisture.

The next waterfall can be found at 13.3 miles along Tooley Pond Road, immediately after the road passes a wide bend in the river. Look for an old tote road to the left, near a NO MOTORIZED VEHICLES sign. This route will lead you in about 600 feet to a large pool at the foot of Bulkhead Falls.

Much smaller and less dramatic than Rainbow Falls, Bulkhead marks an 8-foot drop in the river. The current is funneled through a V-shaped cut in the rocks, and it is very scenic in high water. The pool seems to be an attraction for fishermen. Pink lady's slipper grows here in mid-spring.

At 13.5 miles you have views from the road of Stewart Rapids, where you will often see people angling for trout. At 13.7 miles you reach another dramatic roadside site: Twin Falls. There is room to park on the shoulder and enjoy the northern of the two waterfalls.

Like Newbridge, another 19th-century settlement has long since vanished from existence here. Clarksboro was centered around a sawmill and an iron-mining operation. The channel above the waterfall, as you can see, is lined with manmade rock walls, and no doubt the river's energy was har-

nessed here to drive the millworks. Across the channel on the island are the remains of an old brick iron furnace.

There is no footbridge across the fast-moving channel to the island, so there is no easy way to get to the furnace or the larger waterfall on the main channel. By driving down the road for another 0.1 mile you reach a gravel drive on the left leading to a campsite near the river. This is the best place from which to view both of the cascades at once, across the large pool below the falls.

The next waterfall is also within view of a road. At 14.7 miles Tooley Pond Road meets Lake George Road. The DEC maintains a large parking area at the intersection. Lake George Road crosses the South Branch within sight of the intersection, and immediately downstream is Sinclair Falls. This is a 20-foot, crooked cascade over slanted rocks, with a hairpin bend in the river immediately at the base. A faint herd path leads down beside the falls if you want a closer look.

Basford Falls is the most secluded of all the South Branch waterfalls, and the path leading to it is the hardest to follow. At 15.3 miles, look for a rock barricade off to the left at the entrance of an old tote road. Parking on the shoulder, follow the fading road through fern-filled woods for 0.4 mile to a knoll within earshot of the river. The sound of the falls will lead you to them, but note how you go so that you may find your way back.

Basford Falls is a very scenic 18-foot drop on the river. Open rocks near the top invite you to stay for a while. There is a house across the river, but it is screened by trees and does not interfere with the view of the falls. This has to be one of the most beautiful sites you will visit on the Grass River, for the open rocks allow you to get

Rainbow Falls

close-up views at any time of the year–but do be mindful of the danger of slipping if those rocks are wet.

Tooley Pond Road ends at 16.7 miles near the hamlet of Degrasse, which lies just outside the Adirondack Park. For the final walk of the day, turn right onto Clare Road and follow it for 4.1 miles north to a sign to the left marking the trailhead for Lampsons Falls.

It is a short, 10-minute walk along the well-worn hiking trail to Lampsons Falls, 0.5 mile from the road. Here, the Main Branch of the Grass River slides down a 30-foot smooth and spectacularly broad rock ledge. Below the falls, the trail leads through a marshy hemlock grove and beside a bog and alder meadow before continuing north, close to the river's east bank. At 0.8 mile, near an island, there used to be a bridge that crossed the river to the west bank. The bridge has washed out, and unless it is re-placed this may be as far as you can go downstream on a marked trail. A herd path continuing north along the east bank only proceeds a limited distance before encountering rough terrain.

If you can cross the river, you will find a red trail that heads back south along the west bank for almost a mile to a pine-covered promontory above Lampsons Falls. This spot, with its different perspective of the falls, is a good place for a picnic.

Return to the bridge and continue north on the west bank, now following yellow canoe carry markers. The trail climbs around a marshy area, then descends to a small stillwater that ends in a flume. A second, deeper flume follows almost immediately. Another stretch of quiet water ends at an island that splits the river. West of the island, the river tumbles over rocks and through rapids, while the east side is forced into another narrow flume.

Grass River Waterfalls

Lampsons Falls

This pattern of rocky cascades and deep pools continues. After one deep canyon, the river grows wider with pools and eddies following. A second rock island splits the river, which is turbulent below.

Below one waterfall, the trail enters a reforestation area. The next waterfall leads to a split in the river with the near flow plunging into a deep canyon. Just beyond, nearly 0.8 mile from the bridge, the river becomes more placid. As the excitement ends, turn around and retrace your steps south to cross the river and return to the trailhead.

21

Jenkins Mountain

Distance (round-trip): 8.2 miles

Vertical rise: 780 feet

Time: 5–6 hours

Map: USGS Metric Saint Regis Mountain

Jenkins Mountain is a many-faceted experiment, and a very successful one at that. It is an experiment in building a trail that will not erode, in creating an experience that takes hikers on a circuitous route with many different things to see on the way, and in limiting the number of hikers on the trail to provide the kind of wilderness experience that is so often missing from treks in the more crowded High Peaks. As a result, you have to have a reservation to climb the mountain–30 are issued each day. Some reservations are given in advance; some are available from the Visitors Interpretive Center (VIC) without advance notice. All you have to do to reserve space is call the VIC at 518-377-3000 between 9 AM and 4 PM.

Jenkins is a small mountain that packs a mighty view. Even more exciting for hikers than the view is the remarkably well-designed and varied trail leading to the summit. The trail has everything good trails should have: history, varied terrain, and easy grades. The trail does not head directly toward the summit, but winds about in many different directions, all designed to enhance the walk.

The north and west sides of the mountain burned in the railroad-caused fires of 1903. A fire in 1912 burned the east slopes down to Long and Black Ponds. Thus, almost all the forest you will see is relatively young.

How to Get There

The trail begins from the Adirondack Park Visitors Interpretive Center at Paul Smiths,

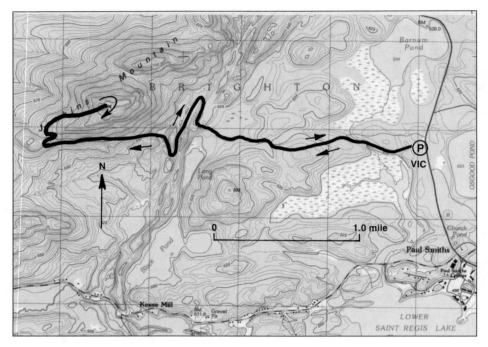

0.8 mile north of Paul Smith's College on NY 30.

The Trail

The route begins along the VIC's Barnum Brook Trail. Follow the blue markers on the north loop of that trail until you reach the bridge over Barnum Brook. Crossing the bridge, follow the blazes right, onto an old woods road that leads toward Jenkins Mountain. Turn west and follow the roadway through nice woods, passing several marked intersections. Markers denote the distance covered every half mile. After 0.5 mile there is a rise through a good hardwood forest, at 1 mile there is a lovely hemlock knoll, at 1.5 miles a balsam wetlands. The road is now heading northwest, and shortly beyond, at a corner where there is an outhouse, the road bends sharply south.

Now begins the best part of the trail, which narrows and winds along the top of a series of eskers, with ferny meadows, stagnant ponds, and one huge beaver meadow below the steep slopes. Over the beaver pond you have a lovely view north to rock slopes of Jenkins's eastern summit. At 2 miles you reach a bridge over the outlet of the beaver pond. The walk along the eskers continues for nearly another half mile. Where the trail makes a hairpin turn back northwest, look through the trees to Long Pond way below the slopes. Notice the tops of the eskers—bracken ferns tell you how dry and disturbed they are.

At 2.5 miles the trail begins a long traverse up Jenkins's steep southern slopes through one of the more unusual forests that you will ever find. The lovely traverse, with some ups and downs, is so gentle you hardly know you are climbing, but the mountainside is so steep that you have wonderful views up to rock ledges, down to a broad valley, and out through the thin forest. Notice how tall, straight, yet small in diameter are the trees that grace the slopes. Notice how the canopy is barely closed so light reaches the forest floor and dries it out. The understory is sparse, not rich as you would find in an unburnt stand. In one place there is a stand of paper birch—sure signs of fire—but most of the trees are maples. Notice how the fields of hay-scented ferns have few young trees—scientists have found that this fern actually inhibits the germination of some tree species.

You pass the 3-mile marker on the traverse. Just short of 3.5 miles, the trail makes a sharp turn to the right and climbs more steeply to a turn back west. At 3.5 miles you are in a small valley between rock outcrops, west of the western summit. The trail crosses to the north side of the mountain. Gradually, the trail curves east to head up the northwest slopes, briefly crossing the one wet meadow on the trail, which is filled with equisetums and jewelweed. As the slopes become steeper, the trail zigzags to keep the grades gentle, thus preventing erosion. Just below the western summit, the trail zags back left, west to the rock knob that tops the far western edge.

From the knob you can see Follensby Jr. Pond to the north, Saint Regis Mountain just south of west, Tupper Lake, and the High Peaks from the Sewards around to Whiteface. The return trip, retracing your steps, takes little more than two hours, but pause frequently to discover what you may have missed on the hike up.

22

Saint Regis Mountain

Distance (round-trip): 6 miles

Vertical rise: 1,235 feet

Hiking time: 3½–4 hours

Map: USGS Metric Saint Regis Mountain

Fire tower

How to Get There

If you drive north from Tupper Lake on NY 30, passing Upper Saranac Lake, you will see the entrances to the Fish Creek Ponds and Rollins Ponds State Campgrounds. Both offer great waterfront camping and access. State maps of the Wilderness Canoe Trail are available from the DEC or campsite headquarters. As you continue on NY 30 past Lake Clear, look for Saint Regis Mountain to the northwest.

At Lake Clear Junction, where NY 86 continues northeast, you turn north, staying on NY 30. When you reach the town of Paul Smiths, home of the college of the same name, 7.3 miles beyond Lake Clear Junction, turn left onto Keese Mill Road. Follow the road west for 2.5 miles to the trailhead parking area.

A narrow gravel road also starts here. It is the access road to the Topridge Estate, which was once owned by Margaret Meriweather Post. She bequeathed the entire property to the state, but in a controversial move the state sold the buildings and a small piece of land to a private individual. The bulk of the tract is now Forest Preserve.

The Trail

Saint Regis is not difficult to climb. You should allow at least four hours for the round trip, although you may meet forestry students from Paul Smith's College who regularly run up the mountain in under an hour, starting from the school's grounds. The trail has been a laboratory for classes

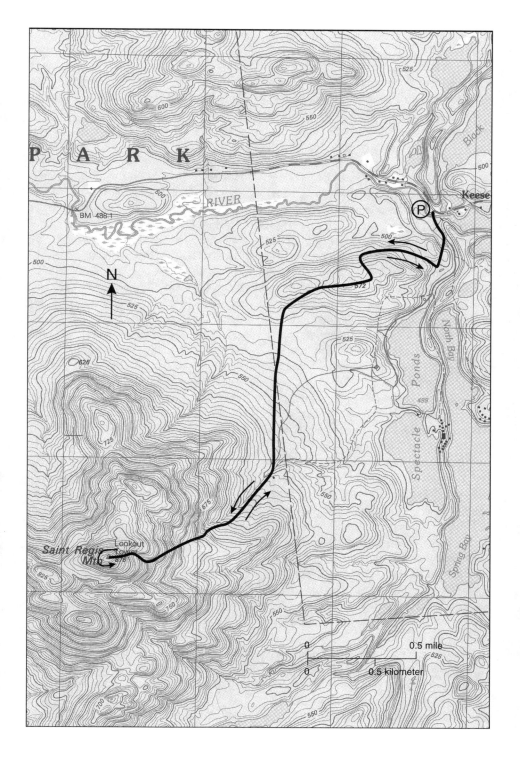

in trail work, and you will appreciate the results as you climb.

The trail, marked with red markers, begins 460 feet along the gravel drive, which is closed to public motorized use. An enormous tamarack tree towers 100 feet above the trailhead register. A bridge carries you across a small swamp, then the trail angles south. There is a short uphill grade followed by a short descent past a small meadow. Then you ascend again through a slight draw and head west along the foot of a steep hill.

At 0.6 mile, about 15 minutes from the start, the trail hooks sharp left and climbs the hill. You follow the ridgeline for some distance, passing through groves of shady hemlocks. The trail slowly descends off the south side of the ridge, and then turns almost due south. For the next mile the trail is notably straight, with a slight ascent as you walk through mixed hardwoods toward the foot of the mountain.

At 2 miles, or just over an hour from your car, you reach a footbridge over a small stream. An older, abandoned trail comes in on the left just before the bridge, and just across the stream a side trail forks left to a small meadow. This was where the observer's cabin stood, from the days when the old fire tower on the summit was manned.

The trail continues alongside the little brook and then turns away. You start to climb in stages at first, sometimes on rock steps built into the hillside. About 20 minutes from the footbridge the timber becomes much smaller, indicating where the fire of 1876 swept the upper slopes of the mountain. Much of the summit is bare to this day.

Rock walls edge the trail to the left, and at times you find yourself walking around fragments that have broken off. The rock is Marcy anorthosite, identifiable by the large, dark-bluish labradorite crystals embedded in it. After 30 minutes of steep climbing, you pass an opening to the right with the first of the views. A minute later you emerge above treeline at the 2,873-foot summit. A total climbing time of 1 hour and 45 minutes reflects a fairly brisk pace.

The summit is so exposed that there is nearly a full 360-degree view without the fire tower. The mountain seems to stand alone, with broad plains below stretching in almost every direction. Saint Regis is a solitary cone in a huge dish of ponds and lakes, edged with mountains on the horizon. Those to the northwest are low, the foothills of the Adirondacks, but from the north the sweep encompasses the rugged range that includes Whiteface, McKenzie Mountain, and the High Peaks through Seward in the south. The High Peaks southeast across Lake Clear are often shrouded in clouds even on a clear day. Saint Regis Pond lies almost due south, with Little Clear Pond to its southeast and Upper Saranac Lake stretching to the distant south. Long Pond is visible a little west of south, with Tupper Lake beyond on the distant horizon (look for the water towers). Fish, Lydia, and Little Fish Ponds, on the Wilderness Canoe Trail, spread out at the foot of the mountain.

To the northwest, the distant mountain with the impressive cliffs is Azure Mountain, with a whole range of knobby little mounds stretching to the west. Jenkins Mountain is to the east of north. Follensby Junior Pond is in the middle distance, and Meacham Lake is on the horizon, with Debar Mountain rising beside it.

Southeast of Upper Saranac Lake, Ampersand Mountain stands in front of Seward and Santanoni, so overwhelmed by those higher peaks that identifying it can be difficult. MacIntyre and Marcy are obvious, with the cone of Colden between them. To the left, north of Marcy, peaks hiked on the Range Trail can be identified, as well as, farther north, Cascade and the Sentinel Range leading around to McKenzie and Moose, which appear from this angle as one long mountain range. Whiteface is just south of east.

The northeastern view is the one most blocked by trees, but enough is visible that you can see a patchwork of lakes and fields, some of them the potato fields for which the northern plains are famous. Both the Post estate and Paul Smith's College are visible on the lakes below. Sand flats and glacial ridges stretch to the northeastern horizon.

Even if you carry only the USGS Saint Regis quadrangle, you can probably name at least two dozen lakes and ponds in view. However, the pleasure of the climb will be enhanced if you also carry the Tupper Lake, Long Lake, Santanoni, Mount Marcy, Saranac Lake, and Lake Placid quadrangles, for most of the area they cover is visible from the summit.

Return the way you came. You will not have much trouble making the trip back in 90 minutes.

23

Debar Mountain

Distance (round-trip): 7 miles

Vertical rise: 1,600 feet

Hiking time: 6 hours

Maps: USGS 7.5' Meacham Lake; USGS 7.5' Debar Mountain

Debar Mountain is the Adirondacks' northern sentinel, offering sweeping views across its dramatic northwestern slopes to the St. Lawrence Valley and neighboring Canada. Rock outcrops covering the mountain's small summit offer views that adequately compensate for those lost when the fire tower on Debar's peak was closed. Stunted spruce frame the cliffs that drop to steep wooded slopes and finally to the broad plain below, plunging more than 1,600 feet in less than a mile.

The entire climb is through a magnificent forest that is as special as the views from the summit. The approach is from the southwest, gentle at first, then steadily uphill, and finally an 800-foot mad scramble up the last 0.5 mile, the steepest and most arduous climb of all New York's fire tower trails.

The trail to Debar begins from the Meacham Lake State Campground, a good place to camp before you climb. There, picnic and camping areas surround part of the 2-mile-long lake, whose cool waters washing sandy beaches will welcome you to a refreshing swim after your climb.

How to Get There

The campground, which is about 18 miles south of Malone on NY 30, is far enough north that signs are in both English and French to accommodate visitors from Canada. To reach it from the south, also use NY 30. You will pass Paul Smith's College and the Adirondack Visitors Interpretive Center. On the way north toward the campground, you drive through level sand plains

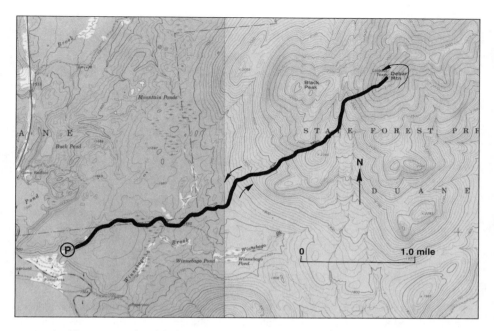

covered with spruce, pine, birch, tamarack, and aspen typical of the forests in the northern Adirondacks. You will see a sign for McCollums 6.3 miles north of Paul Smith's College. It is the site of an old settlement; today the number of tombstones in the cemetery far exceeds the remaining buildings. A historic marker beside the road bears the legend that in October 1908 Debar Mountain and the surrounding land were burned in the wave of forest fires that struck the Adirondacks that year. The local fire consumed over 6000 acres.

The sign for the southern access to the Meacham Lake State Campground is 9.5 miles north of Paul Smith's College. Meacham Road angles right, east, paralleling the lake. A northern access is 2.3 miles farther along NY 30 near Clear Pond. The roads unite northwest of Meacham Lake and continue 0.2 mile southwest to the main gate for the campground. A day-use fee is charged. Ask the gatekeeper for a campsite map—along with instructions, because the

trailhead to Debar is not shown on the map, and signs for it are missing.

The Trail

To find the trail from the campground, look for a dirt road just west of campsite #48. Take it, and turn right at the first intersection in 0.1 mile. In 0.4 mile you reach a sand pit, where you park. The trail commences along the gated dirt fire road heading east toward Debar. (If you start your walk from the campground, this trailhead is 1 mile from the main entrance.)

Walking the soft sand of the fire road is almost like walking on a beach, except that the road is shaded by a tall spruce forest. Beside the road, carpets of Canada mayflowers are punctuated by starflowers, goldthread, wild strawberries, false Solomon's seal, and acres of hay-scented fern. As the forest begins a transition to mature hardwoods, you will spot on a huge maple beside the trail the first of the very few red markers that are supposed to delineate the route. Beneath the hardwoods, sarsaparilla and blackberries edge the road.

After you have been walking about 20 minutes, a glacial ridge appears on your right and a spruce bog opens on your left. The bog should be the first of the detours you take to enrich the trip. A true sphagnum bog, it contains most of the typical flowers: The predominant shrub is Labrador tea, which blooms here about the second week in June. Bunchberry in profusion, cinnamon and interrupted ferns, blueberries, and clintonia continue the great carpet of flowers beneath the tall trees.

Unless you spend some time enjoying the bog, it should take you less than a half hour to walk the first mile to a bridge over a tributary of Winnebago Brook. A barely perceptible woods road heads left from the fire road in the meadow near the brook. Continue on the more obvious road (you will find few markers, but you really do not need them) for 200 yards to a marked fork. Here a sign directs you to turn left and continue on a wide woods road that begins the upward trip so gently that you really do not sense you are climbing.

The first perceptible rise begins shortly in a forest of tall, straight hardwoods that cover a lovely woods floor where *Dryopteris* ferns, mostly the evergreen wood fern, are interspersed with doll's eyes, lady's slipper, crinkleroot, and jack-in-the-pulpit.

As some boulders appear beside the route and rocks pop through the roadway, you will realize how few stones there were in the glacial sand at the trail's beginning. For 45 minutes you follow the road through a forest in which maples become more dominant. Huge boulders edge the route, and a steep hill begins to appear on your right. You will cross several log bridges over a small stream before you reach a height-of-land 1.5 miles from the marked fork. The

roadway descends slightly, and a steep valley becomes visible on your right. You will contour around to the head of that valley, which lies between Black Mountain and the peak of Debar Mountain.

As you begin to climb again, ledges are visible on your left, and you reach a lean-to with a fireplace. Beyond, the trees are shorter and noticeably more dense as the road climbs into a small meadow containing the remains of the fire observer's cabin. The state burned the cabin when it closed the tower, leaving a mess of stone and concrete. As you enter the meadow, the summit of Debar looms ahead of you. Cross the meadow and enter the woods to the left of the stone foundations. The trail is not just a narrow footpath.

The final 0.5 mile makes the first 3 seem dull. Suddenly the route seems to be straight up through a stunted forest. The white of paper birch contrasts with the dark tones of spruce. The mountainside is so steep that stone steps have been built into it. Within 100 yards, a stream crosses the trail. For a time it seems as if the trail is through the stream. Rock stairs lead past boulders glistening with outcrops of garnet. Deadfalls block the narrow trail, and the downed telephone wire leading to the fire tower could trip you. You have to use your hands to pull yourself up some of the small ledges, but don't climb so intently that you fail to stop and look back when the forest opens. A fine view of Meacham Lake and the mountains to its south and east appears through the trees. You can trace your route on the ridge you crossed during the lower part of the ascent, and you will be impressed by the steepness of the knob you are climbing.

The trail levels out in a deep, ferny glen below a moss-covered ledge marking the last short climb. After you cross the last ledge and a short wet level, the sheer rock face of the tiny knob (elevation: 3,320 feet) on which the tower sits seems to block your way. Walk right around the knob to climb it from the north. Fantastic views greet you as you emerge from the forest. Most exciting is the sweep along the mountain's steep-angled northwest face. Only a few more hills break the plain below as it faces into the distance across the St. Lawrence River into Canada. To the southwest you can see Meacham Lake, and in the west a series of small hills barely define the horizon. The view northeast is blocked by a row of small knobs that are a part of Debar itself. The view is less than it was years ago from the tower, but enough openings remain to compensate for the tower's removal.

There are no other rock outcrops with views, but if you walk around the summit your hollow footsteps will tell you that you are walking across exfoliated sheaves, rock slabs that have been broken off by the expansion of ice in cracks in the rock. There is a very small camping spot northeast of the tower. If you climb in June you will also enjoy the bloom of huge clumps of painted trillium brightening the mountain *Dryopteris* that covers the wooded parts of the summit with a lush soft background green.

Going down, you find that the mountain is so steep near the summit that it requires almost as much time to descend as it did to climb up. Be careful on the stairs and rocks. When you reach the height-of-land between the cabin and the marked fork, pause for a moment to enjoy the magnificent forest around you. Notice how many of the yellow birch seem to be growing from boulders. One beside the trail is perched upon a stone with its roots crossed. It so resembles the caterpillar from *Alice in Wonderland* with his legs crossed upon a giant toadstool that I almost expected it to ask, "Who are *you*?"

24

Catamount Mountain

Distance (round-trip): 3.8 miles

Vertical rise: 1,568 feet

Hiking time: 4 hours

Map: USGS Metric Wilmington

If you like to scramble over ledges and boulders, inch along cracks and crevices on steep rock walls, and do a little nontechnical rock climbing, then Catamount is for you. This mountain, one of several with the same name, lies in the northeastern Adirondacks. The climb is great fun, but it will probably take no more than a half day, allowing you time to explore some of the area's attractions on the way to the trailhead.

Driving north from Lake Placid on NY 86, your route is along the West Branch of the AuSable River, past High Falls Gorge, a private scenic attraction for which a fee is charged. Next north is the Wilmington Notch State Campground and Day Use Center, in a very handsome spot near the river. Here there is trout fishing and the best campsites for activities in this area. Beyond Whiteface Ski Center you can stop and walk beside the flume on the AuSable, a wild falls in a deep gorge within sight of the highway. You eventually reach a crossroads where NY 86 turns right toward Wilmington and NY 431 goes left for 2.8 miles to the entrance of the Whiteface Mountain Memorial Highway, a toll road climbing nearly to the summit of Whiteface. That summit, at 4,867 feet, offers some of the Adirondacks' best scenery, but you can get there by car, so for a trek on foot continue straight ahead at the crossroads in Wilmington, onto County Road 19 (unmarked) north toward Catamount.

How to Get There

You will reach a T at the road connecting Black Brook and Hawkeye Road. Turn left, northwest, for 1.6 miles, then turn left again. In about a mile, a third left puts you on Forestdale Road headed southwest. A narrow trail heads right 4.7 miles from the Black Brook–Hawkeye Road intersection. The spot is easy to miss. If you are uncertain, continue for 1.25 miles to the Wilford LaHart Farm and turn around to find the trailhead from the west.

The Trail

The LaHart property borders the trail to the west, and members of that family laid out the very handsome and well-designed route on Catamount. The trail, a narrow footpath, follows an old road that is filling in with small balsams. The path is informal and not marked by the state. You should not let the overgrown condition of the first 0.25 mile deter you. The deadfalls and confusion last only a few minutes, for after 0.25 mile you come to an orange-painted pipe and cairn indicating the corner of the property. Turn left and follow the property line for 0.3 mile toward magnetic north. The straight line is marked with orange blazes and is easy to follow.

Hiking here through an old field, you are on one of the most beautiful and unusual stretches of trail you will encounter. Fires in the northern Adirondacks consumed acres of forestland. The burn on Catamount created a wonderful open-rock summit, but the fires in the valley exposed the sterile, sandy soil, which is only now becoming reforested. Here the ground is covered in a pastel mosaic of soft limey greens, blues, and lavenders, the lacy growth of lichens turning the ground into a fairyland of tinted hoarfrost and sugar icings. Meadowsweet, hardhack, and blueberry shrubs make a colorful middle range.

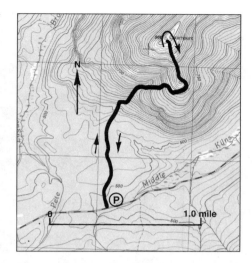

Pine and balsam grow in isolated clumps with the pure white of birch bark for accent.

You can see the mountain ahead as you cross the field. Near the end where you start down a slight grade, a fairly obvious and well-worn footpath angles to the right and heads into the forest. There are few markings, only some rusted tin can lids and an occasional blue plastic ribbon. The path rises quickly into a lovely birch forest and then angles right and levels off as it crosses a small ridge. Within 15 minutes you descend into a slight draw with an intermittent stream. After crossing the streambed at right angles, you head up another incline and cross back to your left.

The footpath becomes less clear as it rounds several large boulders, still rising steeply on bedrock. A sharp angle left below an outcrop is indicated by a white blaze on a tree at a confusing turn where some hikers have obviously gone straight ahead. After rounding the ledge, the trail rises sharply, to emerge on the first of the bare rock patches of the summit. Cairns indicate the way across each patch as the path weaves generally to the east between them and thickets of spruce and balsam.

On the Catamount Trail

The route turns north toward the summit as you walk across the outcrop. You are facing the sheer rock face of the southern summit, with the principal summit behind and to your left. It is an impressive sight, with the height and steepness of the peak exaggerated by the small size of the trees on the outcrop.

The path heads right to climb the lower summit from the east, first ducking into a thicket of large spruce and then emerging at the foot of the rock knob. It only takes a minute to rise above tree line on the knob, which is almost entirely bare except for patches of luscious blueberries. White arrows guide you across the bare rock in a scramble that leads to a southeast-facing chimney. Pull yourself through. Cairns direct you to turn right and back left to follow a crevice up the steep, smooth face toward the first summit (approximately 2,750 feet in elevation).

The principal summit is 0.4 mile away and 400 feet higher, almost due north across a small valley. The scramble over big boulders down into the col is not easy. Large spruce mark the low point, then the trail rises through a wooded slope to emerge again on open rock. Painted arrows and cairns guide you along a route, which zigzags through patches of woods and over sloping bare rock. It should take less than a half hour to reach the summit.

Your initial impression is how small the first summit looks. Beyond it to the right is the sharp cone of Esther, with the summit of Whiteface behind. To the west are Franklin Falls and Union Falls Ponds, expansions in the Saranac River; and in the northwest, Cranberry Pond and Silver Lake. Lyon Mountain is almost due north. The Champlain Valley stretches across the eastern landscape.

To spot the row of cairns for the descent, sight from the summit to the left of the lower summit, and retrace your steps.

25

Pokamoonshine Mountain

Distance (round-trip): 2 miles

Vertical rise: 1,260 feet

Hiking time: 2½ hours

Map: USGS Metric AuSable Forks

Fire tower

The nearly 1,000-foot-high cliff on Poka-moonshine Mountain seems to hang above the Adirondack Northway (I-87) south of exit 33. Rock climbers look very tiny as they challenge the heights of the Adirondacks' "most awe-inspiring cliff." This is the way Bradford Van Diver describes the mountain in *Rocks and Routes of the North Country, New York.* Before you climb Pokamoonshine, you should consult Van Diver's book to learn about the mountain's geological history and the thick, dark bands of intrusions, which etch the fault escarpment.

This is a mountain you will appreciate from below as much as from the summit. The best views of the cliff are from the Northway or from NY 9. Because the trail circles behind it to reach the summit, the major cliff is hidden from view from the trail; however, the tower on top does provide a spectacular panorama of Lake Champlain and the Green Mountains beyond in Vermont.

Seventy years ago, when Walter O'Kane wrote his book *Trails and Summits of the Adirondacks,* he remarked on the unusual display of ferns beside the trail. Today keen observers will be amazed at the variety of ferns that still edge the route. I counted 20 species, ranging from maidenhair and silvery spleenwort to fragile fern and rusty woodsia. With ferns, views, and cliffs to enjoy, Pokamoonshine is a much more exciting climb than its short trail and low elevation would indicate.

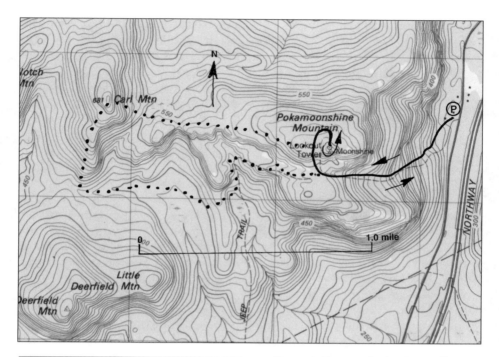

How to Get There

The trailhead is in the Pok-O-Moonshine State Park (the state uses a spelling different from that of the USGS), 3 miles south on NY 9 from exit 33 on the Adirondack Northway. There is a day-use fee at the park. The trail begins its steep climb within 100 yards of the southern end of the campground.

The Trail

The narrow, rooted, and worn trail is marked with very few old red disks, but so many hikers have preceded you that the way is obvious. Tremendous boulders and the ends of ledges rise above the trail. You angle right in a small draw, aiming at a sheer wall, and then turn left below an overhang. The route is fairly steep beneath the cliffs and moss-covered ledges. As the trail turns right along the ridge at about 0.3 mile, look for a side path that heads to a lovely overlook.

Beyond the overlook, the trail turns right, north, toward the mountain and, after a relatively level 0.2 mile in deep woods, becomes steep again. This pitch is fairly short and leads to a level meadow and the site of the fire observer's cabin. An abandoned road heads west in front of the cabin, and there is a lean-to beside it within sight of the trail.

A footpath to the cabin's right leads to a spring on the side of the hill and continues steeply to a chimneylike opening with natural stairs between its walls. Follow it up to a level outcrop and overlook to the east. The path rejoins the red trail about 50 feet farther along.

You might not have even noticed the official red trail, which headed away from the clearing about halfway between the cabin and the more obvious footpath. It leads, after rising 50 feet in elevation, to a lovely outlook through the valley to the northwest.

Then it continues west to climb the summit ridge by a gentler and slightly longer route, meeting the footpath.

Beyond the junction, the trail continues in the woods for 200 yards beside some irresistible blueberries and turns right to approach the tower from the west.

You can appreciate the view east without climbing the tower. From open ledges Lake Champlain stretches from north to south, wrapping around intervening hills, with the Green Mountains defining the eastern horizon. In the southwest and 1.4 miles away is the summit of Deerfield Mountain, which is almost as tall as 2,160-foot Pokamoonshine. Beyond Deerfield is the Jay Range. The fire tower on Hurricane is visible to the left of Jay Range and serves as a guidepost for identifying Nippletop, Giant, and Rocky Peak Ridge, which range to Hurricane's left.

Sighting to the north of Deerfield, you can identify the Sentinel Range, followed by Whiteface, which is due west. Continuing north, the Wilmington Range, the top of Catamount, and Loon Mountain with its fire tower line the horizon. Lyon Mountain, also topped by a tower, is toward magnetic north, 28 miles away.

Rattlesnake Mountain is east of Cata-mount on the shore of Lake Champlain. Sight toward Lake Champlain, just to the left of Rattlesnake's summit, and you will see the Four Brothers Islands, with Willsboro Point reaching north into the lake in the foreground. In the southeast the water of Lake Champlain is interrupted by the cone of Split Rock Mountain. These two mountains should serve to orient the rest of the vast eastern landscape.

Instead of bringing the USGS maps to help you identify the remaining mountains, lakes, bays, and points on Lake Champlain, you might want to use the *New York State Atlas and Gazetteer* or a map of Vermont.

➤ Poka-what?

Settling the spelling of Pokamoonshine seems as unlikely as determining its meaning. No one will probably ever know whether the mountain's peculiar name derives from the will-o'-the-wisp character of its cliffs and crags or from the Algonquin words for "broken" and "smooth," as proposed by William M. Beauchamp in his 1907 treatise, Aboriginal Place Names of New York.

26

Treadway Mountain

Distance (round-trip): 8 miles

Vertical rise: 1,026 feet

Hiking time: 5 hours

Maps: USGS 7.5' Graphite

Pharaoh Lake Wilderness Area

The entire Pharaoh Lake Wilderness is studded with hills and mountains topped by open rock, cliffs, and ledges. Most were laid bare by fires that swept the region in the first decades of the 20th century. Treadway Mountain is perhaps the most dramatic of those open summits. There, the fires burned away the thin soil cover to reveal large patches of quartz, with views from the summit spreading out in almost every direction. The vistas encompassing the many mountains and ponds, and of Pharaoh Lake in particular, are spectacular, as are the views of more distant peaks. The eastern High Peaks are only 30 miles to the north-northwest.

How to Get There

The start of the trail is at the Putnam Pond Campground, at the eastern edge of the Pharaoh Lake Wilderness Area. The campground makes a logical base from which to stage your day hikes in the area. To reach the campground, drive east on NY 74 from Adirondack Northway (I-87) exit 28 for 12.9 miles. Here, at Chilson, turn right onto Putts Pond Road. (Putts Pond is the local name for Putnam Pond.) In 3.8 miles you reach the entrance booth to the campground, where a fee may be charged in the summer. The trailhead parking area is another 0.4 mile beyond. The trail begins at the east end of the lot, just before the boat launch.

The Trail

The first part of the trip to Treadway Mountain follows a yellow-marked trail that passes around the south end of Putnam Pond, con-

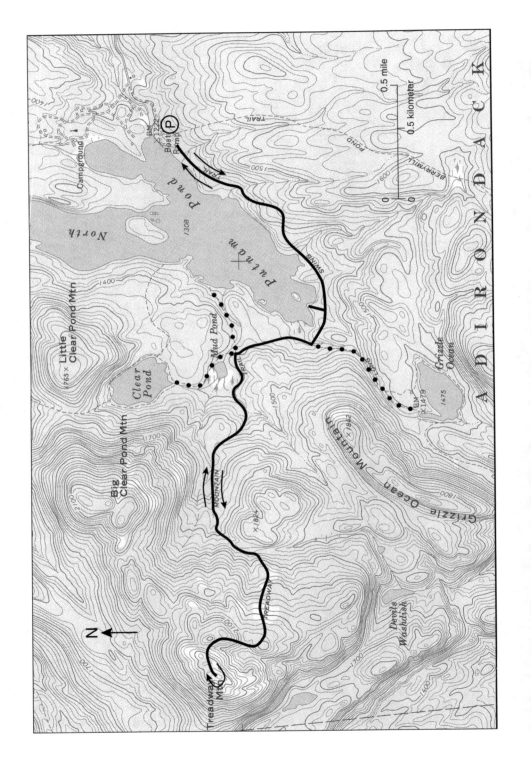

North Putnam Pond

Campground

Little Clear Pond Mtn

×1765

Big Clear Pond Mtn

Clear Pond

Mud Pond

1700

2000

2100

2200

N

Treadway Mtn

TREADWAY

MOUNTAIN

×1824

TRAIL

500

1400

BM
×1479

1475

Grizzle Ocean

Grizzle Ocean Mountain

×1842

1700

1800

Devils Washdish

BERRYMILL

POND

TRAIL

1600

1500

SWING

TRAIL

Boat
Ramp

P

BM
×1222

1308

1400

0.5 mile

0.5 kilometer

0

necting with the Pharaoh Ponds Loop (Hike 27). This section is also the alternate point of access to that loop.

The trail starts by passing through a level hardwood forest, passing the register and then a small bridge in the first two minutes. You start to climb over a hemlock knoll, and just over 15 minutes into your hike you reach a high point in the trail, with a steep, rocky hillside to your left. The trail then makes a long, gradual descent to a log bridge over the outlet of Berrymill Pond, which flows sinuously through a deep ravine. The lively brook and the dark forest cover are worth a brief pause.

So far, the trail has kept far enough away from the pond that there have been no views of it. You round a marshy bay, which constitutes the only view so far, and then cross a second log bridge five minutes after the first. You reach a third bridge in another five minutes. Here, a side trail leads right for 200 yards to a scenic point at the southernmost tip of Putnam Pond, with an island just off shore. This is the waterway access to the trail to Grizzle Ocean, and it is also the best view of Putnam Pond that the trail will offer.

The main trail rises steeply over a rocky little knoll and drops just as steeply down the other side to a fourth log bridge, this one over the outlet of Grizzle Ocean. Immediately beyond the bridge is a trail junction, 1.3 miles from your car. The yellow trail turns left to Grizzle Ocean, but for Treadway you need to turn right onto the blue-marked trail. You will follow this trail for 0.5 mile and 15 minutes to a junction with the red-marked trail to Treadway.

At that junction, 1.8 miles into your hike, turn left onto the red trail. In three minutes you start to see the open wetlands adjacent to Mud Pond. The trail circles around the south edge of the wetland, with views first of the standing dead trees near its center, and then of Mud Pond itself at the far side. You cross a tiny inlet and pull away from the pond, following the stream for a very short time.

The climbing starts ten minutes along the red trail. At first, you ascend in stages: short inclines, followed by brief level stretches, followed by more climbing. After a fairly level, straight stretch through a stand of hemlock and birch, the trail detours to the left around a wet area with blowdown. The detour is well marked. After the next climb, you arrive at a dark birch-hemlock bog to the right. Already you are starting to see quartz embedded in the trail.

After the bog, the trail climbs up to the southwest to a notch on the side of the mountain. You can see a patch of open rock not far above. At one point the notch narrows into a sharp V-shaped portal of sorts. On one side, the hemlock forest shades the headwaters of a stream that flows via Mud and Putnam ponds to Lake Champlain. Stepping through the notch, you are greeted by a forest of red and white pines. Here is the start of a stream that flows through Devils Washdish and Pharaoh Lake to the Schroon River and ultimately the Hudson—to the opposite end of the Adirondack Park from the first stream, just a few feet away!

Once through the V cut, the trail begins to climb in earnest, and forty minutes along the red trail you reach the first of the open burn areas on the side of the mountain. The rocks are carpeted with deep mosses and lichens, with pioneering pines wherever conditions allow. The trail is now marked by a series of cairns, along with the red markers. The only view you have at first is across to the rocky slopes of Big Clear Pond Mountain. The climbing is moderate, but at one point you are expected to

Pharoah Lake from Treadway Mountain

scramble up a five-foot rock wall. If necessary, detour to the left for a gentler way to the top.

After ascending through the open area for 15 minutes, you reenter the woods. A ledge to the side of the trail, to the right, offers the first good view. In this case, you are looking east to the Green Mountains of Vermont. The trail climbs through the woods to a partly exposed knob, and then descends sharply to the base of a rather imposing rock wall. Fortunately, the trail hooks left and finds an easier way up. From the top of this knob you have your first view of the summit of Treadway Mountain across the small cirque to your left. The trail will circle around the edge of that cirque. Also coming into view at this point is Pharaoh Lake, just to the west of south at the foot of the mountain.

As you cross this knob, you will be tempted to leave the trail by the open vistas

you will pass, again looking east toward Vermont. If you do so, keep track of the cairns, for they are all that reliably mark the trail at this point. The trail is routed on the side of the ridge facing Treadway's summit. It descends rather sharply into the col at the north end of the cirque, and then begins the final climb to the summit, with patches of quartz beneath your feet. Finally, you reach the mountain's highest point at 2,248 feet, 4 miles from the campground.

The views range from the east, where Mount Mansfield and Camels Hump are prominent among the Green Mountains, all the way around to the High Peaks of the Adirondacks. To the south are the mountains that rim Lake George, including Black Mountain and the Tongue Mountain Range. To the southwest are Moose, Baldhead, and Crane. The distinctive silhouettes of Snowy and Blue mountains, peaks at the heart of the park, are visible on the distant western horizon. The large range closer in just to the north of west is the Blue Ridge Range, of which Hoffman Mountain is the highest peak. Beyond its north end you can spot Boreas Mountain and Pinnacle Ridge. The High Peaks on the northwestern horizon include Marcy, Haystack, Basin, Saddle-back, Gothics, McComb, Dix, East Dix, Giant, and Rocky Peak Ridge.

Closer in, Pharaoh Lake is the dominant feature, with Pharaoh Mountain, the highest point in this wilderness area, rising beside it. Glidden Marsh, Crab Pond, and a corner of Oxshoe Pond are to the northwest.

The return to the campground follows along the same route. Again, keep track of the location of the cairns as you traverse the ridge, for it is easy to become misled. Once back at the base of the mountain, if you find that your sense of adventure has only been piqued by what you have seen so far, you can extend this hike several miles by passing around the north side of Putnam Pond. This route will take you past Clear, Rock, Little Rock, and Heart ponds. These trails are described in detail in *Discover the Eastern Adirondacks.*

27

Pharaoh Ponds Loop

Distance (around loop): 19.4 miles

Vertical rise: 1,000 feet

Hiking time: 10 hours

Maps: USGS 7.5' Pharaoh Mountain;
USGS 7.5' Graphite

Pharaoh Lake Wilderness Area

Imagine visiting 15 ponds in one day! The ponds are connected by a marvelous network of trails in the heart of the Pharaoh Lake Wilderness Area. Although the map for this area shows only 15 ponds, be prepared for more; beaver have flooded many parts of this wilderness, enlarging ponds, creating new ones, flooding trails, and occasionally making life confusing for the hiker.

Much has been written about the heavy use of the Pharaoh Lake area, but the greatest use is closest to the principal accesses: Crane Pond; the two trailheads on NY 74 in the north; Beaver Pond Road north of Brant Lake, which is the southern access; and the Putnam Pond State Campground, an excellent base when you hike in the area. On this fantastic loop, you reach the heart of the Wilderness and travel far from the popular areas.

In the past, the signs in this wilderness area were notorious for understating the distance between points of interest. As of 2001, the DEC had replaced many of these with newer, more accurate signs. However, if there is still any confusion, the trail description below records only the true distances; beware of any of the older signs that may still be in place.

How to Get There

There are numerous accesses to the Pharaoh Lake Wilderness Area, but the Crane Pond access is perhaps the most interesting. With the new trailhead adding 3.8 miles to the loop, you may want to break this into a backpack trip of 2 or 3 days.

To reach the trailhead, drive south on NY 9 for 0.6 mile from Northway (I-87) exit 28, and turn left, east, on Alder Meadow Road. After passing East Shore Road on the right at 2 miles, the road continues as Crane Pond Road. It is a very pretty drive east, passing a lovely farm shortly before angling south at 4.5 miles. Park on the east side of the road at the turn. People do drive beyond, and motorized access is still tolerated, though shortly it may be restricted. If you have a four-wheel-drive vehicle you may proceed with caution; but to protect the wilderness attributes of the area you should walk. Watch out for vehicles.

Because this route is a loop, you may begin at other points. A logical alternate is the Putnam Pond Campground, which is also the starting point for Hike 26 in this guide. Starting there would actually shave 3.4 miles off the round trip; however, your route would not then pass beautiful Crane Pond.

The Trail

From the official parking area, walk south, climbing beside the small hemlock-covered gorge that surrounds Alder Creek. At 0.6 mile the roadway crosses Alder Creek and, 0.2 mile farther, passes the beginning of the trail to Goose Pond. The road continues level; people have parked along it here. Shortly, the roadway begins to climb sharply through an eroded stretch and you will be glad you are walking, not driving. Descend-ing through a second washed-out stretch to the level of Alder Pond, the road crosses an area that is often flooded. An arrow points left to a yellow-marked path that will lead you around the flooded area. Next, you pass a trail coming in from the north. At 1.9 miles you reach the beginning of the red-marked, 3-mile-long Pharaoh Mountain Trail. The abandoned roadway continues east to a promontory

covered with magnificent pine on the border of Crane Pond.

If you prefer wilderness camping, you will find numerous campsites and fire rings along the west shore of Crane Pond, a truly handsome body of water edged with white pine and huge boulders.

Take the red-marked trail, which begins at the narrow spit separating Crane and Alder ponds. The route heads south across a bridge and immediately plunges into deep woods. Hemlock and pine darken the needle-strewn trail. Even on a bright day, the route can be as dark as night, but the walking may be the best in the Adirondacks. The forest is stately and mature, with pine exceeding 3 feet in diameter.

Within 15 to 20 minutes, at 0.7 mile from Crane Pond, you reach the first interior junction, where the red-marked trail heads to the right toward Pharaoh Mountain. Take the left fork, marked with blue, straight into a small clearing and then back into deep forest on a narrow path.

The route runs past huge boulders and glacial erratics and into a deep hemlock valley, where you cross a stream on a good hikers' bridge. It continues beside a small, boggy marsh with corduroy stretches helping to keep the trail dry. Within ten minutes you cover the 0.4-mile distance to Glidden Marsh, a long, thin, shallow watercourse filled with lily pads and reflecting the tall pines surrounding it. A few steps past your first approach to the marsh you reach another trail intersection. The route to the left leads in 1.7 miles to Horseshoe Pond; you will use that trail on your return much later in the day.

Turn right onto the yellow-marked trail that leads south along the shore of Glidden Marsh. Pharaoh Lake is still 2.5 miles distant at this point. The trail, a narrow footpath showing little sign of use, winds through a

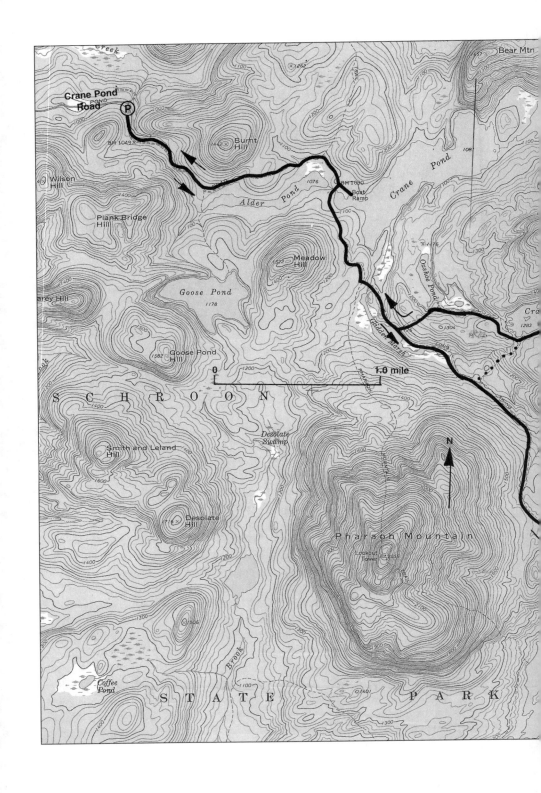

mixed forest of birch, pine, and striped maple—a forest that only fires could have created. It contrasts sharply with the huge hemlock of the first part of the trip. As you round a big boulder, you have a fine view back along the length of the marsh. Continue past the long, thick meadow of cattails, reeds, cedar, and spectacular paper birch whose reflections glisten in the narrow watercourse flowing through the marsh.

After crossing the inlet stream on a slippery three-log bridge, turn away from the flow. The trail climbs into a very dense hemlock thicket, where you should spot one of the forest's giants, a spruce with a diameter exceeding 2½ feet. Again the forest changes, this time to mature hardwoods with tall, straight birch and maple. An understory of horse nettles crowds the trail. You should learn to recognize these plants, for although their sting persists no more than a couple of hours, it is still uncomfortable for an hour or two.

You quickly reach an intersection where a red-marked trail turns back left, northeast, 0.4 mile to Crab Pond. Your route is straight ahead on the yellow trail. As it climbs the lower slopes of Pharaoh Mountain, a deep valley opens to your left. Beech dieback has caused a number of trees to fall across the trail, obscuring it slightly.

After walking for 70 minutes from Crane Pond, you'll find the trail detours right around a beaver flow. It's a good example of the impediments hikers meet in this wilderness, for beaver flooded the trail just a few years ago, causing this realignment. All the valleys here are at about the same elevation. They were scoured by glaciers, and until recently held glacial ponds. This makes it easy for beaver to enlarge or create new ponds, which they do every few years.

Beyond the flow, the trail crosses its inlet stream. You then continue high on the hillside in an area where dead beech have so opened the forest floor that underbrush is filling the trail. You continue beside the stream and a rather eerie little swamp filled with huge clumps of all the osmunda ferns: royal, cinnamon, and interrupted. Stumps covered with lichens and mosses are rotting in the algae-filled water. Beyond it, you begin a fairly steep descent of more than 300 feet to Pharaoh Lake, 3.6 miles from Crane Pond, 5.5 miles from the official trailhead.

A blue trail turns right to circle around the west shore of the pond. You turn left, continuing on the yellow trail, east around the head of the lake. On the way, you cross a small hemlock-covered peninsula dotted with paper birch. Its tip overlooks Split Rock Bay, which serves as a reflecting pool for a group of nature's more handsome sculptures: boulders worn smooth by the last glacier, standing tall above the water. As you round the bay, look for a pipe spring away from the trail spewing cold, clear water. The forest change from open hardwoods to hemlock, cedar, and pine is sudden and dramatic. Within 20 minutes of reaching the lake you arrive at its northernmost lean-to.

The lean-to is in one of the forest's better settings: views of the lake and, overhanging it, Pharaoh Mountain, with its rock slides clearly visible. If you are lucky, you may spot great blue herons nesting nearby. You should surely stop here for rest and lunch. The lean-to is just under 6 miles from the trailhead, and a candidate for a camping stop if you wish to break the hike into segments.

The yellow trail continues behind the lean-to up a small ridge covered with hemlocks and tall white pines. The needle cover is so thick that the foot tread is barely visible. As you approach another of Pharaoh's swampy bays, look for a short waterfall on a small stream entering from the left. The trail continues just east of south to still another bay, this one with a long view of the lake. You reach a pair of trail junctions at 6.7 miles on the bay's shore, less than 20 minutes from the lean-to. First, a red trail leads right for 0.2 mile, past a scenic campsite, to the tip of Wintergreen Point. A short distance ahead, a yellow trail leads left, uphill and away from the pond, toward Grizzle Ocean. This is the route you want. Within 10 minutes you reach the end of Wolf Pond, a dying, swamp-bordered pond filled with water lilies and framed with some of the tallest white pines in this wilderness.

The trail continues along the flow, making a hairpin turn north to avoid swamps. In this vicinity you encounter several peculiar ridges—long, thin, sinuous chains. Because the trail stays high and dry on top of most, and runs up and down and across a few, you enjoy pleasant walking. Glaciers sculpted these ridges, called *roches moutonnées,* or "sheep backs." The residual hummocks of bedrock lying in the direction of the ice flow have smooth, curved edges parallel to the movement of the ice. At the northern end of the hairpin turn, you descend to the level of the swamps and then cross a part of them under a moss-covered ledge. As you climb the shoulder of a small hill, the marsh continues to accompany you on your right, now west.

You now begin to climb the hill east of the swamp, realizing that the hairpin detour took you nearly 1 mile—and 30 minutes—out of your way. First turn sharply left away from the swamp and follow a small stream on a trail that hardly appears to have been used. It passes through a tall and stately hardwood forest, very gradually gaining elevation. You are walking through the long, thin valley between Grizzle Ocean Mountain and Thunderbolt Mountain. This stretch is probably the least exciting in the entire loop, a

dull walk through what develops into an interminable draw. You need more than 90 minutes to walk from the eastern bay of Pharaoh Lake to Grizzle Ocean. Perhaps you can enjoy spending part of the time speculating on the origin of Grizzle Ocean's name. It is certainly one of the Adirondacks' most inventive. One Adirondack historian claims the name derives from the wild bragging of a fisherman named Tom Grizzle. His tales so astounded his listeners that they began to refer to his secret pond as Grizzle's Ocean.

Your first glimpse of Grizzle Ocean at 9.4 miles, 2.7 miles from the intersection at Pharaoh Lake, is at the edge of a narrow, swampy finger of the pond where a forest of evergreen stumps gives a ragged look to the shoreline. A sign by a trail with red markers notes TRAIL AROUND POND. Take that trail right, south, for a better look at the entire pond with its pine- and birch-lined shoreline, but with so many miles to go, you will probably want to go back to the sign and take the left trail for the shorter trek. A loop around the "ocean" would add at least 0.5 mile to the planned route.

Bearing left keeps you on the yellow-marked trail, which almost immediately turns to cross the wide, shallow arm of the pond on a narrow, 80-foot-long plank bridge. It brings you into a forest of hemlock so dense that it can seem as dark as night. You encounter another marked intersection in about 0.2 mile. Here the right fork leads to the east side of Grizzle Ocean and its lean-to, 0.2 mile away.

Stay on the yellow trail, heading north. The trail shows signs of a lot of use and can even be muddy. It descends steeply beside the outlet of Grizzle Ocean through a deep and handsome valley, crosses the stream, and continues beside it to a marked intersection, a distance of 0.8 mile from your first approach to Grizzle Ocean, 10.2 miles into the loop. The yellow trail to the right is the alternate access trail from Putnam Pond. For the route past the ponds less frequently visited, stay left on what is now a blue trail. Within a few hundred feet you glimpse a marshy end of Putnam Pond. In 15 minutes, approximately 0.4 mile, your trail intersects one that leads from a boat landing on the shore of Putnam Pond to the summit of Treadway Mountain (Hike 26).

The loop walk is full of lovely places, and one appears in the next 200 yards, where the trail follows the outlet of Mud Pond. Another marshy lake, it offers lovely views across to part of Treadway Mountain.

The trail continues beside a stream after leaving Mud Pond, this time the outlet of Clear Pond at 10.7 miles. Just south of Clear Pond a red trail forks left across the stream and heads around the west side of the pond. Here you may choose either fork, for distance is no factor. However, the right fork, on the pond's east side, passes a lean-to, a perfect place to rest. It is perched on a small ledge above the pond, which has deep clear water and views of Big Clear Pond Mountain. Swimming is good from the ledge. A trail with yellow markers leads east behind the lean-to to another waterway trailhead on Putnam Pond. This access accounts for the signs of heavier use at Clear Pond.

The route north along Clear Pond has blue markers, and within 10 minutes it intersects the red trail from the west side of the pond. The route north climbs through a deep valley with ledges on either side, facing the long, round-topped ridges that characterize this wilderness. The trail emerges on a saddle in a white birch thicket and then turns right to descend toward Rock Pond. As the trail turns, you can see Rock Pond down to the north through the trees, but the trail reaches it by a roundabout route, head-

ing first almost to the shore of Little Rock Pond. Within 30 minutes from Clear Pond, at 11.8 miles, you reach another trail intersection. This point is 1.1 miles from the Clear Pond Lean-to. The trail that continues north here, eventually leading back to Putnam Pond, may be used to reach a lean-to on the northeast shore of Little Rock Pond. Leave the trail and walk east to inspect Little Rock Pond, with its lovely reflections.

For the loop, however, you turn left, west, at the intersection, on a red trail heading toward Lilypad Pond. From this point, you still have 5.5 miles to go before returning to Crane Pond, and 7.4 miles before reaching the official trailhead.

After the trail passes the marshy end of Rock Pond, it follows closely the pond's southwest lobe. What a surprise the pond is, with rocks and boulders edging and emerging from it. Everywhere smooth, light gray ledges rise from the water. The trail is dry and little used, shaded with tall maple and white birch. The ledges are the best places on the entire loop from which to swim. After you cross a small inlet stream on the pond's southwest corner, you head north where the trail presents views northeast to ledges on Bear Pond Mountain. Small cliffs rise above you on the west shore, and huge pine tower over the hemlock and birch that rim the pond. You walk on ledges thick with carpets of needles and bunchberry, and an opening with a view of the pond may entice you into a short break.

The trail heads west near the outlet, and within 10 minutes you should see an intermittent stream entering from your left, south. In wet times, it tumbles in a waterfall from the high ledges that face Peaked Hill. A short distance farther, less than a five-minute walk, you hear a waterfall on your right at the outlet of Rock Pond. This one

Pharaoh Lake

should be explored, so leave the trail and walk below a small cliff from which the outlet emerges in a series of vertical drops, forming a cascade nearly 50 feet high. Be careful walking on the talus-strewn base of the cliff that leads to the edge of a small pool into which one chute of the waterfall plunges.

Return to the trail and continue downhill to a marsh on your right. Another of the strange stump forests, it has recently been flooded and is full of birds. You should be able to spot Potter Mountain north across the swamp. The walking here is rough, for a new footpath has been worn to avoid the flooded marshes. You leave the marsh, heading southwest, beside a small stream along a trail choked with maple seedlings and viburnum, the new growth on the forest floor filling the open spaces created by the dead beech. The relatively obscure trail from the outlet of Rock Pond to Lilypad Lean-to requires 35 or 40 minutes of walking. You may want to stop at the lean-to for a brief rest. Just remember to keep at least three more hours of daylight to walk the remaining distance. Lilypad Pond is minute and choked with lily pads, but nevertheless it is a beautiful camping place.

The red trail ends at 13.8 miles, 0.1 mile from Lilypad Pond, within sight of the pond's outlet. Here it intersects a blue trail. The right fork leads north toward NY 74. The sign points to Tubmill Pond, which you will not find on your map. It is another of the wilderness's newcomers, a beaver pond filling the huge marsh east of Crane Pond. The area is shown accurately on topographic maps, but they do not give it a name. Take the left fork, continuing southwest up a short, steep pitch through low scrub on a trail that could become overgrown in the future as the beech that cover it continue to fall.

The trail crosses a high, pine-covered ledge with a crunchy lichen tread. Fires have opened the hillside, and a sign on the ledge points toward 2,248-foot-high Treadway Mountain and 2,551-foot-high Pharaoh Mountain. As the trail descends around a marsh, you begin to notice steep ledges below on your left and a stream, which flows toward Crab Pond. If you are making the walk in summer, you can enjoy a few blueberries on the ridge before descending to Horseshoe Pond.

Horseshoe is a half-hour walk from Lilypad. A small rock promontory jutting into the pond from the west gives it its horseshoe shape. The peninsula has been used for camping. The trail zigzags down a sharp, almost vertical, drop beside the rock wall over which the outlet flows. Immediately at 14.7 miles you see Crab Pond; only a stone's throw separates the two ponds.

Crab Pond's picturesque shoreline hosts the trail for over 0.5 mile. Giant pines topping rounded boulders that seem to rise from the water provide delightful companions. But before you walk beside its shores, you have to cross its inlet, and there is no bridge. In low water you may not believe this could ever be a problem. Suitable stepping-stones can be found, even in high water, but you may have to walk away from the trail to do so.

All of the ponds are lovely, in their distinctive ways, but Crab is especially beautiful. Cliffs and ledges on its northern shore are accentuated with pine and white birch. You will spot at least one beaver lodge. This marvelously handsome section of trail is sometimes close to the pond and sometimes above it on a hemlock-covered knoll overlooking a new beaver flow. You will find a lovely rocky knoll for a brief rest about halfway along the shore, this one surmounted with red pine and white birch, lady's slipper and lichen, and within sight of the sheer rock face of Peaked Hill.

For a time the trail takes a course transverse to the ledges, so the route is up and over and down and up again. There is a short spur trail that continues southwest, but the signpost may be missing. In any event, you should continue around the western end of Crab, heading west toward Oxshoe. This route takes you through a mixed forest and past another unnamed swamp with a pine-crowned knoll. Within 20 minutes you reach the southern end of Oxshoe Pond, at nearly 16 miles, where a lean-to caps a ledge covered with enormous white pine. There is a beautiful view up the pond's length across to wonderful ledges.

From here it should take less than 10 minutes to climb over a height-of-land west-southwest to the lean-to, and drop over 100 feet, the last of it fairly steep, to Glidden Marsh, at roughly 16.4 miles. Here you take the right fork, the blue trail, north. You only have 0.4 mile to go on this trail before reaching the wide and easy 0.7-mile stretch that takes you to Crane Pond, at 17.5 miles. It is surprising how muddy stretches and a little corduroy can trip you up at the end of a long walk. However, retracing the last 0.7 mile is so easy that you will feel almost refreshed as the trail emerges at Crane Pond with birches glistening and reflecting the setting sun. Be sure to allow time for the remaining 1.9-mile walk back to the official trailhead, bringing the entire length of the route to 19.4 miles.

28

Severance Hill

Distance (round-trip): 2 miles

Vertical rise: 880 feet

Hiking time: 1¼ hours

Map: USGS Metric Schroon Lake

The walk up Severance is so short and gentle that you can easily make it your first climb in the Adirondacks, even after a long day's drive. If you are planning several days of hiking in the eastern Adirondacks, this small mountain is an ideal place to become acquainted with the region's hills.

The summit of Severance Hill offers several rocky open perches with commanding views of Schroon Lake and the Pharaoh Lake Wilderness Area to the east. The 880-foot climb to the 1,693-foot summit is scarcely more than 1 mile long and takes 45 minutes at most. The summit is a perfect place for a picnic, perhaps in the evening to watch the rays of the setting sun play across the normally dark summit of Pharaoh Mountain. From here you can understand why that mountain was first known by Native Americans as Ondewa, or the Black One.

From Severance, Schroon Lake stretches out to the south between the hills. The origin of that lake's name is still shrouded in mystery. Alfred Donaldson, in *The History of the Adirondacks,* wrote that early French settlers at Crown Point "named it in honor of Madame Scarron, young and beautiful wife of the famous wild and comic writer Paul Scarron . . . I am not alone in wishing the story might be true—this humble but fascinating goose-girl, who became wife of a physically misshapen poet, and later, as Madame de Maintenon, the wife of a morally misshapen king, had given the imprint of her memory to a lovely lake in the American wilderness."

Severance itself bears the name of settlers who reached the area in the early 1820s. Walking the hills in the Adirondacks you cannot help but be fascinated by the origins of the names, and the histories of the families who once lived in what is now the Forest Preserve. Most of the early-19th-century settlers were loggers and lumbermen. The few farmers eked out a meager subsistence in the cold north. Many early families in the Schroon Lake area were attracted by work in the iron mines north of Paradox Lake.

How to Get There

Take the Northway (I-87) to exit 28 at NY 74, north of Schroon Lake Village, and head south on NY 9 toward town. Driving less than 0.6 mile south, you pass Alder Meadow Road on your left. Immediately beyond that road, turn right into a parking area. From the parking area, a trail heads west and through a tunnel under the Northway.

The Trail

Before starting, make sure you have water, for the summit is very dry. The trail, denoted by yellow markers, takes you through a narrow culvert under the Northway and then through a flat area on a broad trail covered with pine needles and shaded by a low forest of pine, maple, birch, spruce, balsam, and aspen. After five minutes you start to head gradually up into a tall cedar forest. The broad, smooth trail soon becomes steeper. A small stream gurgles in the valley to your right, and you may notice an old roadway entering from that side. Continue straight, and within 20 minutes the trail briefly levels out. Here the forest is open enough for you to see the top of Severance Hill ahead. You may still hear traffic noises from the highway below as you enter a patch of wet woods that throbs with birdsong. I spotted a scarlet tanager and a

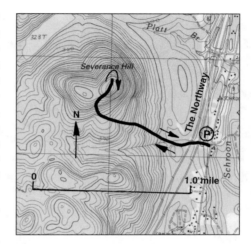

black-throated blue warbler, both at the side of the trail.

Beyond a hikers' bridge you come out of the cedar swamp thicket to begin climbing again, this time into a forest of magnificent tall trees with huge pine and hemlock shading ground cedars and other club mosses on the forest floor. You may want to stop and study the pines spared by early loggers. Most of the largest have double or triple trunks, which were spurned by loggers, but a few significant single trunks may be found. The route seems straight up through evergreens and immense paper birch. You cross a second level, angling south, then zigzag back to the north and begin to climb again. The trees, now mostly oak and considerably smaller, open out to rock ledges from which the views begin.

The first lovely promontory you reach looks across to Pharaoh Mountain and down the full length of Schroon Lake. Patches of wild columbine grow beneath the scrub oak that cover the summit. You will find several stone fireplaces on the open rock. Walk north to a second opening that overlooks Paradox Lake and the mountains to its north. High water brings Paradox Lake two outlets—hence the name,

---

Severance Hill

to explain that peculiar phenomenon.

The summit in early spring is a choice place for watching migrating warblers. Within a half hour I identified the Blackburnian, the blackpoll, the yellowthroat, and an ovenbird.

Because the walk is so short, consider combining it with a visit to the Natural Stone Bridge and Caves at Pottersville, west of the south end of Schroon Lake. The caves are a privately owned tourist attraction, and an entrance fee is charged. Plenty of signs direct you from NY 9 at exit 26 off the Northway, west 1.7 miles to the caves and adjacent lunch and picnic facilities. More than enough signs point out the scenic wonders along the self-guided tour through the site. The path winds past caves cut out in the Grenville bedrock and beside huge potholes scoured out in the streambed by giant grindstones. Trout Brook, whose waters created the caves, disappears into clefts in the rock, reappearing again in the gorge below to provide reflecting pools for the handsomely sculptured rock walls.

The Pottersville caves are a great place to begin learning the geology of the Adirondacks, and the owners can tell you much about the area's more common minerals. Their gift shop has a range of literature on geological subjects to enhance all your walks through the mountains.

29

Crane Mountain

Distance (around loop): 4.8 miles

Vertical rise: 1,300 feet

Hiking time: 4–5 hours

Map: USGS 7.5' Johnsburg

Crane Mountain is my favorite Adirondack peak. I have introduced many people to its trails, and because they share my enthusiasm, they, too, return almost yearly to enjoy this perfect hike.

Crane is a massive mountain, isolated from surrounding peaks and commanding great views in all directions. Its steep slopes offer a challenging climb, and its bare rocks provide unrestricted overlooks.

How to Get There

If you are coming from the north or west to climb Crane, which lies in the middle of the southeastern Adirondacks, you will find that the easiest approach is from NY 8.

From the south and east, the most direct route is from the Adirondack Northway (I-87), exit 25, southwest on NY 8 through Chestertown to Johnsburg.

Turn south at Johnsburg onto Oven Mountain Road and continue on South Johnsburg Road to Thurman. There, take Garnet Lake Road, which is marked with a sign for Crane Mountain. Shortly after turning onto Garnet Lake Road, you are treated to a lovely view of Crane. Drive west from Thurman 1.2 miles to a fork and bear right, continuing west on a newly widened dirt road (Ski Hi Road) whose condition depends on the amount of recent rainfall, despite constant care. After 1.5 miles the road turns sharply left toward the Ski Hi Lodge, but you continue straight for just under 0.5 mile to the marked trailhead.

Were you to continue on Garnet Lake Road to circle Crane Mountain by car, you would have a dozen places to view its sheer rock faces and its companion peak to the north, Huckleberry Mountain, which appears to have been split off Crane by some giant cleaver. The name Huckleberry should be your clue to plan your trip in midsummer, for some of the best blueberrying in the Adirondacks is on Crane and Huckleberry Mountains.

The Trail

The trees near the trailhead are reminders that Crane, like so many other Adirondack mountains, was ravaged by fierce fires. Aspen, maple, and birch saplings are sprinkled with white pine, all pioneering trees. Both ends of your loop meet at this trailhead. By the eastern route, on which you start this hike, it is 1.9 miles to the summit. You return on the western spur, a trail that bypasses the private land and leads quickly to Putnam Farm Road and another trail up the mountain. By this route, which takes you past Crane Mountain Pond, it is 2.9 miles from the summit to the trailhead. You may, of course, walk the loop in the opposite direction.

Following the red disks of the right-hand trail, you soon enter a forest with a deep canopy cover of white and yellow birch interspersed with beech and maple. Within 10 minutes, the grade becomes quite steep. You are about to climb 700 vertical feet in 0.4 mile.

As the grade steepens, the trees become smaller, with pine emerging dominant. Many rock outcrops appear, and very early on you come to openings with views back to the southwest.

After a 40-minute walk and a climb of about 600 feet, the trail approaches ledges of anorthosite gneiss, where you find good views to the west. Within another five minutes you reach a second large rock outcrop,

where the continuing trail is poorly marked. Walk about halfway out on the open rock before heading up across it. You should see a marker a little east of north on a dead pine. Within another three minutes you reach a trail junction. The left fork is a spur trail leading 0.4 mile west to Crane Mountain Pond.

Turn right for the 0.8-mile continuing climb to the 3,240-foot summit. Your route is toward the east, moderately uphill at first, but steep enough in one place to require use of a 6-foot ladder. The trail enters a balsam and spruce thicket and heads almost southeast below the cliffs that face the summit, trending northwest to southeast. Less than 15 minutes from the junction, you will have covered most of the distance to the summit, leaving only a bit more than a 100-foot scramble up the cliff. The trail turns sharply left, climbing on almost bare rock. A 15-foot ladder attached to the rock wall may be shaky, so it may be safer to climb using the good handholds in the rock ledge to the right of the ladder. As you reach the uppermost rock ledge, head left about 100 yards to the actual summit.

You will find views from almost every point along the summit ridge. The first view east stretches all the way to the southern end of the Green Mountains of Vermont, with the mountains on the east shore of Lake George clearly identifiable in between. To the south, Moose and Baldhead almost conceal the summit of Hadley. Walking west along the ridge you can enjoy the view across the valley defined by Garnet Lake Road. Garnet Lake is southwest, and the string of sharp hills on its western shore leads to the rocky cone of Mount Blue.

Views to the west and north improve as you continue west. The best are from a large outcrop at the end of a short spur path branching left, south, 0.2 mile from the sum-

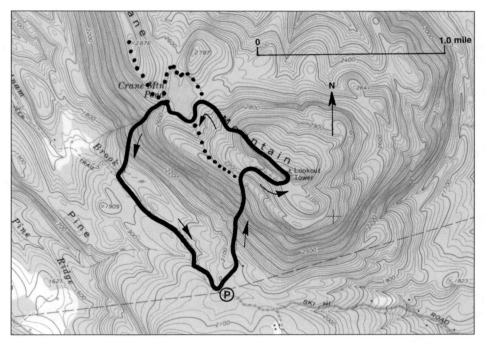

mit. So many hikers have walked this part that you should have no difficulty finding the unmarked turn, which is just before the trail descends steeply into the woods. The outcrop overlooks Crane Mountain Pond. Across the pond, in the northeast, lies massive Eleventh Mountain. Use it to orient the distant horizon. Over it and 24 miles away lies Snowy, the knob and cliff face of its summit always easy to identify. To its left is Speculator Mountain; Pillsbury is a little north of east, between Speculator and Snowy on the horizon. North of Snowy and 7 miles farther is the summit of Blue Mountain. To the right of Eleventh Mountain is the steep and unmistakable cone of Height of Land Mountain, and next, toward magnetic north, is Gore.

In the small angle between Gore and due north, the High Peaks are visible. It was easier to name individual peaks before the new tree growth began to crowd the vista, but Santanoni on the west and Nippletop on the east offer the easiest profiles to identify. Dix and Giant are to the right of Nippletop. Marcy, Haystack, Basin, and Gothics are prominent between Santanoni and Nippletop. If you want to be certain about the peaks you see, you will need the USGS quadrangles for the area and good binoculars.

Continue descending the main trail toward Crane Mountain Pond. When you reach a muddy stretch at pond level, turn left to continue the loop. The intersection is frequently flooded. (If you are adventurous, turn right on the unmarked path, which dwindles as it approaches a small knob north of the pond. You can easily wind between rock outcrops to a point on the southern side of the knob that has a special view across Crane Mountain Pond to the outlet, with the summits of several distant mountains rising unexpectedly over treetops in the south.) Heading generally west on the

Granite outcrops face Crane's summit ridge.

trail around the southern edge of the pond, you pass the intersection with the spur trail, several places campers have used, and a smooth rock that leads to a good swimming spot.It is just 1 mile from the summit to the outlet of the pond, and if you have time, you can easily make your way north-northwest along the top of Crane's western summit ridge toward several other outcrops with good vantages south and west. Crane, like all the mountains west of the Hudson, was scoured by a glacier, which left a gentler slope on the northwest but scraped smooth the cliffs on the southeastern flanks. And like many neighboring mountains, Crane was ravaged by forest fires so intense that the thin organic topsoils that had accumulated since the last glacier were also consumed. The pattern of open rock interwoven with pockets of shallow mineral soils is typical. From the pockets spread the pioneering lichens and mosses that slowly create soil to support scrub balsam, spruce, and birch. In June, pink lady's slipper thrives beneath the evergreens. And along the sunny edges, blueberries produce abundant crops.

Watch carefully as you begin the steep descent toward Putnam Farm Road from the west side of the outlet. This is a dangerous place: the descent is steep, slippery when wet, and the trail angles across open rock. Be careful! Stay on the trail beyond the outlet crossing; the smooth, rounded slopes are deceptively steep. This trail is steeper than the route up, dropping nearly 900 feet in little more than 0.5 mile. It heads west-southwest, generally following the outlet and crossing it again after about a 200-foot drop in elevation from the pond. This is the only place where you may have problems on the descent. Stay close to the stream and do not venture out on the escarpment. The trail reenters the woods just a few feet from the stream.

Old-timers tell stories of cranes nesting in the vicinity of the pond, so perhaps that is how it got its name. Just as likely the name is attributable to a surveyor named Crane who laid out the "line of mile trees" 55 miles from the Hudson to the north line of the Totten and Crossfield Patent. That survey line passed over Crane Mountain. The mountain's namesake pond, which lies nestled on a shelf west of the summit, has generated rumors that it has no outlet or that it has two outlets. There is some truth to both. Midsummer droughts can so reduce water draining into the pond that no water flows from it along the principal outlet to the southwest, which you will soon cross. A swamp on the north of the pond drains into Crystal Brook, and in high-water times water sometimes also flows into the brook, seeping from the swamp as if from a hidden outlet of the lake.

After 0.4 mile the trail heads south, away from the stream, to intersect Putnam Farm Road. Just before reaching the road, about 0.8 mile from the pond, the trail crosses a stream on a natural stone bridge. The tiny stream disappears into a cave of Precambrian marble, and reemerges about 50 feet away, only to disappear again in a still larger cave. The cap of granitic gneiss that constitutes the bulk of Crane Mountain overlies a belt of marble. There is a second layer of marble and easily eroded rock at the level of the pond; it has been worn away to create the bench that contains the pond and gives Crane its distinctive stepped profile.

Beyond the cave, turn left to follow the old road toward your car. Both the roadway and a bypass, 0.2 mile from the parking area, are marked. The bypass circles private land to reach the trailhead.

You can make the circuit described in four hours, but I have never spent less than six hours on the mountain. There is so much to see and enjoy that you may want to plan an even longer trip.

30

Siamese Ponds

Distance (round-trip): 13.2 miles

Vertical rise: 600 feet

Hiking time: 7 hours

Map: USGS Metric Bakers Mills

Siamese Ponds Wilderness Area

The Siamese Ponds are a favorite southern Adirondack camping destination. They lie at the heart of the eponymous Wilderness Area, a region so remote that the trails to the ponds are the only formal routes in some 50 square miles of surrounding forest. Most other destinations in this forest are reached by either informal paths or bushwhacks (see *Discover the South Central Adirondacks* for details on over 90 nearby trips).

Hikers carrying a pack for overnight camping need as much as four hours for the roughly 6.6-mile trek into the ponds, but day-hikers can make the 13.2-mile round-trip in seven hours. That is just walking time, though. You should add at least three more hours for exploring, swimming, and picnicking.

How to Get There

This trip shares its beginning with the East Branch of the Sacandaga access trail. The trailhead is on the north side of NY 8 between Wells and Wevertown. If you are traveling from the south or west, turn east on NY 8 at the intersection of NY 8 and NY 30 north of Wells, and drive 13.5 miles northeast. This section of highway follows the East Branch of the Sacandaga River and is one of the prettiest drives in the mountains. Coming from the east or north, the trailhead is 4 miles southwest of Bakers Mills on NY 8, south of Wevertown. The trailhead is designated by a state historical marker, and the trail is marked with both the blue hiking and the yellow ski-

Diamond Brook Flow on the East Branch of the Sacandaga Trail

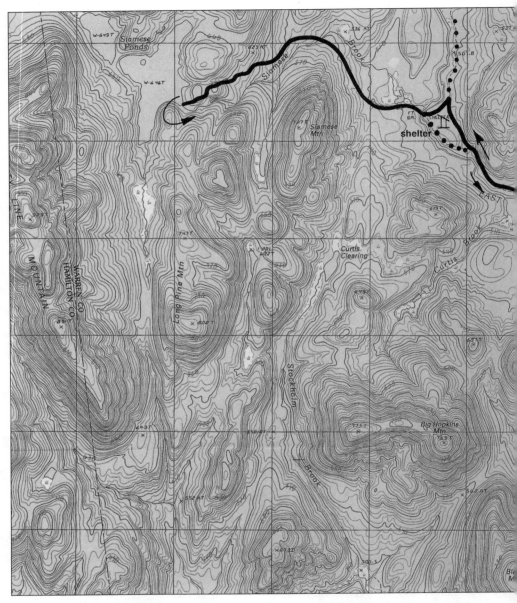

touring disks used on state-maintained trails.

The Trail

At the start of the trail, you climb 200 feet up the shoulder of Eleventh Mountain in 0.5 mile and then drop 400 feet to the valley of the East Branch of the Sacandaga at 1.2 miles. The short pitch on the latter rise always seems formidable to tired hikers on their return.

The trail reaches the confluence of Dia-

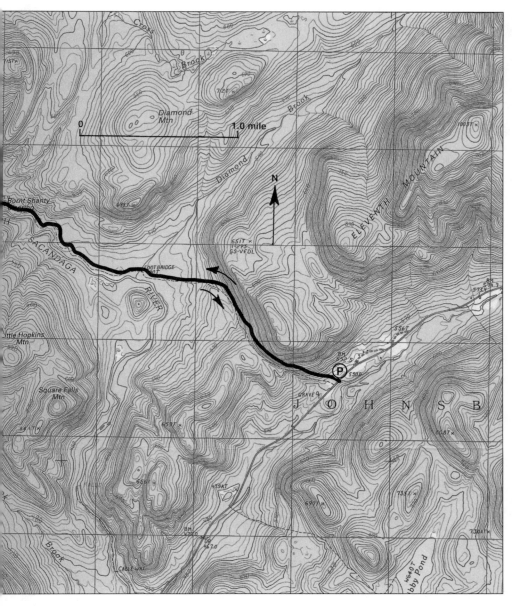

mond Brook and the Sacandaga in a most attractive beaver meadow. From the flow you can see the cliffs on Diamond Mountain to the north, those on Square Falls Mountain in the southwest, and the highest of all, those ranging across Eleventh

Mountain back to the southeast.

The trail continues east-northeast beside the river for a little over 2 miles to a junction. Occasionally, where the valley is very narrow, you walk close to the water, but most of the time the route is back from

---

the river on slightly higher ground. The trail you are following was once a principal route north, used by loggers and tan-barkers to transport logs and hemlock bark from the interior to mills along the river at Oregon and Griffin or east to settlements in the Town of Johnsburg. The trail was thus designed for practicability, not for the scenery.

You see few signs of the early settlers; only their names survive. Big and Little Hopkins Mountains to the west were named for two brothers who joined the settlement near the Curtis Clearing. The clearing was named for Norman and William Curtis, who settled in the area after 1865 and whose sisters, Eliza and Electra, married the Hopkins brothers. Later, John Sawyer harvested timber in the area now called Burnt Shanty Clearing, which is halfway between the Diamond Brook crossing and the intersection.

At the trail junction, at 3.4 miles, the right fork heads due north toward Thirteenth Lake. You want the left fork, which continues near the river for 0.5 mile to a lean-to by an enormous modern hikers' bridge, a few feet upstream from the ford used by outfitters who transported hunters and their camping gear into the wilderness via horse and wagon.

The trail to the ponds heads west; the trail straight ahead rejoins the north-south route. Heading west toward Siamese Ponds, you circle the southern edge of the flows that edge Siamese Brook. The trail then swings north around Siamese Mountain. After the trail crosses Siamese Brook, it begins to climb toward the west-southwest, rising 300 feet to a plateau before dropping to the shore of the eastern pond. You will probably notice the climb only if you are carrying a heavy pack.

Several campsites edge the trail and the eastern lake's western shore. Another choice camping spot can be found on the spit separating the ponds. Occasionally, you will find a rowboat on the eastern lake suitable for the trip across to the western lake. Many campers bring inflatable boats to Siamese Ponds, a wise move for those who wish to fish or simply to get away from other campers.

As you explore the ponds, you may find it hard to believe that the area was once heavily logged, and that not too many years ago a guest cabin for hunters was maintained on the eastern lake shore. If you are spending the night, you may have to share the lakes with other campers, but it is usually possible to find a camping spot in a hidden cove or bay, away from everyone else.

31

Chimney Mountain

Distance (round-trip): 2.5 miles

Vertical rise: 900 feet

Hiking time: 4 hours

Map: USGS Metric Thirteenth Lake

Siamese Ponds Wilderness Area

Chimney Mountain serves as an excellent introduction to the story of the rock mass that underlies the Adirondack landscape. Nowhere is that geological tale more vividly depicted. Hiking Chimney Mountain takes you back millions of years to the birth of these mountains and allows you to confront directly the results of many of the forces that shaped today's Adirondacks. This adventure to columns, caves, and crevices is as exciting as any other climb up a "big" mountain.

Beginning about 2.3 billion years ago, limestone and sandstone sediments were deposited in an area known as the Grenville Sea, a shallow body of water. Slowly, throughout the Precambrian period, sediments accumulated in the sea until about 1.4 billion years ago.

In the next 200 million years, there followed a period of mountain building known as the Grenville Orogeny. Some speculate that its cause was the collision of continental plates. Whatever the reason, the event changed all the area's rock. The sediments were intruded by magma, which cooled into syenite, gabbro, and granite. The entire mass lay several miles below the surface of the earth and the resulting heat and pressure metamorphosed any rocks that predated the Grenville Sea as well as the sediments and intrusions. The metamorphism produced syenite gneiss, granite gneiss, and metagabbro (or metanorthosite, as the feldspar-rich variety of Adirondack metagabbro is known).

These are among the rocks visible in the

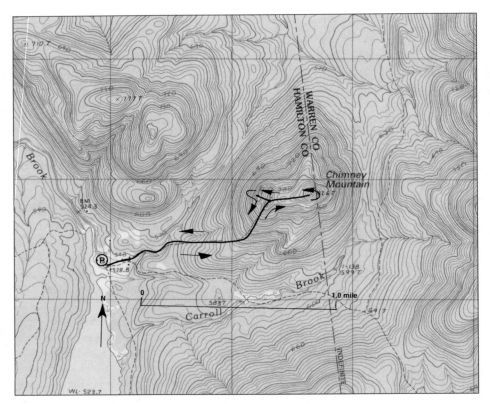

Adirondack dome today. Only the rocks persist from this ancient time, for the landscape is new. Erosion gradually carried away the overburden. About 400 million years ago, a period of upheaval created faults in the rock mass. Further erosion deepened the north-east-trending faults into the valleys and lakes we see today. Indian and Thirteenth Lakes were created in just this way. Finally, the period of glaciation sculpted the landscape into its present form.

It is possible that a part of Chimney Mountain, composed of Grenville rocks, took on its present form as recently as the retreat of the last ice age, a mere 10,000 years ago. It is theorized that in the period of erosion that culminated in the last ice age a layer of resistant rock was stripped from the mountain, revealing an upturned sand-wich of syenite gneiss, metamorphosed Grenville sediments or marbles, and a topping of layered granite gneiss. As the overburden was worn away, the release of pressure created fractures in the top layer. Erosion of the exposed surfaces was most rapid in the relatively softer middle layer; and as the top was undercut, a huge triangular block broke away, creating the rift on the mountain. Smaller blocks were moved along the fracture zones by ice and by the collapse of the triangular block, creating caves in the rift and in its western wall.

The rift valley is 600 feet long, ranging in width up to 250 feet and in depth to 200 feet. The Chimney itself rises 35 feet above the eastern rim, which falls beneath the Chimney, presenting a vertical drop of over 80 feet. Some of the openings are only cracks and crevices, but others are true caves and should be explored only by those with spelunking experience and equipment. A detailed map of the caves and paths through the valley is given in my *Discover the South Central Adirondacks.*

How to Get There

Drive south on NY 30 from Indian Lake Village for 0.6 mile to Big Brook Road, on the left, and continue southeast on Big Brook Road across the Abanakee Causeway. At 1.5 miles, turn right, south, continuing on Big Brook Road. There is a second, unmarked right turn about 2.2 miles farther. Continue 2.5 miles from that fork to the end of the road at Kings Flow, by a former Scout camp. Hikers are still permitted to park in a designated area for a fee, currently $1, and cross the private lands to the edge of the field where state land begins. Remember, camping, fishing, and hunting are prohibited on the private lands. Be very respectful of the property so that the owners will continue to extend this privilege of access to the public.

The Trail

After parking, walk east through the field beside a large barn that occupies the camp's northeast corner. The trail leads east-northeast into the forest and continues relatively level for a five-minute walk to a sign-in register beside a small stream. Cross the stream by hopping rocks and continue uphill. The 900-foot, 1.25-mile climb takes less than an hour.

At 1.1 miles, you reach the first overlook, just south of the rift valley, with views back across Kings Flow. At the overlook, the trail goes straight ahead, steeply uphill to the east rim and the Chimney. A path left becomes indistinct and branching; it leads to various caves and can be followed partway to the west rim. There is currently no good single route to the west rim; in fact, the whole area is a maze of paths. If you continue to the Chimney and study the landscape, you should be able to plot a route that will enable you to explore the rift as well as find your way to the west rim.

So stay straight, and in less than 10 minutes from the intersection you enter a walled corridor beneath ledges that extend from 8 to 15 feet above the path. Just as you enter this draw, note the small path heading down into the rift on your left, for you return here after inspecting the Chimney and absorbing the view. For starters, climb now to the top of the ledges on your right, from their northern end. From here the views of the mountains north of NY 28 are spectacular, with Vanderwhacker's cone silhouetted against the High Peaks. For an even more spectacular view north to the High Peaks, you can continue east following a faint path to Chimney's true summit, 0.25 mile away.

Return to the end of the draw and make the 8-foot climb over the ledge to your left. It leads to an outcrop that overlooks both the valley below and the Chimney above. Be careful near the cliff edge. If you walk around the Chimney on its eastern side, by first descending from your outcrop directly to the Chimney's base, you find a window in the boulders that artfully frames the view of the western rim.

When you return to the draw to find the path into the rift, be careful. Although it is not quite as steep as others, it is still a precipitous drop to the rift floor. Diverse paths lead through the valley, and you will want to poke about as much as time and ability allow. In summer, blasts of cold air emerge from the deeper crevices, and sometimes bursts of fog alert you to their presence. The walking is very rough, and it is easy to jam a foot in a crack between rocks.

The Chimney

The north end of the rift is a jumble of broken rock and talus rising about 18 feet from the valley. You can climb its western corner and find several large holes and a cave with ice in early July. If you walk across the valley floor on any of the many footpaths to the southwest corner, you will pass several large openings. Shine a flashlight into them. One cave has a distinctive round opening about 4 feet in diameter facing north at the edge of a huge, freestanding boulder. It drops 6 feet to a ledge from which you can almost always see ice and icicles in late summer.

After you have explored the valley, continue southwest, walking behind the rock that shields that ledge-cave, to find the unmarked path up the west wall. (Remember, all of this is really bushwhacking, improvising your own route, for no path in the valley is marked. It is a small area, so you are not apt to lose your way, but do watch your footing at every step.)

As you climb out of the valley toward the west wall, a narrow spine of rock, look for a clearly delineated but still unmarked footpath. Turn right, uphill, on it to find the highest overlook along the wall. Here, the view of the Chimney is spectacular, with easily discerned lines showing the variations in the Grenville deposits.

There is also a great view to the southwest. Beyond Kings Flow, Round Pond is visible, flanked on the north by Crotched Pond Mountain and on the south by Kunjamuk Mountain. Farther south, the split cone of Humphrey Mountain rises over the end of Kings Flow. Only the tops of Snowy and Squaw Mountains on the west side of Indian Lake show above the intervening range. From the northern end of the west wall, you see a panorama of the High Peaks that ranges from Santanoni to Giant.

A faint path leads south along the west rim for a quick descent to the fork above the first lookout. Several paths diverge from it, some leading back along the west face of that rim to deep and usually ice-filled crevices. You continue angling to the east to rejoin the path to Kings Flow.

Only the main footpath up the mountain is formally marked, so you should have a map and compass for this trip. You will also want a flashlight. Do not attempt to go in any of the caves without proper equipment, and knowledgeable and experienced leaders. I cannot stress enough that the majority of the caves are for experts only.

32

Pillsbury Mountain

Distance (round-trip): 5.6 miles (from Sled Harbor) or 3.4 miles (from Pillsbury trailhead)

Vertical rise: 1,677 feet

Hiking time: 4 hours

Maps: USGS Metric West Canada Lakes; USGS Metric Page Mountain

West Canada Lakes Wilderness Area

Pillsbury Mountain's summit gives an intimate view of the West Canada Lakes Wilderness, one of the Adirondacks' most remote, inaccessible, and hidden lake and forest regions. Hikes and camping trips in this wilderness core are described in *Discover the West Central Adirondacks.* There are five gateways to the West Canada Lakes Wilderness: a long trail from the north that begins after a tedious drive along a dirt road into the Moose River Plains; the Northville-Placid Trail from the northeast starting at the Cedar River Flow; the Northville-Placid Trail from the south starting at Piseco; the Sled Harbor access from the east through International Paper Company lands; and a connector to the Northville-Placid Trail from the southern extension of the road to Sled Harbor.

Inaccessibility has always enhanced the romantic aura surrounding the West Canadas, but the exploits of one of the region's former inhabitants, trapper French Louie, have added spice to that image. French Louie's traplines were strung between the region's lakes, circling the interior wilds. He knew every fishing hole in the wilderness and harvested hundreds of deer, bear, marten, beaver, mink, and otter skins. Each year, using part of the route you will follow on your trek to Pillsbury Mountain, he walked from his home on West Lake to Newton Corners, now Speculator, pulling a sled piled high with skins. These he exchanged for money, which in turn was exchanged for the whiskey that fueled some of the North Woods' most notorious drinking

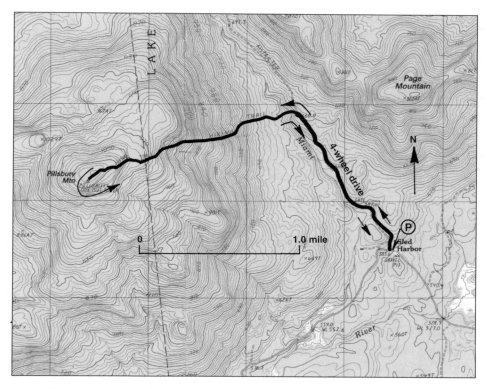

bouts. Stories of his excesses and antics survive in tales that contemporaries related to Harvey L. Dunham. His book, *French Louie: Early Life in the North Woods,* is your best introduction to the West Canada Lakes Wilderness, as well as a most amusing account of 19th-century life in the backwoods.

The road north from Speculator to Indian Lake originally passed through Perkins Clearing before heading west into the wilderness. Beyond Sled Harbor, the roads were so bad that wagon loads had to be shifted to sleds or sledges before continuing to distant lumber camps. Then the road, following precisely the one laid out in 1812 to open up the territory between Albany and Sackett's Harbor, headed north through the Miami River Valley between Pillsbury and Page Mountains. The trail along that stretch of road has been named the French Louie Trail.

How to Get There

To reach Sled Harbor, drive north on NY 30 for 8.4 miles from Speculator. Just after you pass Mason Lake, turn west along the shore of the lake on a dirt road (Jessup Mountain Road) that heads back south and southwest. There are a number of camping places along the lake, all popular and often full. The road angles south and at 2.4 miles traverses a swamp dominated to the west by views of Page Mountain. Turn right, west, at the intersection at 3.4 miles. This is Perkins Clearing. This logging road, which is easily passable by ordinary cars, heads due west, crosses the Miami River at 4.4 miles, and reaches the first parking area—an old gravel pit at Sled Harbor—at 5.1 miles. The main road continues to the left; for the road/trail to Pillsbury, take a sharp right, uphill. With a

---

high wheelbase, you can drive the 1.1 miles to a second parking area opposite the Pillsbury trailhead.

The Trail

At Sled Harbor, the road/trail heads west and uphill. Shortly you begin to hear the Miami River as the trail begins to follow the river quite closely through a lovely valley. The way is now gently uphill. At 1.1 miles from Sled Harbor, you pass a small field on your right, which is the new parking area. Just beyond, at 1.2 miles, the trail to the tower is a left turn. The intersection is marked with a guide board, and the trail has red markers.

You descend nearly 100 feet to cross the Miami River, here no more than a small stream. Then you immediately begin to climb, for you have over 1,500 feet to go in 1.6 miles.

The handsome woods surrounding the Miami River soon give way to groves of beech that have been decimated by the dieback. At first the trail does relatively little traversing across the hillside; it just heads straight up. Within 30 minutes you notice many blowdowns—the beech, of course, but also good-sized birch and striped maple—making the mountainside a scene of desolation. As the trail begins to zigzag up the slopes, you may tangle with the fallen telephone line that used to serve the tower. Along the steady climb, you pass a few erratics perched on the hillside. You may want to pause beside the stump of a huge yellow birch that once grew from a boulder beside the trail. Beyond this large boulder, the trail levels in a fern meadow, remarkable for the lack of forest cover. Grasses, sorrel, and hay-scented fern grow beneath the few spruce.

The trail becomes steep again, and on the next rise is worn to bedrock with seepage, so the footing is slippery. The worst of the climbing ends as the trail levels, then dips slightly before rising again, a last, sharp pitch. Suddenly the cover opens, providing a spectacular view northeast past Indian Lake to the High Peaks. A little more climbing brings you through a narrow trail beneath stunted spruce to the tower. The summit elevation is 3,597 feet.

Many points on the horizon should be obvious. Due north lies Wakely, and to the left, west-northwest of its tower, Manbury and Little Moose Mountains rise above portions of the Cedar Lakes. Both mountains have open rock slides. To the right of Wakely, Blue Mountain presents its rocky southern slopes. In the foreground to the northeast, Blue Ridge and Cellar Mountains lead to cone-shaped Lewey Mountain. Panther is the peak to the right of Lewey, and next, Snowy's unmistakable profile rises above the valley of Indian Lake.

To the right of Snowy, over the north end of Indian Lake, stretches one of the most exciting views in the Adirondacks. The eastern High Peaks, 50 miles distant in the northeast, are clearly visible above the lowland valleys of Indian Lake and the Boreas River. Only a couple of intervening mountains interrupt the string of summits.

Rock faces, scars, and slides present clearly recognizable patterns on the far peaks. To the left of Indian Lake, the mountain with two big open rock patches flanking its bare summit is Gothics. Between it and Snowy, but hardly obvious, lie Mount Marcy and Haystack. To the right of the foot of Indian Lake lies Vanderwhacker, and to its right on the horizon, the outline of a range of mountains traces the shape of a bracket pointing skyward. The apex of the bracket is Hough, with McComb and Dix flanking it, each baring rock slides that appear nearly identical at this distance.

Closer to Pillsbury, the mountains east of Indian Lake are readily identified. These include Bullhead, Puffer, and Gore with its rock cut. Crane Mountain lies due east on the horizon, almost in line with Dug Mountain. Whitaker Lake is visible southwest of Dug's summit, and the Kunjamuk Valley is outlined beyond it. A little east of south, Speculator Mountain rises behind Lake Pleasant. Much of Sacandaga Lake is also visible. Southeast from the lakes lies the valley of Piseco Lake, and you should be able to recognize the mountains on its western shore.

In the west you can see the valley of West Canada Creek stretching to the horizon. Nearer the tower you can spot a corner of Pillsbury Lake, with Noisey Ridge beside it. Mountains beside West Canada Lakes have more open rock ledges. Kitty Cobble is the highest peak to the north of "Big West" Mountain, the peak with cliffs that guards the lakes' northern shores.

33

Snowy Mountain

Distance (round-trip): 7.5 miles

Vertical rise: 2,100 feet

Hiking time: 6 hours

Map: USGS Metric Indian Lake

West Canada Lakes Wilderness Area

Some trails require and deserve rich and detailed descriptions. Others need only be located, for the route is obvious once you have arrived. The trail to Snowy Mountain is of the latter kind. The mountain is, after all, the Mount Marcy of the southern Adirondacks—it is the tallest and the most popular, with an overly worn trail to prove it. However, while this guide omits the trail up Mount Marcy on the grounds that it is often "as busy as a walk down 42nd Street," Snowy cannot be overlooked. Its views are too spectacular, and its striking profile too important as a reference from every other mountain in the southern and eastern Adirondacks. You have only to see its angular summit or its cliffs reflecting white in the sun from NY 30 driving north from Speculator to know you must climb it. And even though you can no longer climb Snowy's closed fire tower, you will be able to pick out a vast number of the Adirondacks' mountains from Snowy's clifftop vantages.

So choose a brilliant day, midweek if possible, and be rewarded with a solitary walk to this magnificent peak. Though long and precipitously steep near the summit, the trail is easy enough to follow. Rising 2,100 feet in just 3.7 miles, the trail is the most challenging in the southern Adirondacks; allow plenty of time.

How to Get There

The trailhead is on NY 30 opposite a parking turnout 17 miles north of Speculator and 7 miles south of Indian Lake Village. A sign marks the beginning of the trail.

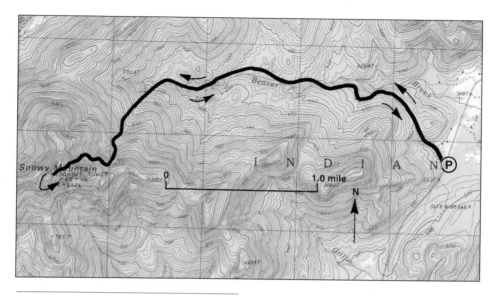

The Trail

The sign-in register is located about 0.2 mile from the highway along the red-marked trail. The first 2.5 miles of trail is over rolling terrain, and the climb is gentle, as you gain only 800 feet in that distance. In the past few years, Adirondack Mountain Club (ADK) trail crews have built many boardwalks over the muddy areas of the lower trail as well as stone staircases on particularly washed-out places along the lower slopes.

The trail heads northwest at first, through a mature forest of aspen; white and yellow birch; striped, red, and sugar maple; and beech interspersed with balsam, spruce, and hemlock. Within 1.1 miles you approach Beaver Brook, which accompanies the trail at varying segments for another 1.5 miles. The trail crosses that braided stream several times, at one point traversing an island between branches. After the last crossing at 1.9 miles, the trail continues quite close to the brook for 0.6 mile.

It is in the last 1.2 miles that you encounter steep pitches, with the last 0.5 mile so steep that you have to use your hands. The trail is essentially a rocky streambed, and much work remains to be done to rehabilitate it on the upper slopes. The DEC is currently considering a major relocation near the top, which will follow in part an older trail, not the straight ascent that currently follows the route of the old telephone line. ADK has proposed ladders or other devices for the last pitch to the summit.

In the last 0.5 mile, the trail is worn to bedrock, deeply cut through the soil in places, with water coursing down most of the upper trail. In wet weather, danger exists for both trail and hikers, for then you are forced off the slippery rocks to the sides. Pulling at trees and roots for support further erodes the trailsides. Here, the forest changes dramatically from tall to scrub trees, mostly balsam, mountain ash, white birch, and striped maple. Long before you reach the summit, you can enjoy glimpses of the mountains to the east side of Indian Lake. One open stretch of trail offers views to the northeast, revealing a High Peaks profile that is among the best available on the mountain. As it approaches the summit, the trail climbs through a draw between two cliffs and emerges on the top of the eastern cliff, with its easterly views. This grassy knoll, where no sign of the fire observer's cabin remains, is a nice spot for a picnic.

In the past few years, hikers have worn paths to vantages that look out in every direction, so even if you cannot enjoy the tower's broad panorama, you can find overlooks for every point on the compass. You should be able to pick out Crotched Pond and Kunjamuk Mountains a little south of east, across Indian Lake. Behind them range Bullhead, Puffer, and Humphrey, the latter a distinctive, regular cone. On the horizon between Crotched Pond and Kunjamuk Mountains, the slash of the Barton garnet mine clearly identifies Gore Mountain. Farther to the right, south, is the broad summit of Eleventh Mountain, and beyond, to the right, is Crane Mountain, whose summit is 24 miles distant. You may be confused by the jumble of hills farther south; the view of them was better from the tower.

Walk west from the cabin site to an open rock ledge on the west side of the summit. Narrow footpaths winding across the scrub covering the summit lead you to it. The rock surmounts a cliff, so wooded that it is scarcely noticeable from western vantages; however, the opening provides my favorite vista from Snowy. The dense row of hills, in which Snowy is almost central, is cut with a deep cleft valley trending northeast to southwest. The heavily wooded and remote valley is really not obvious from many other points, but it is one of the Adirondacks' deeper ones. Two brooks rise in the valley: Squaw, which flows northeast into Indian Lake, and Little Squaw, which flows southwest into the Cedar River Flow. The valley is bordered on the east by Squaw, Snowy, and

Lewey Mountains; on the west by a steep little knob called Onion Hill on the USGS map; and by Buck, Buell, and Panther Mountains ranging to the north. The latter's summit is only 34 feet lower than Snowy's 3,899-foot elevation. Panther's peak is toward magnetic north from Snowy, and to its right is Burgess Mountain.

Beyond Lewey Mountain is a chain of mountains. Cellar is to its left, south, with Blue Ridge Mountain between them. Farther to the right of Cellar you can spot Pillsbury Mountain, which lies, as does Snowy, on the edge of the West Canada Lakes Wilderness.

Farther to the south you can see Lewey Lake, and the long finger of Indian Lake that fills the valley through which the Jessup River once flowed. To the east of south, Dug Mountain is obvious.

Returning to Panther, look to its south for Buell Mountain. Immediately south of Buell, in the distance, is Wakely, which also has a fire tower. To its right on the horizon you should be able to spot West Mountain exactly 20 miles away.

You need a really clear day and good binoculars to pick out the High Peaks. While views from the north summit both east and west are marvelous, the tower certainly did enhance the most distant views.

To name the High Peaks, start again with Panther. To its right and 12 miles away lies the top of Blue Mountain. Moving around to the right, on the far horizon, you should be able to identify the Seward Range, in which Seymour presents the most obvious shape, a steep cone. Santanoni is next, a huge mountain on the horizon. It is reported that the top of Whiteface can be seen above the right side of Santanoni, but it is 51 miles away and requires a perfectly clear day. I have never been certain that I could see it.

Moving to the right, east, MacIntyre is

obvious, as is the cleft of Indian Pass, which precedes it. The sharp valley to the right of MacIntyre is Avalanche Pass, and to its right range Colden, Marcy, and Haystack, 36 miles away. The jagged summits that follow are the Gothics and Sawteeth, then Nippletop. Vanderwhacker is the isolated mountain in the middle distance; it lies between the Hudson Valley and the High Peaks, in line with the eastern range of the High Peaks and the end of Indian Lake. In all, 32 of the 46 High Peaks are visible from Snowy Mountain, though without the tower you have to move about the summit to find openings that duplicate the tower's views.

Even with this outline and the appropriate USGS maps, you may at first have trouble recognizing the profiles of far-off mountains. In your climbs you will find that the change in perspective from one crest to another completely alters the distant profiles, so it may take several trips before the mountains become familiar. Snowy is a marvelous place to begin to make their acquaintance.

34

Wakely Mountain

Distance (round-trip): 6.4 miles

Vertical rise: 1,636 feet

Hiking time: 5½ hours

Maps: USGS Metric Indian Lake; USGS Metric Wakely Mountain

Fire tower

In 1978 only 200 visitors made the climb to Wakely, while 5,200 made the trek up Blue Mountain, just 11 miles away. Today the disparity is even greater. Perhaps the long drive to the trailhead on Cedar River Road deters some people, but that trek is part of the fun of discovering Wakely.

The Cedar River Flow, a long, man-made lake, begins 0.3 mile beyond the Wakely trailhead, and it is a popular camping spot as well as a gateway to the Moose River Plains. Consider camping there when you climb Wakely. You will find details of many adventures in the area in *Discover the West Central Adirondacks.*

Hikers who become acquainted with the Adirondacks by approaches from the south and east are often unaware of Wakely's existence, because from that direction it is hidden by the range of mountains west of Indian Lake. However, if you hike the low hills in the northern and western Adirondacks, you soon discover how commanding a position Wakely holds. The panorama from its summit includes the only overview of the Moose River Plains, which reach to the southwestern horizon.

The fact that Little Moose and Manbury Mountains block the view to the southwest, and to Cedar and West Canada Lakes, is more than compensated for by the view to the east over the Cedar River Flow and Valley, which leads up to the western profiles of Panther and Snowy Mountains. Best of all, the Cedar River Valley opens out to permit a view north-northeast to the High Peaks.

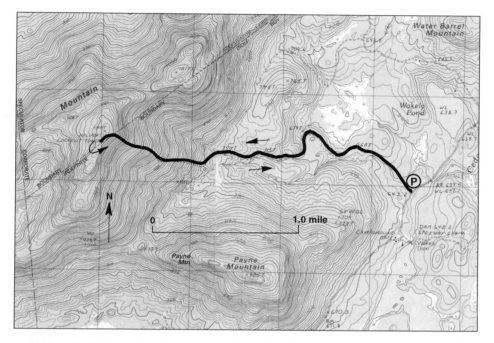

William D. Wakeley, for whom the pond and mountain are named, apparently spelled his name with a second *e*, unlike the USGS map. Wakeley was a British-born hotel-keeper who pushed this road through to Cedar River Falls, where in the 1870s he built a dam, a sawmill, and a hotel. His Cedar Falls Hotel was "so remote that each night bonfires were required during his first season to keep the wolves from his tethered oxen. The impressive hotel had a three-story main building, with two-story wings, and sported a bar." According to his advertisements in *Wallace's Guide to the Adirondacks* of 1878, his hotel was located in the finest sporting grounds of the Adirondacks, and his table abounded with game and fish. The hotel burned in 1878 and was rebuilt on a smaller scale, only to burn again in 1884.

Throughout the late 1880s Wakeley ran a stage from North Creek to Blue Mountain, with connecting coaches to the Cedar Falls Hotel. At that time, the main road from Indian Lake followed the Cedar River Road south to a dirt road that is now the route of the Northville-Placid Trail between McCanes and Lake Durant.

How to Get There

To reach the trailhead, drive west from Indian Lake village on NY 28-30. You cross the Cedar River in just under 2 miles. Cedar River Road is a left, west, turn at the point where the highway turns north, 0.2 mile beyond the bridge. There is a cemetery near the intersection.

On the drive to the trailhead, the Cedar River is mostly out of sight, with the exception of a short stretch within 1 mile of NY 28-30. Near McCanes the handsome view southwest across nearby fields is of Burgess and Panther mountains. Other guideposts along the road are a series of short hills to the west: Round Top is first in the north; Sugarloaf with its dramatic rock face is next; and Water Barrel is just north of Wakely Pond. Sugarloaf's resemblance to an old-fashioned cone of sugar is so striking that the mountain actually looks like a miniature of its Brazilian counterpart. Your best view of it is looking north from the road, 2 miles north of Wakely Dam. The road intersects the Northville-Placid Trail at McCanes. From McCanes south, that trail follows the road for the 7.1 miles to the flow.

Cedar River Road changes from macadam to dirt within 3 miles from NY 30. You will cross the outlet of Wakely Pond 5.5 miles south of the Northville-Placid trailhead. Pause a moment on the causeway to view Wakely and its tower, then continue about 0.7 mile to a dirt road on your right. This former logging road, at 12 miles from NY 28-30, is the trailhead for Wakely Mountain. Allow for 45 minutes to navigate the length of Cedar River Road. There is a large parking area at the start of the side road. The Wakely Dam camping area, ranger station, and entrance gate for the Moose River Road are located only 0.3 mile further down the main road.

Lands on both sides of the trail and even up the steep lower slopes of Wakely Mountain were logged in 1986 and 1987, just before the state purchased this tract from International Paper Company. The state purchase included Wakely Pond and a portion of the Cedar River downstream from Wakely Dam. Both have good fishing.

The Trail

From the trailhead parking area and register, the trail follows a narrow gravel lane that is still used by those vehicles capable of doing so. You will not see any trail markers at first. The road leads west from Cedar River Road through a young forest of aspen, beech, and cherry, interspersed with spruce thickets. The road fords a small stream at 0.2 mile and continues with the stream close on

the left, south. As you walk, you have occasional glimpses of Wakely. Some of the surroundings appear to be former staging areas returning to forest, and you may spot the remains of several buildings and an old truck. The trees along the road are uniformly young, but they do manage to shade the trail in summer.

After 1.1 miles and 20 minutes of walking, you reach a barricade where motorized access ends. Beyond is a small footbridge. The trail now follows the stream you have just crossed. You continue to the right of it and its merry, tumbling course. As you continue gently uphill, you can sometimes see the tower ahead. You cross a second, smaller stream without the benefit of a bridge and begin another gentle climb.

You may notice several logging roads branching off, but none are so obvious as the main trail, even if there are no trail markers in this section. At 2 miles you reach a sign pointing to a foot trail on the right. Here, at an elevation of 2,530 feet, you have climbed about 400 feet from Cedar River Road, but you have over 1,200 feet left to climb in under a mile. Before you begin that climb, walk a few feet farther along the abandoned logging road and enjoy the view over the weedy beaver meadow.

Beginning right at the sign, the trail begins its relentless climb, which will not moderate until you reach the summit. Red markers guide your way on the narrow footpath, a dry, hard-packed trail up the logged hillside. A mixture of beech, maple, and yellow birch gives way to spruce and balsam the higher you climb.

Just past halfway to the summit, the mountain is so steep that the trail begins to zigzag back and forth across the side of the mountain. A straighter, steeper route that cuts through the middle of the zigzags was where a telephone cable once connected the tower with the rest of the manmade world. The trees become smaller, with balsam predominating. Finally the grade eases, and you can see an opening to your right with the aging helicopter pad that served the tower for years.

You should reach the tower on the 3,744-foot summit after walking 2 to 2½ hours from Cedar River Road. You have to climb a few flights of stairs on the unmanned tower for the view, as the broad summit is mostly tree covered. The tower is 92 feet tall, the tallest in the Adirondacks.

Blue Mountain lies beyond the helicopter pad north of the tower. If you are lucky enough to have climbed on a really clear day, you should spot Whiteface in the distant north to its right. The eastern High Peaks range farther to the right, and you can name Santanoni, MacIntyre, Colden, Marcy, Haystack, Gothics, Giant, and Big Slide.

The view east is not as distant, for the range of mountains west of Indian Lake Valley blocks the horizon. From north to south they are Panther; Snowy, with its tower; Lewey; Cellar; and Blue Ridge. Directly south lies Pillsbury Mountain, also topped by a tower.

The view west and northwest encompasses many lakes, with Fourth Lake, the largest of the Fulton Chain, beyond Lake Kora; Sagamore Lake north of Kora; and Raquette Lake to its north. West Mountain is visible across Raquette. The wooded summit of the Blue Ridge, the second group so named and visible from Wakely, shuts out a view of Blue Mountain Lake, but the tower on Blue is clearly visible. Rondaxe Tower on Bald Mountain is visible on the rocky ledge overlooking Fourth Lake, and Goodnow Tower can be seen in front of the High Peaks.

For the first part of your descent, you will find you are walking almost as slowly as you climbed, because the way is really steep. Still, a half hour should see you past the worst, and 45 minutes suffices for the descent to the main logging road. You should be able to make the return trip to your car in less than another hour.

35

Rock, Cascade, and Stephens Ponds

Distance: 7.5 miles or 9.7 miles (alternate loop)

Vertical rise: 370 feet

Hiking time: 4 hours

Map: USGS Metric Blue Mountain Lake

Blue Ridge Wilderness Area

Lake Durant Campground is an ideal location from which to discover the heart of the Adirondacks near Blue Mountain. If the weather is not clear enough for a mountain hike, you will enjoy the variety provided by a visit to three remote ponds. A handsome loop connects Rock, Cascade, and Stephens Ponds, all in the Blue Ridge Wilderness just south of Lake Durant.

The entrance to the Lake Durant Campground is on NY 30, 8.5 miles north of Indian Lake Village and 2.5 miles southeast of Blue Mountain Lake and the junction of NY 30 and NY 28. On part of the loop you follow the Northville-Placid Trail, New York's famous trail that winds along both footpaths and roads from Northville in the south, through Wilderness Areas and villages, to Lake Placid in the north, a distance of 119 miles.

How to Get There

The eastern end of this hike terminates at the Lake Durant Campground; if you park here, there is a day-use fee. A parking area for the Northville-Placid Trail is immediately west of the entrance to Lake Durant Campground, and day-hikers may wish to begin there to avoid the campground's day-use parking fee. The western end is at the opposite end of Lake Durant, down a side road; walk or drive along NY 30 for 2 miles and turn left onto Durant Road, then immediately left again in 0.2 mile, following signs to the Rock Pond Trailhead. If you do not have two cars, one to leave at each end of the hike, you can make a full circuit by walk-

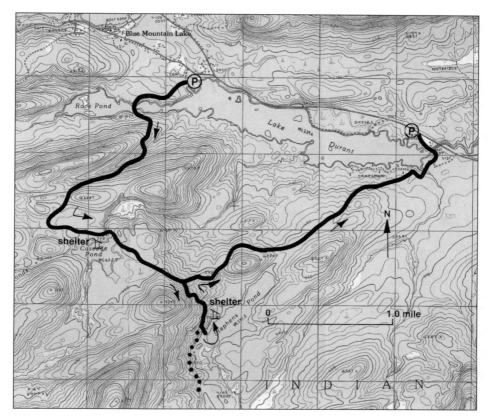

ing along the highway between the two trail-heads, adding 2.2 miles to the trip. On the way, just 0.2 mile west of the Northville-Placid trailhead, a dirt road, the old highway route, circles south bordering Lake Durant's marshes. Including this nature walk on a trek along the highway really enhances a loop from the western parking area.

The Trail

This hike begins from the western trailhead and follows a dirt road alongside a cemetery. The road goes to a picnic spot on the shore of Lake Durant, passing a big glacial erratic and an outhouse. The intersection is not well marked, although there are some informal red blazes to indicate the trail, which immediately crosses a small stream

on a footbridge. Now you see the first of the official red trail markers.

It is only 0.8 mile west to the long bridge separating Rock Pond from Lake Durant. From the bridge, Blue Mountain appears to loom over the water. Across the bridge, the trail becomes a narrow footpath heading up and over a ridge. The route is little used; you really need the red markers here. As you cross the ridge, you see a second hill across a small valley. A short, steep descent into that valley takes you to a small stream. Cross it and turn right to parallel it, climbing through the valley along the prettiest section of the day's hike. Tall, straight hardwoods make a forest so open that you can see the hills on both sides.

At the head of the valley, the trail turns

Rock, Cascade, and Stephens Ponds

The view across Lake Durant to Blue Mountain

left for the short climb southwest over the end of the ridge. A long, almost level stretch through a hemlock thicket follows before you reach a trail junction. The right fork is unmarked, but the left is designated as being 0.9 mile from Cascade Pond. The sign says it is 1.8 miles back to Rock Pond and 2.3 miles to Blue Mountain. The mileages on signs you see on this trip do not quite add up, but the walking time to this point is about 75 minutes.

Bear left. The trail turns southeast to follow an obvious old road walled in with tall, straight hemlock and spruce. As you first approach Cascade Pond, a path forks right to an evergreen-covered promontory. The trail continues to a lean-to at the foot of the pond and there crosses the outlet on a narrow log bridge. Below you is the small cascade that lends the pond its name. There are parting views of the pond beyond the bridge, and then you plunge back into the woods.

Southeast of Cascade Pond the trail is good and broad, offering a lovely 20-minute walk through a forest with many white birch and lots of spring flowers. Then, for the next 15 minutes, you descend slightly to an intersection 1 mile from the Cascade Pond Lean-to, and 0.6 mile from the Stephens Pond Lean-to to the right via the blue-marked Northville-Placid Trail. The left fork, also marked blue, heads 2.5 miles northeast to the Lake Durant Campground.

Bear right to Stephens Pond. The walk is very pretty, heading east and then southeast down a long hill to the lean-to. You often find nesting loons and sometimes good fishing in the pond, though reputedly not as good as at Cascade Pond. Much of the shoreline is swampy, but there are several good campsites near the southwestern corner.

As you head back to the intersection and then on toward Lake Durant, you will be impressed by the width of the Northville-Placid Trail. The route northeast from the intersection runs moderately downhill a short distance and then slopes more gently the rest of the way to the campsite. Here the forest is less exciting, and the trail is fairly heavily used. It is typical of that trail's passage through the Adirondacks; in comparison, nearby routes are often much more fun. Unless you parked at the campground, continue through to its entrance on NY 30, and head west to your car.

36

Blue Mountain

Distance (round-trip): 4 miles

Vertical rise: 1,560 feet

Hiking time: 3½ hours

Map: USGS Metric Blue Mountain Lake

Fire tower: Manned in summer courtesy of private donations

A combination of extraordinary views and easy accessibility attracts thousands of hikers yearly to the 3,759-foot summit of Blue Mountain. The 2-mile climb of 1,750 feet requires less than two hours and is not overly strenuous. The walk down usually takes only 90 minutes, so even with a picnic stop, exploring Blue Mountain is a half-day outing, allowing you plenty of time to visit the nearby Adirondack Museum at Blue Mountain Lake.

If you make the climb in the early morning, you can enjoy the play of sunlight across the Eckford Chain of lakes that stretches west from Blue Mountain to the distant horizon. If you visit the museum first and then climb the mountain, the western sun will better illuminate the distant crest of the eastern High Peaks. Either way, the museum is a good introduction to the Adirondacks. Hikers will find the museum's large relief map of the region especially appealing. Lights can be switched on to indicate many of the more famous mountains.

The Blue Mountain region was one of the early areas in the Adirondacks to be developed as a resort. The first hotel was started on the lake's shores in 1874 by John Holland. The principal developer of this part of the Adirondack interior, however, was William West Durant, the son of the Union Pacific railroad baron who was also responsible for getting the first tracks to North Creek. The younger Durant invested his time and enthusiasm for the North Woods in acquiring huge tracts of land, including all of Township 34, in which the Eckford Chain

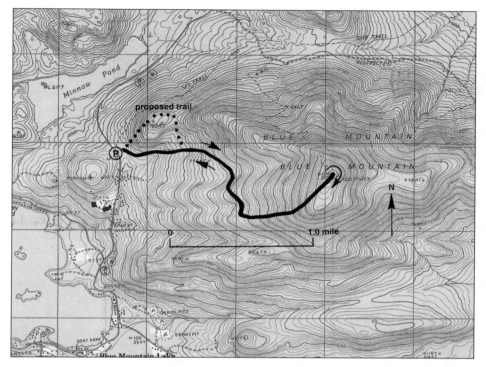

of lakes lies. Blue Mountain Lake is the northernmost in that chain; Eagle and Utowana stretch to the southwest and are connected, via the Marion River and its famous carry, to Raquette Lake. Durant built for himself the magnificent Camp Pine Knot on Raquette Lake as well as several homes in the style the noted Adirondack writer Alfred Donaldson calls "camp beautiful" on nearby lakes, among them Uncas on the lake that now bears that name.

Durant also encouraged the development of Blue Mountain Lake. But while Raquette Lake was "dominated by the camp beautiful idea, Blue Mountain succumbed, structurally, to the hotel horrible." The lake's original hotel took its name from the mountain that rises to the lake's east, and Blue Mountain became the dominant feature of the landscape in name as well as fact.

The mountain looms over the surrounding countryside, almost always appearing in shades of blue, a dark, imposing hulk, scarred on its southern face with rock slides and presenting a distinctive silhouette as a reference from almost every direction.

How to Get There

The Adirondack Museum is 1.1 miles north of the intersection of NY 28N and NY 30, and the trailhead is 0.4 mile north of the museum, at the height-of-land on the east side of NY 30.

The Trail

This trailhead replaces the traditional beginning, which crossed private lands. The new route, slightly longer than the original, saves about 200 feet of climbing. It commences from the same parking area as the trail to Tirrell Pond.

The trail still crosses private lands—those of Finch, Pruyn, and Company, which has granted public access. The beginning follows a logging road for 300 yards to a sign-in booth. Land on both sides of the road is posted. The trail heads generally east and already shows signs of being rutted and eroded by hikers' boots. You cross a stream on a half-log bridge, then begin a fairly steep climb. After 20 minutes, the route levels out beneath huge paper birch with a lush fern understory. In the next few minutes you will cross two streams and, shortly beyond, turn steeply uphill. This pitch leads to a level in an especially beautiful wooded area. As you wind in a southeast direction across the saddle, you encounter another stream. After a 40-minute walk, climbing 600 feet in 1.1 miles, turn east to join the old route. You have nearly 1,000 feet to climb in less than a mile.

Blue Mountain's famous steep pitches begin almost immediately. The route is worn to bedrock, smooth slabs that at times seem like an almost vertical sidewalk. The route is so steep that the sky seems to emerge deceptively through the evergreens, prematurely alerting you to the summit. The cover has shrunk to scrubby balsam and birch, dense growth clinging to the mountainside. Look for the intrusion of quartz crystals in the rock beneath your feet. The steep section levels out after a half hour of puffing, unless you rest to catch your breath. New and old corduroy lines the trail through a sphagnum area on the level summit. Forty minutes from the intersection, you should see the tower.

The best views are from the tower. The sweep of ponds and lakes fading into the distant west is amazing. Blue Mountain's isolation from surrounding hills means the views are especially good. The closest summit that exceeds it in height is more than 12

➤ The Adirondack Survey

When Verplank Colvin, often called the father of the Adirondack Park, began the first survey of the region in 1872, measurements were still made via chains and elevation was determined by comparing barometric pressure among mountain peaks. It was Colvin's careful way of using these simple tools, inventing others, and filling in with triangulations that enabled him to measure the location and height of Adirondack summits, correctly place the lakes and ponds, and determine the contours of the rugged slopes. One key to his work was establishing sight lines between peaks. His crews cleared many summits that remain bare even today (although the top of Blue Mountain has regrown to scrub spruce and fir). Colvin's crews also had to coordinate their measurements precisely, so it was essential that everyone know the exact time. Because Blue Mountain was the center of much surveying work, each night at nine a charge of gunpowder was set off from it to alert observers on distant summits. In this way all observations were synchronized.

miles away. Most spectacular is the vista northeast across Tirrell Pond to the outcrops of Tirrell Mountain. Beyond them rise Dun Brook Mountain on the right and the Fishing Brook Range on the left, with many of the High Peaks recognizable on that far horizon.

To the west you have the lovely view across Blue Mountain Lake and its sisters in the Eckford Chain. "Sisters" is appropriate, for originally all three lakes were named by the surveyor Emmons for the daughters of Henry Eckford: Janet, Marion, and Catherine. Eckford first visited the lakes while participating in the 1811 state waterway survey.

You need an atlas or a large-scale map and a good pair of binoculars to help identify individual mountains. Private funds have been raised to staff the tower in summer, and the tower ranger can help you identify points on the 360-degree horizon. From right to left beyond the north side of Dun Brook Mountain are Dix, Colvin, Marcy, Colden, the MacIntyre Mountains, and Santanoni. The most distant identifiable peak is Whiteface, which appears behind Sawtooth, with Deward, Kempshall, and Ampersand filling out the row of significant summits to the north.

South of Dun Brook Mountain you can pick out Vanderwhacker and, if conditions are right, Pharaoh Mountain on the far eastern edge of the Adirondacks. In the south, Wakely is obvious, but Snowy is harder to spot because you see only a small portion of it behind Panther. Immediately south lies Lake Durant, with Stephens Pond visible behind it. Completing the panorama back to Eagle and Utowana Lakes are the Metcalf Mountains and the Blue Ridge.

Looking northwest across South Pond with its several islands, the double summit of Owls Head, with Mount Sabattis to its north and a little closer, completes the view back to the north and Kempshall. Once you have picked out the major peaks, you can more easily name the numerous bodies of water.

The northeast face of the summit is bare, so you have good views without climbing the tower. There is a picnic table north of the tower, and several other places along the ridge are ideal for a meal, offering a panorama of the sweep of mountains beyond Tirrell Mountain and Tirrell Pond. In 1853, Irish immigrants were brought to the shores of Tirrell Pond from Ticonderoga by a Catholic priest, Father Olivetti. The rigors of the woods proved too much for them, and they quickly moved on, abandoning the 16 log cabins they had erected, but leaving the name of their foreman, Pat Tirrell.

To the north of the summit rises a radio relay tower, but there are no good views from the exposed rock that covers the summit in that direction. The slides you see while driving north on NY 30 are all well below the summit on the south face and fairly difficult to reach.

Return by the same route. For the first half hour of your descent, watch your footing; the trail is steep and rugged.

37

Owls Head Mountain

Distance (round-trip): 7.2 miles

Hiking time: 3½ hours

Vertical rise: 1,060 feet

Map: USGS Metric Deerland

From NY 30 along the eastern shore of Long Lake, you can spot the double peak that inspired the name of Owls Head Mountain. Owls Head overlooks the southern end of that 14-mile-long lake, which is really just a widened section of the Raquette River. South of the lake on the river is Buttermilk Falls, one of the Adirondacks' choicest spots. Since the climb up the mountain should take no more than a half day, plan a morning visit to the falls before you reach the trailhead and a late afternoon trek from the mountain trail to Lake Eaton for a swim (that 1-mile detour is included in the hike total above). With all these opportunities, you are sure to remember the day as one of your great ones in the Adirondacks.

If you are coming from the south, certainly visit the falls first. Drive north on NY 30 from Blue Mountain Lake for nearly 8 miles, where the highway angles right and another road turns sharply left. A state sign designates the road as the access to the Forked Lake Campground, a good base for explorations near Long Lake. The sign indicating that the road also leads to Buttermilk Falls is visible only if you are driving south from Long Lake Village, 3.5 miles to the north.

In 2.1 miles there is a small unmarked parking turnout, which is not even 100 yards from the falls. No camping is allowed in the vicinity, but there are picnic tables and fireplaces. The light in early morning, shining through the pine, is especially good for photographing the falls, whose roar is evident even at the parking turnout. The falls

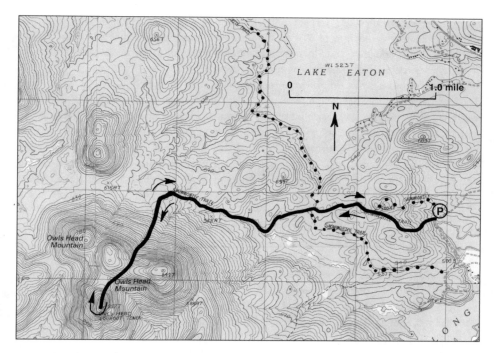

are so handsome that you may want to return for a picnic after you climb Owls Head.

How to Get There

To reach the Owls Head trailhead from the bridge over the Long Lake narrows on the northwest side of the village, continue north on NY 30 for 0.6 mile to Endion Road and turn left, southwest, on it. Follow it for 1.5 miles to a parking turnout on the right. A trailhead sign indicates distances on the red-marked hiking trail to Owls Head and to several destinations reached by snowmobile trails, which intersect the hiking trail at several points.

The Trail

From the trailhead register, the Owls Head Trail begins a moderate climb over a small ridge, followed by a gentle descent. After 25 minutes, at 1 mile, you reach a three-way intersection. The way right is a snowmobile

trail leading to Lake Eaton, along which you will return if you make the detour to the lake. For now, turn left (the sign says 2.1 miles to Owls Head) and in 200 yards a second trail forks right back to the lake. In another few minutes, an abandoned snowmobile trail forks to the left.

There are no more snowmobile markers along the red-marked route straight ahead. It continues through a good, deep forest of yellow birch, spruce, hemlock, and maple. The trail is generally level for a bit longer; it's a great dry route, hard-packed and smooth through a mixed forest of mature trees and smaller saplings.

The trail starts uphill 45 minutes into your walk, gently at first, then more steeply. The trail enters a little draw with a small stream.

Follow the stream on its right bank; perhaps you will spot signs of both bear and deer. You walk for another 20 minutes before you realize that you are really beginning

---

Owls Head Mountain

to climb. Fifteen minutes later you encounter the first rock-strewn section of trail as the old logging road joins an intermittent streambed. A deep valley begins to appear on your right and a small one on your left. The trail becomes noticeably steeper with a water-washed, rubble base. Stay left of the watercourse, in a shallow draw; the trail disappears in a section of deadfalls. A few huge maple and beech have fallen across it, and higher up there has been a significant blowdown of striped maple.

As you emerge from the draw you will see high ground on your left. You cross a height-of-land and descend nearly 100 feet in elevation to a valley that lies below the summit of Owls Head, with its abandoned tower. The remains of the ranger's cabin occupies a portion of the meadow of hay-scented fern that fills the valley.

Immediately beyond the cabin site you climb again, now on a much narrower and steeper trail. The footpath zigzags across the steep face of the summit knoll. A few of the rock stairs and ledges constructed by the tower's first ranger survive, although all the railings are gone. The route is just steep enough for you to need an occasional handhold.

As the trail swings west just below the summit, you catch glimpses through the trees of the watery panorama that stretches to the southwest, including Raquette and Forked Lakes. You should be able to climb the small summit knob in 20 minutes or less, in spite of the route's steepness.

The fire tower is still standing, minus its lower staircases, but the tower is not necessary to take in the spectacular view to the east. A cliff faces the mountain's eastern side, keeping the vista open through more than 180 degrees of the compass. To the southeast you can see Blue Mountain across South Pond. Owls Head Pond is the

dark emerald gem a little west of south just below. Due south, Snowy and the mountains adjacent to Indian Lake stand out on the horizon.

Not much of Long Lake is visible from the 2,780-foot summit; the lake is narrow and tucked between mountains that range to the northeast. A little south of east, East Inlet and Sabattis Mountains rise above one of the few parts of the lake that can be seen. Over it in the northeast you can spot Kempshall Mountain, with Santanoni in the distance beyond. Just to the right of Santanoni you should be able to discern Marcy and the eastern High Peaks fading into the distance.

The northern spur of Owls Head bisects the range of the High Peaks in the northeast. To the left of the spur lies Seymour, then the Seward Range.

These views from the cliffs are the best the 2,687-foot summit has to offer, for there are no really good vantages from which to survey the sweep of lakes lying to the southwest. The drop below the tower summit is several hundred feet, a distance that provides a marvelous updraft for soaring hawks and a windswept perch to keep the bugs away.

When you descend, even if the day is not warm enough for swimming, consider visiting Lake Eaton. Within three minutes from the marked junction, you intersect a snowmobile trail from Endion Road (you use a shortcut to this route on the return). It hardly takes 10 minutes to reach the lake, so the 0.5-mile distance stated on the sign must be a bit exaggerated.

The road approaches the lake and then turns west to round it. Walk to the first opening you see, a lovely grass-covered spot below tall spruce. The lake's sandy shores invite you to swim. The opening is a landing site and access to the trail for boaters from the Lake Eaton Campground, which could also serve as a base for hiking in the Long Lake area. The campground is off a right fork from NY 30, 1.4 miles northwest of Endion Road.

On your return to the Owls Head Trail, bear left on the more obvious fork. (If you were climbing to the summit from Lake Eaton, you would probably miss the right fork completely.) You will intersect the trail that takes you back to Endion Road in less than 10 minutes. Without the detour to Lake Eaton, the descent should take little more than 1½ hours.

38

Nehasane Preserve

Distance (round-trip): 9.4 miles

Vertical rise: 460 feet

Hiking time: 5 hours

Maps: USGS Metric Beaver River; USGS Metric Little Tupper Lake; USGS Metric Forked Lake; USGS 7.5' Wolf Mountain

Since 1894, land that the state has acquired for the Forest Preserve of the Adirondack Park has come from many sources. A few parcels have been outright gifts and some have been purchased by conservation groups, but the vast majority have been bought with state funds. In the early years of the Forest Preserve, most of the Adirondacks had been heavily logged, so huge tracts with depleted value were frequently offered for sale to the state or taken by the state to cover back taxes. Over the years, though, the most exciting purchases have been the huge tracts of land, encompassing thousands of acres, amassed by private clubs or wealthy individuals during the second half of the 19th century. One such acquisition by the state is Nehasane Preserve, once the private park of Dr. William Seward Webb. Parts of Webb's lands were acquired by the state in the 1890s; Nehasane did not become state land until 1979.

This major addition places within the public domain the largest wholly state-owned lake in the Adirondacks and a huge preserve that offers great opportunities for hiking, camping, canoeing, and fishing. The walk described here only introduces you to the area; I am certain that once you have visited Nehasane, you will want to return for a longer stay to explore other parts of the preserve.

Nehasane originally encompassed over 140,000 acres, and even with the sale years ago of 50,000 acres in what is now the Five Ponds Wilderness Area, Nehasane was still larger than either Litchfield or

Whitney Parks. The lands around Lake Lila have not been logged for more than 50 years, so this addition is a true wilderness gem.

Dr. Webb was the builder of the Adirondack & St. Lawrence Railroad. It stretched across the Adirondacks, connecting Utica in the south with Malone in the north. That railroad once carried Webb's guests by private railcar from New York City to his personal station just north of the lodge.

At Nehasane, you can enjoy the woods as the railroad baron might have, for parking restrictions limit the total number of hikers and campers in the area to approximately the number of visitors Webb could entertain at one time at his huge, 20-bedroom lodge and a cluster of guest houses on the shore of Lake Lila.

The land around Lake Lila has been classified Primitive, while the rest of the estate has been given Wilderness protection. This means that no motorboats are allowed on the lake and only DEC vehicles or those of owners of adjacent private land are permitted on the road/trail that continues from the parking area around the north shore of Lake Lila. In addition, special rules govern the former estate. Parking is permitted only at the designated area, not along the access road. Where the road/trail passes through private lands still held by Webb's heirs, you must stay on the road. No trailers are permitted in the parking area, and you may not camp within 0.25 mile of it. At the lake you must camp at designated sites only, or at sites at least 150 feet from water.

How to Get There

Turn west off NY 30 onto County Road 10 a little over 6 miles north of Long Lake Village. A second road, similarly designated, also heads west from NY 30 farther north, approximately 11 miles south of Tupper Lake Village. The roads intersect near Little Tupper Lake and continue west past Whitney Headquarters toward Sabattis. CR 10 is a good macadam road and fairly attractive, for it follows part of Little Tupper Lake's shores after crossing its inlet.

In 7.5 miles a sign points left, indicating ACCESS ROAD TO LAKE LILA 5.8 MILES. This dirt road leads southwest across private land. It is closed during part of the winter and apt to be muddy in very early spring. If you are planning a trip then, check with the DEC ranger in Long Lake to see if it is usable. The road ends in the designated parking area, which accommodates 25 cars. If it is filled, you may want to reschedule your trip, because there is no parking along the 5.8-mile access road.

The Trail

After you have signed in at the registration booth, walk west from the parking area along the road/trail. If you plan on canoeing, notice the path heading south from the trailhead. The shortest portage to Lake Lila, it takes you in 0.3 mile to a northeastern arm of the lake.

Your hike is an easy 3.2-mile walk along the roadway to the lodge site. Part of the time you see the lake through a screen of hemlock, spruce, and yellow birch. To vary the tempo, look for a large boulder on the right side of the road with a red marker indicating STA. 230 a bit more than 1 mile from the parking lot. Beyond it, the trail starts to descend to lake level, but instead climb the ledges on the shoulder of Harrington Mountain. As you walk along them, parallel to the roadway, enjoy the excellent views of the lake. Return to the roadway by following the ledgetops as they descend toward Lake Lila.

The road first approaches the lake at 1.5 miles. You cross Harrington Brook about 2 miles from the trailhead. This very pretty little brook drops over a series of large boulders

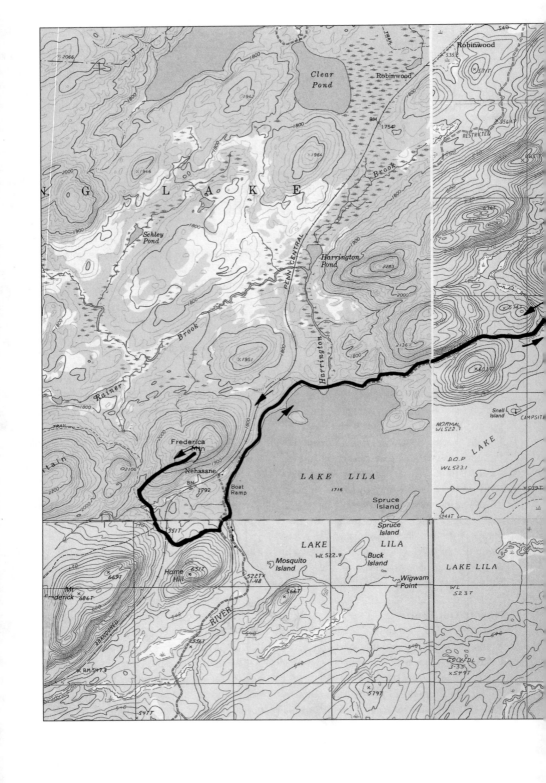

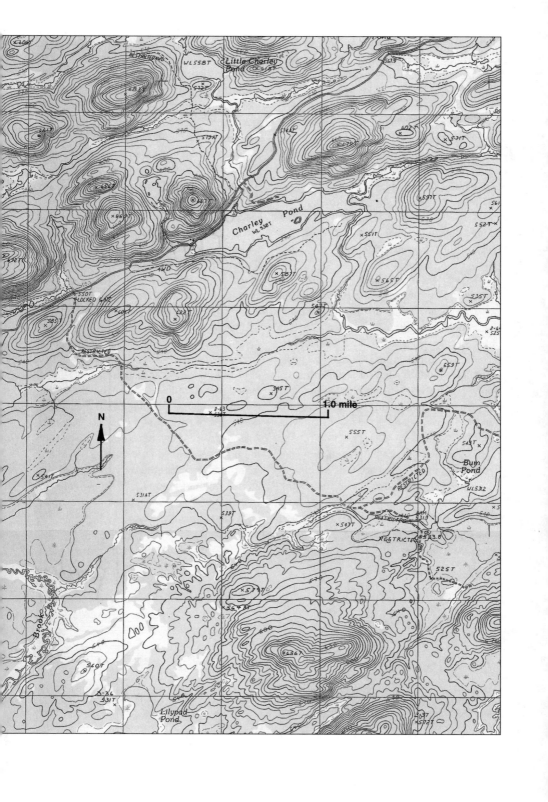

in its final rush to reach the lake. About 400 yards beyond the brook, an old logging road forks right, north. It is typical of the many logging roads that lace the estate, allowing you to explore the preserve's recesses.

At the first main intersection, just before the lodge, a road forks right, north, to the old railroad station. The lodge site faces east, commanding a fine view of 3-mile-long Lake Lila, named for Webb's wife, who was the daughter of William Vanderbilt. The estate's inclusion in the Forest Preserve meant that all the buildings were removed, even the fireplace of the main lodge, with its stones nearly a yard square.

Many of the lake's sandy beaches are suitable for swimming. The fishing is as good as in any other of the Adirondacks' rapidly acidifying lakes. There is an excellent stock of lake trout as well as land-locked salmon and brook trout. Be sure to bring binoculars; the lake's remoteness makes it a good spot for viewing the bald eagles and ospreys that nest in the area. There are many loons as well as other shore- and waterbirds.

For the best view of the estate, continue south along the gravel road. At the intersection just before the lodge site, bear right. This roadway, now marked as a hiking trail, heads west, crosses the railroad tracks, and then swings north into the draw between Webb and Frederica Mountains.

Climb into the draw to the height-of-land, about 1 mile from the lodge. A sign marks the trail as it turns northeast and climbs gently for less than 0.5 mile to the open rock ledges on the south face of Frederica Mountain. Older maps designate that mountain with the name Smith, after the region's first settler, a trapper who arrived about 1830.

The view is outstanding from the southeast through the southwest, encompassing all of Lake Lila and the Beaver River Valley through to Nehasane Lake. You should spot the fire tower on Mount Electra a little south of magnetic west. From clifftops a little below the end of the trail, there are distant views east to the High Peaks.

Notice the open ledges on many of the surrounding mountains. All are the result of fires that swept the area in 1903 and 1908, after the period of heaviest logging. Those fires created another unusual feature on the Nehasane estate, one that has few counterparts in the normally heavily wooded Adirondacks. Many huge, open fields dot the preserve, and you will want to return another day to visit the larger ones. They stretch north of Frederica Mountain beyond Rainer Brook and are most easily reached from the old railroad track.

39

Ampersand Mountain

Distance (round-trip): 5.6 miles

Vertical rise: 1,790 feet

Hiking time: 4 hours

Map: USGS Metric Ampersand Lake (a short distance at the beginning of the trail is on USGS Metric Saranac Lake)

High Peaks Wilderness Area

Ampersand stands almost isolated from other mountains in the center of one of the Adirondacks' great expanses of mountains and water. To the north and west, ponds and lakes stretch to the horizon; to the east, the High Peaks range north to Whiteface; and to the south beyond Ampersand Lake, Seward, Seymour, and Santanoni form an impressive chain. Ampersand is a mountain to enjoy as you would a great painting, to savor leisurely as you would sip a rare vintage wine. The walk up it is as beautiful and special as are the views from the summit.

Its 3,352-foot summit is entirely bare. That clearing is the work of man: in 1873, when Verplank Colvin was making his mountain survey, he had paths cut to expose triangulation lines to other mountaintops. Erosion did the rest. The removal of the fire tower does not limit in any way the full panorama you can enjoy from Ampersand's bald crest.

How to Get There

Trailhead parking is on the north side of NY 3, east of Tupper Lake and precisely 7 miles east of the intersection of NY 30 and NY 3. The turnout is just over 8 miles southwest of Saranac Village.

The Trail

The trailhead itself is on the south side opposite the parking area. NY 3 has become a very busy highway, so cross carefully. The sounds of the highway may pursue you most of the way to the summit.

The trail enters the woods on an old

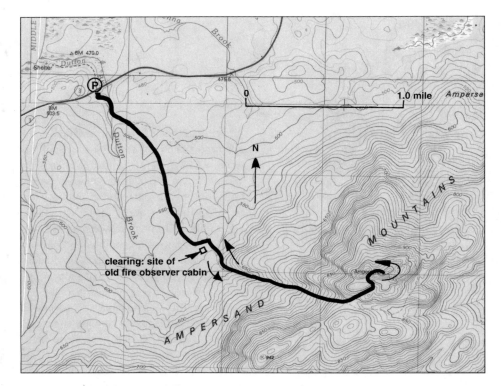

clearing: site of old fire observer cabin

roadway blocked by a stone barrier. The barrier seems to provide an immediate separation from the civilized world, for crossing it you enter a deep, quiet woods. Large and stately hemlock mingle with maple and yellow birch to shade the rich understory of oak fern, long beech fern, goldthread, sarsaparilla, and almost the complete array of the spring-blooming flowers typical of eastern forests. Moss-covered rocks edge the rolling trail, with its soft, root-free tread. Much of the forest surrounding Ampersand Mountain has never been logged; it is Adirondack old growth at its most beautiful.

You cross a stream on a log bridge, and a stretch of old corduroy leads you to a fantastic hemlock grove with a view of the mountain through the trees. Few trail markers guide your way, but none are needed. A long boardwalk elevates you above the

muck of a thriving deep spruce swamp. Huge trees tower over an understory of ferns, bunchberry, and sorrel growing in the sphagnum moss. You may find yourself walking more slowly than usual, in spite of the easy trail; the woods are worthy of an observer's pace.

You begin to climb gradually and cross several intermittent streams. You cross a larger stream, this one not shown on the USGS map, and continue east of south. Within 40 minutes, you notice you are really climbing. Before long, the hemlock and spruce have virtually disappeared from the forest. This is the mountain's hardwood zone, where sugar maple and yellow birch share dominance in the canopy.

At 50 minutes, after climbing a steep pitch, you enter a small clearing, the site of the fire observer's cabin, 1.4 miles from the highway. From here an abandoned trail veers slightly left to cross McKenna Brook. This was the old trail up the mountain, which was maintained by the fire observer Walter Channing Rice, who earned the nickname of the "Hermit of Ampersand." Wooden steps and railings, log and earthen risers, and stone stairs once provided an easy way to mount the nearly 1,500 feet remaining.

Today, the trail bears right through the clearing, but then swings back toward the brook, crossing it above the cabin site. Shortly, the way becomes steep. The next section of trail, once called the worst in the Adirondacks, has been improved with rockwork and stone steps. The uniform abruptness of the mountain's profile precludes rerouting the trail, so the steps are an important element in preventing trail erosion. While the flanks of the trail are still recovering, remember to keep on the rocks to avoid trampling the fragile vegetation.

As you climb, note how red spruce, balsam fir, and paper birch are beginning to appear more frequently. Keep an eye out for a solitary cedar tree growing to the left of the trail. Cedars are more accustomed to lakeshores and swampy habitat, such as that found near the trailhead parking area, but at the same time they are not deterred by high elevations. Cedars are willing to grow wherever water is close to the surface.

The cedar tree grows at the lower edge of a pure stand of balsam fir, which signals your arrival at the upper slopes of the mountain. But don't start looking for the summit opening yet! As of 2002, the rockwork ends within this balsam fir zone, and from here on you can see what a difference there is between the improved and unimproved sections of trail. The way is now rooted and rutty, with slippery muck in a few precipitous sections. Erosion has widened the trail be-

yond the standard 18 inches, and several detours and "shortcuts" around some of the worst sections may actually mislead you from the real trail. The red markers play an important role here.

At times the trail is a scene of destruction, and at others it takes on the romantic aura of wilderness that pervades some early Adirondack photographs. The trail reminds me of old pictures of mountain gorges, with a jumble of trees lying across huge boulders. It needs only a few women in long skirts, their escorts encumbered with wicker packs, to complete the illusion.

The trail passes a moss-covered wall on the right, with ferns dotting the ledges. You will probably have to pause for breath, leaving plenty of time to enjoy the scene. Beyond the top of the rock, a view opens up through the trees, with glimpses of island-studded waters hinting at what is to come.

The washed-out trail continues. The nearly vertical slopes make you pause and question the proper route, but in most cases your choice will not matter, for you have to scramble in any case. By this time you have climbed enough manmade steps and stared at enough eye-level, mud-covered ledges that the thousands of hikers' footsteps before you have destroyed any notions that this could be a pristine wilderness.

Just about the time you despair, in a terrible, steep section where the average slope must exceed 45 degrees, you emerge in a level valley filled with exquisite paper birch and ferns. Huff-and-puff hikers may need an hour to reach this spot from the cabin site, a distance of 1 mile. The 1,000-foot climb is excuse enough for the slow pace.

A few spruce and balsam dot the glen, which is edged on the left by the cliffs that ring Ampersand's summit and on the right by an unbelievably large boulder. "Boulder" is hardly adequate; the rock might better be called a miniature mountain. Moss clings to its nearly vertical sides, ferns fill its crevices and fissures, and spruce trees perched on the top have managed to grow to a mature size. If you are planning a full day on the summit, wait until your return to photograph the birch glen; then afternoon sun highlights the trees against the gray cliff walls.

The trail continues through the glen, rising to pass under an overhanging rock. If you are curious, look for a footpath leading to the right around a massive pile of boulders, just before the overhang. Follow it to explore a cave concealed in the rocks; a razor-thin shard of rock is wedged above it between the two halves of this ice-fractured monolith. Cold air emerges from this and several other openings, hinting at deeper crevices. Take time to clamber around the rock, looking for little caves and openings.

Continuing, you pass the other end of the fissure that splits the rock into halves. (The entire rock is literally the size of a house when seen from above!) Beyond the rock, the trail dips, veers right, and leads to the foot of a rock wall. Your exuberance (and the roots of a tree) should carry you up and over the ledge, following yellow arrows painted on the rocks.

You arrive at the summit on the westernmost of the three knobs, each of which offers different exposures. The truly great emerging views reward you for your climb of 2 hours and 15 minutes. Turn around first to look back the way you have come, past a series of ledges to a cone that is a part of the flank of Ampersand, and then to Stony Creek Mountain. To the south, at the foot of the mountain, Ampersand Lake is nestled in the center of a giant handful of mountains.

Everyone who writes about Ampersand Lake reminds you of the brief role it played in the life of a distinguished group of Boston scholars that included Ralph Waldo Emerson, James Russell Lowell, and Louis Agassiz. The story of their choice of Ampersand Lake for an Adirondack camp, the "philosopher's camp," is beautifully told in Alfred Donaldson's *The History of the Adirondacks.* Donaldson also discusses the origin of Ampersand's name as deriving from a corruption of Ambersand Lake, which in turn was inspired by the "bright yellow sandy shores and islands which make it truly Amber-sand Lake."

An atlas or large-scale map will help identify distant mountains. Directly south across Ampersand Lake, the Seward Mountains climb impressively skyward, rising 1,000 feet higher than your perch, but nowhere commanding a finer view. To the right of Seward lies Kempshall, its long and rounded summit in the distance beside Long Lake. Between the two, on the horizon, lies Blue Mountain, its profile a narrower one than is usually seen from other vantages. To the west of Long Lake lies a mountain that appears so large from this perspective that its lack of name is peculiar.

In the distance, immediately left of Stony Creek Mountain, lies Mount Morris, topped by a fire tower; Buck is the long mountain to its left and farther away.

Looking back again beyond Ampersand Lake, a narrow cleft separates Seward and Seymour Mountains. In front of them, extending from the lake, a valley stretches southeast toward the Duck Holes. On the far side of the valley, Santanoni stands next to Seymour to the east, with Henderson beyond it. Continuing to your left, Mount Adams is the small peak in the distance next in line.

East, between Ampersand and its pond, lies Van Dorrien Mountain, and if you follow beyond its summit you see the Sawtooth Mountains, whose peaks dip down to border the northern edge of the valley leading

Ampersand Mountain

to the Duck Hole. On the horizon beyond the Sawteeth range Nye Mountain in the north; Street Mountain next, right or south; and then, overshadowing everything and blocking farther views east, the MacIntyre Mountains.

Walk east along Ampersand's summit to the middle knob, from which the views north are best. Immediately below the mountain is Middle Saranac. Upper Saranac begins on its left and curves around it to the north, with Boot Bay Mountain between. Lake Clear is due north, with Saint Regis and its tower to its left. You can see only a little of Tupper Lake in the west, with Raquette Pond to its north. Mount Arab, also a fire tower mountain, can be spotted west of Tupper.

The best eastern views are from the farthest perch, beyond the knob that once held the tower. As you walk across the summit, you will enjoy the magnificent feeling that the mountain drops away, with cliffs facing all exposures.

Lower Saranac Lake is just east of north, with Kiwassa and Oseetah Lakes ranging east. Over Lake Oseetah lies McKenzie Mountain, with Whiteface and its distinctive white slide behind it. Slide, Hurricane, and Cascade complete the eastern skyline back to Nye. With binoculars and a clear day, you can spot three more fire tower mountains in the north, from left to right: Debar, Loon, and Lyon.

The huge dark crystals of labradorite embedded in the anorthosite exposed on the peak are fascinating to geologists, but to ordinary mountain climbers, the mountain is a gem by itself. You see so much: water expanses to the north and west, impressive peaks to the south and east, and all so separate from your perch, as if placed to form a perfect panorama. None of the higher peaks with their barer summits is as open and expansive as this.

Ampersand Mountain

As you start back across the summit to return, look for the plaque erected to the memory of Ampersand's hermit, facing the ledge below the tower knob. Be careful to retrace your steps all the way west across the summit ridge to pick up the trail. The ranger reports that a few hikers have headed north through the draw and become seriously lost as they entered the woods just a few feet from the summit rocks.

40

McKenzie Mountain

Distance (round-trip): 10.6 miles

Vertical rise: 1,221 feet

Hiking time: 6 hours

Map: USGS Metric Saranac Lake

McKenzie Wilderness Area

McKenzie is an isolated peak rising north of the High Peaks between Saranac Lake and Lake Placid. Its wooded summits do not permit a single complete panorama, but overlooks on the east and west sides of the northern summit cover a surprising portion of the compass. Moose Mountain, a slightly taller peak, lies in the northeast, blocking views and creating the impression that the two are part of one long mountain range. From the overlook west of McKenzie's summit, the panorama extends from Moose Mountain through the north with low hills, fields, and ponds; the west with Saint Regis Mountain; and the southwest across the Saranac lakes to Ampersand and Scarface Mountains. The views from the second overlook, on the east, encompass Whiteface, the Sentinel Range across Lake Placid, and the High Peaks. That view includes the MacIntyre Mountains and ends with the eastern flanks of Scarface.

How to Get There

The relocated McKenzie trailhead is on the north side of NY 86, 1.6 miles east of the DEC office in Ray Brook.

The Trail

The beginning of the trail, which once crossed private land, has been rerouted, adding considerably to the distance to the north summit. The new trail is well marked with blue disks. The first half mile heads generally a little east of north, first through a reforestation area, around a small wetland, then uphill to change to a more westerly course just before crossing a small stream on a rock-ledge bridge. The next half mile or so is relatively level, contouring a little north of west on the side of Little Burn Mountain. A gentle descent due west follows. The cover of mostly small white birch is broken by occasional glacial erratics. A 40-minute walk takes you to a split-log bridge at 1.5 miles. Beyond, the trail angles along the top of the ridgeline of a small esker and reaches a rock outcrop with through-the-trees views of Scarface to the south. The trail curves north to northeast following the contour of the hillside and descends to meet the old trail at 1.8 miles after a 50-minute walk.

The trail, now following an old road, continues northeast, beginning a gentle rise along the valley of Little Ray Brook. Much new trailwork makes the walking easy. Small waterfalls and rapids mark the stream, which tumbles through a very handsome gorge covered with tall hemlock and a sprinkling of huge yellow birch and cedar.

Ten minutes later, at 2.4 miles, you reach a fork. Blue disks now mark the left turn to Haystack. Stay straight ahead, on the red-marked route, uphill for a time, but continuing through the valley on an almost level stretch. At 2.6 miles, you cross one stream; 100 yards farther, a second; and at 3.4 miles, a third. Here you meet a bad stretch of trail, rocky and washed out, with exposed roots.

The ski trail from Whiteface Inn to McKenzie Pond crosses your route 0.2 mile farther. Continue straight on a gentle rise for 10 more minutes. Then, at 3.8 miles, the trail appears to hit a sheer wall. You start climbing, straight up and then angling across bare rock and mucky slides in a slow zigzag pattern. To scramble up the long slope to the northwest as far as the first overlook will take you more than 30 minutes, but you will have

➤ Mountain Wood Fern

Mountain wood fern, Dryopteris campyloptera, is a lacy gem that is among our most ornamental ferns. This Dryopteris is common from the subarctic through Canada and into northern New York State, but it is rarely seen and even then only at high elevations south of the northernmost Adirondacks. The species constitutes most of the tall fern cover on McKenzie. You can identify it by its broadly triangular form (and by the fact that the lower subleaflets are obliquely triangular).

climbed nearly 900 feet in 0.6 mile.

Walk to the right of the trail at the overlook, then turn left to follow the trail below more ledges, descending a few feet into a deep, ferny glen. This walk along the wooded summit ridge is McKenzie's most attractive feature. Stands of sorrel and mountain Dryopteris fill every niche below the open balsam cover. The top of McKenzie has one of the state's most handsome stands of mountain wood fern. The trail winds northeast through the fern woods, climbing two short rises before reaching a path that leads a few feet left to an overlook atop a cliff. The northern summit is visible on your right, still over 0.4 mile away.

The trail ducks back into deep woods, climbing a few feet in 0.1 mile across the narrow ridgeline to the southern summit, which has a limited view southeast to Scarface. Then at 4.9 miles the trail slides down a steep pitch into a col, reaching the bottom in 0.1 mile and crossing a second beautiful, wooded glen. You encounter two steep pitches on the climb to the north summit.

At 5.2 miles, about 100 feet past the last rock scramble, a path turns left for the western overlook. In the foreground, the view of McKenzie Pond is neatly framed by Little

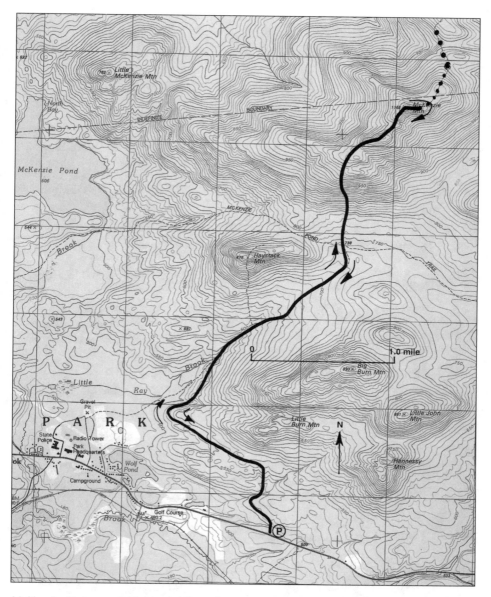

McKenzie, Baker, and Haystack Mountains. You will probably want the Saint Regis and Santanoni USGS maps to help you identify the distant mountains.

The second overlook is scarcely 100 feet to the north. That intriguing sharp cone to the right of Whiteface is Moss Cliff Mountain.

The Lake Placid and Mount Marcy USGS maps will help you identify the rest. From both outlooks you will marvel at the way the mountain drops steeply away from the summit ridge, which is 3,860 feet in elevation.

Your return trip should take you just a bit less time than the ascent.

A view of the High Peaks from Pitchoff Mountain

41

Pitchoff Mountain

Distance (one-way): 5.2 miles

Vertical rise: 1,440 feet

Hiking time: 5 hours

Maps: USGS Metric Lake Placid; USGS Metric Keene Valley

Sentinel Range Wilderness Area

Pitchoff Mountain lies immediately north of the High Peaks Wilderness Area between Lake Placid and Keene and offers some great views south to the High Peaks and north to the Sentinel Range. Pitchoff is not a simple mountain; it is actually a series of small summits, which are connected by a range trail as varied and exciting as you could wish. The unnamed tributary of Cascade Brook rises in a spring on the side of Pitchoff near the end of the trail. Unfortunately, it is the only water you encounter on the trip. You will need water long before you reach the spring, so be sure to carry plenty.

How to Get There

The trail begins and ends on NY 73 in the Cascade Valley, its two trailheads 2.6 miles apart. The best way to enjoy Pitchoff is to walk the full length of the trail, leaving a car at each end; you will have nearly 300 feet fewer to climb if you begin at the western end. The eastern trailhead, where you drop off your second car, is a little over 4 miles west of Keene; this end of the trail starts on a bridge over the tributary of Cascade Brook. Then, in your first car, drive to the western trailhead, 4.4 miles east of Heart Lake Road, directly opposite the trail to Cascade and Porter Mountains. This upper, western trailhead is less than 0.5 mile west of Upper Cascade Lake.

The Trail

One of the rewards of this climb is the rapidity with which you gain the first views of the Cascade Lakes and the sheer cliff faces of the Cascade Range bordering them on the southeast. The trail is marked by red disks and begins by traversing the steep bank of the road cut. Then there is a steep pitch through a forest cover that indicates that the area burned almost a hundred years ago: Small spruce and balsam are filling the spaces between striped and red maple and white birch. The short pitch north for 0.2 mile is followed by a level trek northeast along a ridge parallel to the road. You drop down into a spruce thicket and then climb gently over rock outcrops to reach the first overlook, a boulder 0.8 mile from the highway and less than a 25-minute walk from your start.

Standing out on the boulder here, the sheer drop makes you feel as though you could easily jump into Upper Cascade Lake. From this spot you can see the spit that separates it from Lower Cascade Lake. This overlook also offers the most dramatic view of the cliff behind the lakes. Even though you've barely begun your hike, take time now to enjoy this view.

The trail clings to the side of the hill around the boulder, climbing a small pitch, then a modest rise, and then another pitch above steep ledges to the right. Birch, balsam, bracken, and dry, scrubby growth mark the way. A second outcrop appears within five minutes, offering another beautiful excuse to pause.

As you descend from this outcrop, a wall of rock rises ahead of you across a small, damp woods with large red baneberries. The trail heads almost straight up, and it is slippery with loose dirt. You angle left, below a ledge, and then climb, steeply again, on an almost polished marble base.

About an hour into your hike (if you have stopped to enjoy the views) and 1 mile from the start, the trail angles west. The trail used to go straight up the rock ahead, on a dangerous route that is now closed. The newer route to the left will take you to the same vantages that the steeper one did. The newer trail, a narrow footpath, hugs the outcrop, heading almost west, then north, and finally, after descending a little, northeast again. You pass under an overhanging rock that looks like the entrance to a cave. Here the trail climbs again. A smooth, vertical rock rises above you as you traverse the wooded back side of the ridge. In 15 minutes you intersect the older route.

Turn right across the ridge on the old trail for a detour to one of the day's best promontories. Stepping on parts of a giant jigsaw puzzle made of huge, angular, flat slabs of interlocking rock, some with deep crevices between, walk west to three huge, reddish boulders. Glacial erratics, they are precariously perched on a beaklike rock. To the south, the views west from the shoulder of Cascade include Basin, Haystack, and Marcy, Colden, and Avalanche Pass. The MacIntyre Mountains are to the right of the pass, with Santanoni, the Sawtooth Mountains, and Ampersand filling the horizon around through the west.

A half hour will suffice for the detour, unless it is blueberry season, when you will just have to stop every other step for another handful. Your trip will have covered about 1.7 miles when you duck back into the woods and pick up the trail again. It continues northeast between scrubby patches and open rock, circling left around a bare outcrop and then angling right on open rock. Intervening clumps of balsam have a good, rich, spicy smell. You walk through a birch glen with a fern meadow beneath and then rise through mountain maple and taller spruce. As you climb between two boulders, you reach a wooded height-of-land, the highest point on the

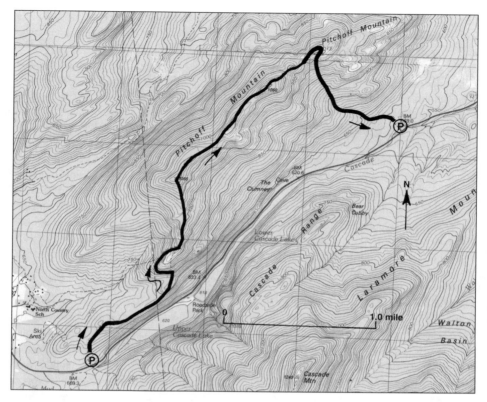

range walk. You have to leave the trail, walking to the left, for even limited views, which begin to include the Sentinel Range to the north. In spite of a leisurely pace, it has probably taken you less than two hours to walk the more than 2.2-mile route to the summit, which is just over 3,600 feet in elevation.

Continue northeast along the ridge, descending a little through a fern glen and then ascending 0.2 mile to a rock ledge with a spectacular overlook to the north. What a drop to the valley below! There is a big slash on Slide Mountain to the north. Pitchoff's ridge is so narrow that you can see most of its length, a series of knobs and summits that appear as high as your perch.

Blueberries, ledges, balsam, and gorgeous views continue before the trail drops into a wooded glen. Within a half hour of the wooded summit you reach a narrow spine of open rock. The trail turns left at 2.9 miles to climb the highest rock along the spine. Now you can enjoy the view back, past the spectacular ridges you have traversed, to the summit of Cascade. The knobs ahead are equally impressive. The view north is across the deep valley to Black Mountain and North Notch and South Notch Mountains, which are about as tall as Pitchoff.

Again you descend, but the roller-coaster trail immediately climbs to follow a cairn-marked route across open rock at 3.3 miles. In the northeast, another summit in the chain appears; and to its right, across Cascade Valley, range Hurricane Mountain and, on a clear day, the Green Mountains of Vermont rising above Lake Champlain. Farther right, just to the left of Cascade, Giant and its distinctive slides are clearly visible.

Northern views continue as you walk across ledges that hang steeply above the valley on the north. Prostrate spruce and tall blueberries cling to the thin soil on the summit. At 3.6 miles, you should glimpse a small, steep knob in the valley that separates you from the last summit. Walk about 15 feet to the left, off the trail, to enjoy the view of the last summit across the peculiar knob.

Next, yellow arrows painted on the rock guide you into a steep gully below and north of the ledge. Be careful; it is slippery! After dropping to the col, turn sharply left, below the outcrop, then climb through a cleft, head down a slide, and cut sharply up a ridge for a view northeast to the last summit in the range. It takes 15 minutes to cover the distance from the col, just over 0.2 mile.

You are climbing on bare rock now, guided by more yellow arrows. Do not forget to look back; those views are great, too. You approach the last summit from its northern side: The south and west are too steep. You reach it just short of 4 miles from your start and after 3 hours and 15 minutes of walking. Stop, rest, and enjoy the curious rock formation below you to the south; it is easy to see why it was named the Sleeping Elephant. You have a slightly different perspective on the eastern views you enjoyed from the previous summit; this last knob is only a little more than 300 feet below the highest one. You will marvel at the steep drop to the south and east to Cascade Valley, with Owls Head Mountain a little north of east across it.

Your route down is as steep as the way up. To find the continuing trail, walk a short way northeast, following arrows and cairns on the open rock. A few of the signs are concealed by the spruce and balsam that fill the crevices. The trail makes a sharp, hairpin turn to the right, dropping below the ledge and doubling back southwest beneath ledges into a draw below the summit. Rocks and rubble fill the steep and difficult trail. It is really a scramble to descend through the birch-covered slope. Erratics cover the hillside and boulders fill the trail. It is so steep that you probably need an hour to cover the final 1.25 miles to the highway.

About halfway down, you cross an intermittent stream, and within a few feet you can hear the spring emerging from below a boulder about 50 feet east of the trail. Below this point, the slope is noticeably gentler. Your route is close by a small stream on the right, across it, and then across the main stream. Following a fairly steep section, you cross and recross the stream. Finally the route levels out, just before emerging from the woods on the bridge by NY 73, where you have left your second car.

You will agree that this is not a long or difficult trail, but there is a fair amount of climbing between the summits. Be sure you have allowed at least an hour a mile for the trek and extra time for picking blueberries and enjoying the changing views.

42

Blue Ledge on the Hudson

Distance (round-trip): 5 miles

Vertical rise: 230 feet

Hiking time: 3 hours

Map: USGS Metric Dutton Mountain

The Hudson, New York's mightiest river, has more beautiful vistas than the fabled and historic rivers of Europe. But from its birth at Lake Tear of the Clouds high in the Adirondacks, to its passage through the Hudson Highlands, and then to its mouth below the skyscrapers of New York City, no more inviting place exists than the narrows of Blue Ledge in the heart of the Adirondacks. The towering cliffs that give the gorge its name rise above one of the river's wildest stretches of rapids. The boiling white foam contrasts with the deep blue shadows of the rock. On a sand beach opposite the ledges you can picnic and in spring watch the noisy antics of a pair of nesting ravens. Their nest is usually secreted in a dark niche high on the cliffs, and the black young birds would be totally concealed if they did not reveal themselves with gaping brilliant red mouths, screeching for food.

How to Get There

Drive north on NY 28N from North Creek for 9.4 miles, then turn left, west, on North Woods Club Road. Paved for the first 2 miles only, this road bridges Deer Creek, heads west, and then swings south through the valley between Kellogg and Venison Mountains. The road descends a steep side hill to a one-lane bridge over the Boreas River 3.8 miles from NY 28N. The trailhead is 3 miles from this bridge over the Boreas. Park at the marked turnout at the east edge of Huntley Pond.

The 5-mile, round-trip walk to Blue Ledge can itself be made in less than three

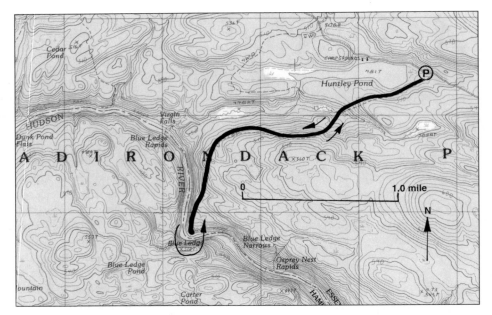

hours, but you should allow twice as long to appreciate the gorge's uniqueness. On the way north on NY 28N, you pass a lovely view of Moxham's slide 3.5 miles above North Creek and go through the hamlet of Minerva at about 7 miles.

Then, on the North Woods Club Road—handsome but rugged and in a high, open forest typical of this part of the Forest Preserve—you pass a picnic area at the bridge over the Boreas from which several informal fishermen's paths head along the river. Beyond the bridge you cross the abandoned railroad tracks of the line that served the titanium mine at Tahawus. In the early 19th century, iron was the raison d'être for the mine's existence. It was the failure to build a good road or railroad that prevented the mine's development then, and impurities, namely titanium, made the mine a marginal operation. In 1871, Dr. Thomas Clark Durant completed the Adirondack Railroad, which was first chartered in 1839, from Saratoga to North Creek; however, it

was not until the early years of World War II that the road was extended all the way to Tahawus to ship out the titanium, which turned out to have greater value than the Adirondacks' fabled iron.

From here to the trailhead, the dirt road can be rugged; you have to drive so slowly that you can easily spot some of the lovely clumps of wildflowers that edge the road.

The Trail

The first part of the trail south crosses a boggy area covered with huge yellow birch and hemlock. Blue trail markers denote the route, which heads up and away from Huntley Pond along a dry and narrow footpath. The easy, gradual climb through mixed forest is followed by a gentle descent into a little valley through a sort of natural gate formed by two huge boulders and two enormous yellow birches. The valley is filled with many spring-blooming plants, which form a multicolored carpet of wild oats, trout lilies, and spring beauties.

After crossing a small stream, you continue generally southwest to an area of low scrub and brush beside an old shanty, all signs of logging. The place is about 1.2 miles in, and here the footpath intersects an old roadway with a stonework base. The trail continues on the roadway toward the Hudson, passing to the south of a long beaver flow with extensive signs of both old and new beaver work. The high, open canopy of huge trees (through which the old road passes) creates a parklike setting. The Hudson was used to flood logs to sawmills throughout the last 70 years of the 19th century and into the 20th century, and this road was undoubtedly a principal route for dragging logs to the river.

Just about the time you first hear the Hudson, the trail reaches a section with posted signs designating North Woods Club property. You turn away from the property line and head straight up a narrow pathway that traverses a knoll bearing old blazes on the trees as well as the blue markers. The low shoulder of a hill separates you from the Hudson. As the roar of the river grows louder, the trail turns due south to wind along the nose of the ridge. You are approaching the area opposite Blue Ledge. The trail is covered with the tall white pines that rim the entire gorge here. The route is up and down along the ledge, past a pine point that affords a small glimpse of the crest of Blue Ledge on the opposite shore. The crest rises higher than your perch on the north shore. You will have walked for no more than an hour, but pause to enjoy sounds from the promontory overlooking the Hudson: the wind in the tall pines and the din of the rapids. With the exception of the Harris Rift west of the confluence with the Boreas, the most violent of the Hudson's rapids are the ones you now hear.

They churn and boil the river both above and below Blue Ledge.

Now the trail drops rapidly to the Hudson, past rattlesnake fern, boulders, and ledges, right down to the shore of a large pool. There is no camping here, but signs direct you past the sandy beach downstream to campsites. Blue Ledge rises 300 feet above you on the opposite shore. The blue cliffs are surrounded by other ledges colored gray and green and even various hues of orange and salmon. Pines and cedars cling to tiny crevices in the cliff faces. The marvelous colors and the variously eroded bands reflect Blue Ledge's geological structure: a series of banded gneiss beneath bands of schist interstratified with gneiss and limestone.

Short, informal paths head both east and west along the riverbank. Cedars rim the shoreline, which is barely flat enough for a picnic site, though it is obvious that several places have attracted campers. The Hudson is only 150 feet wide just below the cliffs. Huge rocks break the water into swirling rapids and crests of foam, both upstream and downstream. The deep pools for swimming are deceptive, for the Hudson can have a mighty current. Be careful if you do enjoy the cooling waters.

In spring, in high water, you may glimpse a kayak or rubber raft shooting the rapids. Eagles and hawks are often sighted riding the updrafts above Blue Ledge. And, of course, this is one of the few places in the Adirondacks where in spring you can expect to see ravens.

Allow at least a full day for the trip to Blue Ledge even though you will spend no more than three hours of it walking. The drive in and out may take another hour and a half, and you will want plenty of time to picnic and admire the cliffs.

Blue Ledge on the Hudson

43

Vanderwhacker Mountain

Distance (round-trip): 5.8 miles

Vertical rise: 1,700 feet

Hiking time: 5 hours

Map: USGS Metric Newcomb

Fire tower

Vanderwhacker Mountain stands alone, the only peak in a rough rectangle of Wild Forest land outlined by the Hudson River on the south, west, and a portion of the north, and the Boreas River on the east. Neither river is visible from the summit of Vanderwhacker, but the broad expanse they define separates the mountain from any other that approaches its height. Enormous Vanderwhacker sits in isolated splendor, offering commanding views of distant summits in all directions.

The mountain's tower is not manned at present, and its lower flight of stairs may be removed, although there are no current plans to remove the tower. If the stairs are there, permitting you to climb the tower safely, you can enjoy all the distant views described; but if not, you may have to scramble about the summit to obtain all the views. You can enjoy the spectacular panorama of the High Peaks to the north, framed by stunted spruce trees, without climbing the tower.

Vanderwhacker's trail is very steep, rising sharply 1,700 feet from the surrounding valleys. The trail generally follows a long, narrow ridge that leads to the small summit cone. The 2.9-mile climb is strenuous enough to make a good day hike.

How to Get There

Take time to enjoy the sights on the way to the trailhead. Drive north from North Creek on NY 28N, which is also called the Theodore Roosevelt Highway. A sign beside a deserted frame building 14.6 miles north of NY 28 explains why that highway

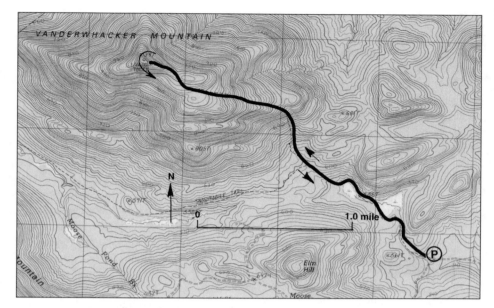

has been named after him. On September 4, 1901, when then Vice President Theodore Roosevelt heard that President William McKinley was on his deathbed, Roosevelt stopped at the inn here on his wild dash from Mount Marcy, where he had been vacationing, to North Creek, where he caught a train to Buffalo to be sworn in as president of the United States.

The highway bridges the Boreas River at 16.2 miles; if you are not in a hurry when you reach this bridge, you might enjoy walking 0.5 mile south on an informal path that follows the eastern shore of that river past rapids and a small falls. (Other destinations along the Boreas and NY 28N are described in *Discover the Central Adirondacks.*)

Immediately north of the bridge, turn west on an unmarked dirt road. It has a firm gravel base and even in early spring is safe for ordinary vehicles, but still use caution. A parking area is on your left near the start, and many camping places are tucked beneath the tall pines lining the road. Huge hemlock stand out in the dense mixed forest

off to the sides. The dirt road is so beautiful that you might enjoy walking along this stretch. Particularly good camping spots are at 1.1 miles in and 1.5 miles in, near Vanderwhacker Brook. Just beyond, you cross the railroad track from the Tahawus titanium mine, which trains use at irregular intervals, so look before you cross. The road continues west, more interesting than many other trails in the Adirondacks. Beyond the tracks, it climbs a small, spruce-covered bank bordered with bunchberry, blueberry, and pipsissewa. It reaches a fork at just over 2.6 miles from the highway. The way left leads to a private club at Moose Pond. Your route is to the right. There is a parking spot 150 feet along the right fork, but the road is not good, so a safer parking turnout is on the north side of the dirt road 200 yards before you reach the fork.

The Trail

The trail's beginning is marked with a sign giving Vanderwhacker's elevation, 3,385 feet, but no mileage. Red disks mark the

---

trail, which begins by following an old road that leads in 1.5 miles to the fire observer's cabin. In the late 1990s the old road portion of the trail was bulldozed to widen it for part of a snowmobile trail. This section has been partially rehabilitated so the trail is almost as it was. Shortly after the beginning, the trail angles right away from the roadbed to higher, drier ground. You are following a small stream, and 0.3 mile from the trailhead there is a lovely spot where the water slides over a small ledge and tumbles into a sheltered pool. Chains of logs make for dry crossings over the few wet places on the new route, which climbs up and over a couple of knolls before rejoining the roadway. Good bridges span the streams that flow from the north.

In 15 minutes you see a lovely wetland to the right of the trail, and a few minutes later you approach a large, drying marsh whose stumps frame views of the mountain to the northwest. The trail, now a narrow route again, skirts the marsh to the north. Only those who have walked the route before will be aware that the trail strays from the old roadway that used to circle south of the marsh. Beyond the marsh, you cross a small stream flowing into it, then begin to climb. There is a larger stream to your left. Another stream joins the trail and makes it wet. Here you see cabins ahead of you. After 45 minutes you reach the cabin sites (elevation: about 2,050 feet). A large sign warns that there is no camping here.

Walk between the cabins uphill to begin the strenuous climb up the lower and much steeper flanks of Vanderwhacker. You are headed more northerly on a narrow but well-marked route that traverses the almost vertical slopes. A 20-minute struggle suffices to reach the first crest, and the gradient eases. You cross a draw and a small stream flowing to your right, and shortly other small streams join the trail. It is wet going as you traverse the southern slopes for nearly 30 minutes. The moderately steep climb is straight up through a narrow defile, walled by spruce and balsam. Much of the route is on bedrock.

It may take you an hour to climb a mile from the cabin site and reach the next crest, where the trail is drier and the climb becomes more gentle. Soft mosses line the corridor and host goldthread, bunchberry, and sorrel. You continue west along the south slopes below the narrow ridgeline, still climbing. The mountain continues to drop steeply away from the trail to your left. The narrow passageway is really pretty, and it even smells good, but it does seem interminable.

As you descend from a small rock ledge (the only noticeable descent on the climb), walk south to an opening just a few feet from the trail with a view to the south. The spot overlooks Moose Pond down on your left. The trail is now on the top of the knife-edge ridgeline, going up only slightly through trees that are progressively smaller, when, suddenly, you are at the tower.

When you reach the summit, your first impression of the view north is of the looming, massive hulk of Santanoni and the enormous spread of the MacIntyre Mountains. If you can climb the tower, you can see west to Kempshall and the mountains that line Long Lake. To their south is Blue Mountain. You will need binoculars to pick out Goodnow's tower as it is silhouetted against Kempshall.

The rest of the panorama to the north is visible from the tower or from the rocks below it. Straight below lies the village of Newcomb, identified by the town's water tower, with Lake Harris to the west of it. Santanoni, with its long, curved slide, is beyond Newcomb, and to the left of Santanoni lie the Seward Mountains, with Couch-sachraga and Little Santanoni between. To the right of Santanoni on the horizon lie the Sawtooth Mountains and Henderson, and beyond them are flat-topped MacNaughton and Wallface, with its cliff bordering Indian Pass and leading up to the broad sweep of the MacIntyre Mountains. Continuing to the right, the cone of Colden is impressive behind Mount Adams, whose rock outcrops can be seen with field glasses. Next is Redfield, with Marcy peeping over it, and then Skylight and Haystack on the horizon. In the foreground, the North River Mountains lead up to Allen and on to Haystack.

Farther east range Colvin and Nippletop, then the cleft of Hunters Pass, with Dix, Hough, and McComb rising behind Boreas Mountain. You feel you are on top of the world, surveying the broad valley to the north and the sweep up to the Adirondacks' most impressive range.

To the east, you can spot Texas Ridge and Hoffman Notch, with Hoffman Mountain beyond. Pharaoh Mountain can be seen over Hoffman's right flank.

From the tower, you can enjoy views to the south. There are openings on the summit ridge east of the tower that give you pieces of the view visible from the tower. The tower view includes Indian Lake and the mountain on its western shore. Immediately below the tower lies Moose Pond; spotting clockwise (west) from Moose Pond, you can identify Little Beaver Mountain in the foreground, and Beaver

and Split Rock Ponds. Directly over them lies Panther Mountain, with Wakely to the west. Panther defines the western side of the Squaw Brook Valley, which you look straight through from this angle. Snowy Mountain with its sharp profile punctuates the eastern side of that valley. Next is Indian Lake, and to the left, or east, lies the heart-shaped summit of Humphrey, then Puffer, and finally Bullhead. Between the latter two, and closer, is one of the rare views of the chimney on Chimney Mountain. The dominant mountain in the south-southeast is Moxham, which appears like the back of a closed fist, its string of summits ranging off to the left. From the stairs on the tower, you can easily identify the mountains to the southeast. Gore, with its tower, is clearly defined a little east of south over Moose Pond. On a really clear day, you can even discern the mountains edging Lake George.

You will need about 1 hour and 40 minutes for the descent. The way across the ridgeline is so gently downhill that you seem to fly along, but watch for slippery, wet places as you descend through the walled corridor. After you cross the draw, you may catch a through-the-trees glimpse of the marsh that seems very close below as you approach the crest of the steep flank. The short descent along that flank is steep; you will need to proceed slowly down to the observer's cabin. The newly marked trail beyond makes the rest of the hike seem very easy.

The view south from Goodnow Mountain

44

Goodnow Mountain

Distance (round-trip): 3.4 miles

Vertical rise: 1,030 feet

Hiking time: 2½ hours

Map: USGS Metric Newcomb

Fire tower, staffed in summer

Some wonderful things have happened recently in the Adirondacks and in particular in the center of the park near Newcomb. First of all, the Adirondack Visitors Interpretive Center just west of Newcomb has opened with some of the park's most handsome trails, which circle a peninsula on Rich Lake and follow Sucker Brook. Winding along heavily wooded shores, beneath tall evergreens, with spectacular stands of cedar and lovely boardwalks, rustic bridges, and canopied benches, these trails set a new standard for nature trails.

The second wonder is that the new standard in trails is being applied to Goodnow Mountain. Not only has part of the trail been redesigned, but the tower and its support buildings have been restored as well, in a joint effort between the State University College of Environmental Science and Forestry, which manages Huntington Preserve where the tower is located, and the Town of Newcomb. Both signs and a booklet describe the natural history of the mountain and the fire tower's history. From the restored fire tower, you can enjoy one of the park's finest views of the High Peaks. Even the fire observer's cabin is destined for restoration so it can show how rangers lived on the mountain. Further, the restoration of the historic fire tower is a harbinger of efforts to restore all Adirondack Wild Forest towers.

How to Get There

The trailhead is off NY 28N, just over 1.5 miles west of the Visitors Center (11.4

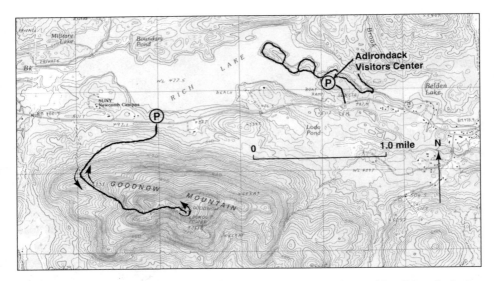

miles east of the intersection of NY 28N and NY 30 in Long Lake).

The Trail

The trail heads southwest from the parking lot. After the first steep pitch, gentle rises and level stretches with log stringers and numerous log bridges enable the trail to traverse the previously logged mountainside gradually, in a way that forestalls future erosion. Within 40 minutes the trail reaches a T-intersection and turns left, southeast, along the old trail. This well-trodden route has water bars, bridges, and rockwork that make it a fine example of good trail maintenance. The trail winds to the east, climbing steadily. A long, curving boardwalk leads past an old foundation where, after just over an hour of walking, there are views to the west.

In another five minutes, a path forks right to an old well. The cabin is 100 feet farther along the trail. More boardwalk follows, then the final pitch begins. A rock outcrop offers views to the west, then the tower appears.

The fire tower has the traditional circular map that will help you identify peaks in the surrounding panorama. In the summer a guide is often on duty to help you spot peaks. Views to the north are spectacular; the most impressive feature lies to the northeast, through Indian Pass. Wallface and the MacIntyre Mountains clearly define the pass. Following along to the right, east, Avalanche Pass is also outlined, with the MacIntyre peaks on the left and Colden on the right. Next, Marcy, Skylight, and Haystack define the horizon, with Marcy almost hidden behind Redfield and Skylight. The jagged crest of Sawteeth leads up to a part of the series of peaks that Adirondackers call the Range Trail. That route connects the summits of Basin, Saddleback, Gothics, Armstrong, and Upper and Lower Wolfjaw. Here the eastern peaks of the Range lead around to Giant, which is barely visible. To the right of Giant, Colvin, Nippletop, and Dix are easily spotted.

A little north of east lies Boreas Mountain and south of east is Vanderwhacker, both with fire towers. The Goodnow River flows south along the western edge of the mountain, and beyond its flow lie the little-

---

known and rugged slopes of Dun Brook Mountain and the Fishing Brook Range. Around to the south, Snowy, 21 miles away on the shore of Indian Lake, is unmistakable. In the south, beyond the small hills that rim the Hudson River Valley, Humphrey, Puffer, and Bullhead range east on the southern horizon, with the mine cut on Gore making that mountain most distinctive in the south-southeast.

Looking back north, Mount Adams, topped by a tower, rises south of the MacIntyre Mountains. To the left, west, of Indian Pass, you can see Henderson and then Santanoni. To the west of Santanoni, and over several intervening hills, lie Couchsashraga and Little Santanoni Mountains. Farther left, the Seward Mountains define the northern horizon. To the northwest, Kempshall Mountain lies between you and Long Lake. Harris Lake, with its state campground, is visible in the northeastern foreground, just beyond Newcomb. Due north, below Goodnow, is Rich Lake and the Visitors Center. Since an hour suffices for the return, you should have some time to enjoy the summit and to visit the center and walk some of its trails.

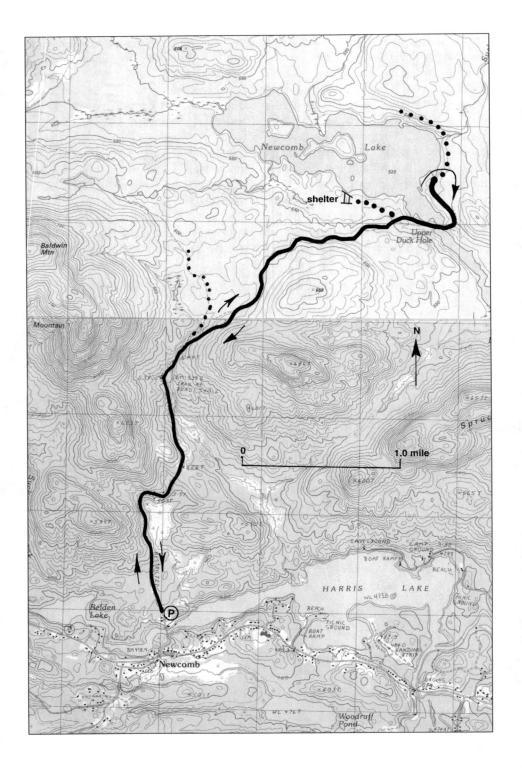

45

Santanoni Preserve

Distance (round-trip): 10.2 miles

Vertical rise: minimal

Hiking time: 4 hours

Maps: USGS Metric Newcomb; USGS Metric Santanoni Peak

High Peaks Wilderness Area

Picture yourself camping near or canoeing on a remote lake surrounded by beautiful mountains and having the spot almost to yourself. You can arrange this in the Santanoni Preserve, and you may not even have to carry your own canoe.

Santanoni Preserve was once a huge private estate. Now it is managed as a wilderness retreat, with no motorized vehicles permitted along its access road. Both hikers and campers must sign in at the trailhead registration booth. Camping is limited to a couple of lean-tos and a few isolated and primitive tent sites around the shores of Newcomb Lake. Campers rarely fill the designated campsites. In spring and fall it is possible to enjoy the handsome lake in almost complete solitude.

You may arrange with local drivers to have your canoe transported to the lake on horse-drawn carts for a nominal charge. This will let you explore the islands and bays of Newcomb Lake.

Hunting, in season, is permitted, subject to the usual state regulations. Fishing for both brook and lake trout is restricted to artificial lures, with catches of a minimum size of 12 and 21 inches, respectively, and there is a day limit of three brook trout and one lake trout.

Day-hikers and canoeists can easily make the 5.1-mile walk to the estate boathouse in two hours. The trail follows the old state road, which is broad and fairly level and still used by the DEC. You should plan a fairly early start in order to spend a full day on the lake, and then walk out after a picnic supper. That way you can enjoy birding in both early morning and late evening, when it is best.

Campers find that walking with a pack takes a bit longer. They may resent carrying packs when the road appears to be suitable for vehicular traffic; in fact the road is in such good shape that bicyclists can and do use it.

How to Get There

To reach the entrance to the preserve from the east, use either Blue Ridge Road from the Adirondack Northway (exit 29 off I-87) or NY 28N northwest from North Creek. It is about a 40-minute drive along either road to their intersection. Continue on NY 28N west, passing the Harris Lake Campsite in 3.1 miles and crossing the Hudson River in 3.4 miles. The entrance to the preserve is in Newcomb, 5.2 miles from the intersection. If you are driving from the south or west along NY 30, turn east on NY 28N at Long Lake, and drive 14.7 miles to the entrance.

Drive north along the entrance road across the outlet of Rich Lake to the parking area. Beyond stands the gatehouse near a farmhouse, one of the oldest buildings in the village of Newcomb. Dark brown shingles with red trim and fieldstone distinguish all the estate's buildings, including the magnificent home that still stands on the shore of Newcomb Lake.

A sign near the parking area tells the estate's history. Robert C. Pruyn, one of the state's wealthier foresters, assembled the Santanoni Preserve from several smaller parcels in the late 1880s and early 1900s. He used the property until 1953, when it was sold to the Melville family. Through efforts of The Nature Conservancy, the DEC, the Federal Bureau of Outdoor Recreation, and anonymous donors, the land was ac-

quired and given to the state to manage as a wilderness retreat.

The Trail

From the entrance, many foot and horse trails emanate into the preserve and on into the High Peaks area. All routes begin along the estate road.

A parklike area greets you just beyond the gatehouse, a forest of large hemlock, spruce, tamarack, cedar, and birch. Down on your right you can spot a beaver flow through a spruce thicket. Within a half hour you pass the shingled barns and silo of an old farmsite. Stone walls still edge the fields, which lead east to an open flow. The meadow beside the flow is a good place to watch for birds.

The roadway winds past other fieldstone buildings through woods to open fields, across which you can see a small hill to the north; you will circle it to reach the lake. Watch for hawks and owls near the fields. If you make the walk in spring, say late May, you should be able to identify a dozen different warblers. They migrate into the area before the leaves are fully out, making it easy to spot them in the mature forests that edge the road.

The road follows a stream on the right for a time, crossing it on a beautiful stone bridge, passing a wet meadow, and rising on a gentle incline to a fork 2.1 miles and less than an hour's walk from the gate. The way left heads to Moose Pond, but you keep straight on the principal road toward Newcomb Lake, 2.7 miles away. The road begins a very pleasant and gentle descent around the hillside. In very little time you see the lake through the trees. Keep circling, now to the east, above the lake, crossing two stone bridges. At 3.7 miles, a red-marked trail heads left through the woods along the south shore of the lake to a lean-to. The road now descends to a promontory where a picnic table overlooks the lake. Beyond, the bridge carries you over a narrow neck of the lake. The bridge separates the flows called the Upper and Lower Duck Holes from the western, principal part of the lake. Continue on the road, which turns west, past numbered campsites along the lakeshore for 0.4 mile to the estate and boathouse. The most beautiful campsites are beyond the buildings.

The high, open forest along the eastern shores appears undisturbed by any logging. Most of the western shoreline and all of the islands are densely covered with cedars. The islands range in size from 0.3 mile long to tree-covered boulders. Even if you are not a fisherman, you will enjoy exploring the lake's bays and coves. You can easily spend four hours paddling around Newcomb Lake and the Duck Holes, all of which abound with birdlife. The shoreline is partly edged with boulders, often with huge pine capping the rocks' promontories, and the lake bottom is generally sandy and perfect for swimming. Standing at the boathouse, you can see Moose Mountain in the west, with Baldwin on the left and Santanoni peeking over the trees on your right. As you move out into the western end of the lake, Santanoni becomes most impressive, with its long, thin, curved slide glistening in the sunlight.

You will certainly want to poke about the buildings of the estate. They are massive log structures connected by wide porches and covered breezeways, which seem to attract the slightest winds from the lake. The doors, inlaid with rustic logs in a variety of geometric patterns, are truly fascinating. Huge fieldstone fireplaces warmed every room of this lodge, which was typical of the Adirondack retreats built in the late 19th and early 20th centuries by those whose wealth permitted "camping" in such a grand style. Efforts to preserve the buildings as examples of the Great Camps are continuing, and volunteers have helped restore roofs and stabilize parts of the buildings.

You can follow a yellow-marked trail to the north beyond the buildings, around the eastern end of Newcomb Lake. It passes a number of campsites situated behind some of the most beautiful sand beaches in the Adirondacks. Huge, old, gnarled and twisted cedars rim the shore, providing a lovely backdrop for a refreshing swim that is free from the leeches that inhabit the water nearer the bridge.

The return seems a bit steeper than the trip in because of the height-of-land on the shoulder of the hill, less than halfway back to the gatehouse. It is mostly an illusion, for the road never rises more than 200 feet above the level of the lake. Maybe the fact that you notice a climb and the length of the trip out reflects displeasure at leaving so lovely a spot.

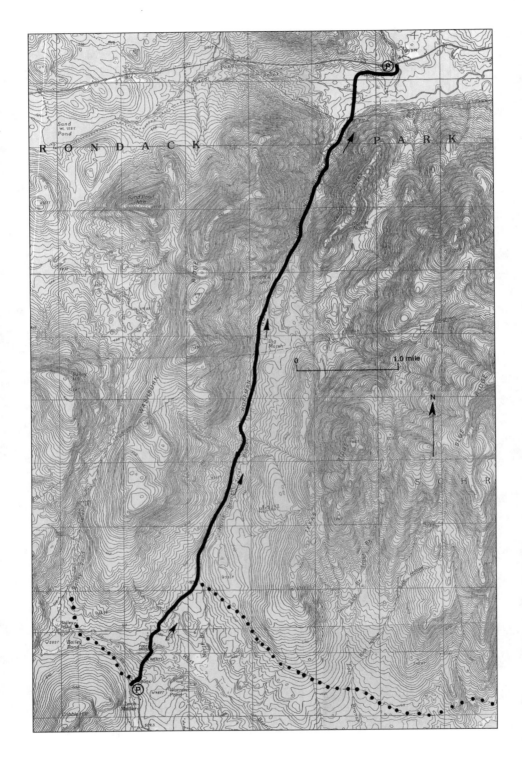

46

Hoffman Notch

Distance (one-way): 7.5 miles

Vertical rise: 300 feet

Hiking time: 6 hours

Maps: USGS Metric Blue Ridge; USGS Metric Schroon Lake

Hoffman Notch Wilderness Area

The Hoffman Notch Trail is a beautiful and little-used route through a high mountain pass. Handsome streams, waterfalls, and upland marshes edge the trail its entire length. You can walk into the notch from either end of the trail and then simply retrace your route, but if you want a full day of great hiking, walk it all at once, traveling from south to north. The logistics of leaving cars at both ends are time-consuming but not impossible.

Your route north follows some of the roads early settlers used as they moved into the mountains to harvest the virgin timber and farm the rugged countryside. This isolated and remote valley has been settled since the early 19th century.

Walking from south to north through the notch, you have less of a climb and also gain an enhanced sense of the transition from a southern Adirondack forest to a northern one: the hemlock at the southern edge of the notch give way to balsam on the north. It also puts the greatest excitement, as well as the possibility of getting wet, near the hike's end, where there are several brook crossings. The streams are certainly more beautiful in high water. I think it is worth risking wet feet toward the trail's end just to make sure there is enough water in the flow that plunges from Washburn Ridge, partway along and not far from the trail. The waterfall is spectacular.

How to Get There

This is a through-walk, so two cars are necessary. The northern trailhead, where you leave your second vehicle, is on the south side of Blue Ridge Road, the western spur of the road at exit 29 of the Adirondack Northway (I-87). Here, Blue Ridge Road follows The Branch, which flows south from Elk Lake and then east to the Schroon River. In 2.5 miles you reach the small settlement of Blue Ridge, where lodgings and campsites on private property overlook a set of falls you will certainly want to stop to view. Continuing west, you pass the marked turn for Elk Lake Road in 1.8 miles and 1.5 miles farther come to a small parking area just beyond the bridge over The Branch. Here an abandoned road heads south along The Branch. Although there are no signposts, the road and the continuing route south are marked by new yellow DEC disks.

Finding the southern trailhead is an adventure in itself. From the Northway, exit onto the parallel highway, NY 9, and drive to Schroon Lake Village, about halfway between exits 27 and 28. There take Hoffman Road right, west, climbing steeply away from the highways. In just over 5 miles it crosses Trout Brook, shortly beyond which a road forks left to Olmstedville. Less than 0.2 mile farther, Potash Road forks right. You could turn here, but natives warn that its condition can be marginal. Instead, turn right at the Loch Mueller sign, 0.8 mile beyond. Loch Mueller Road intersects Potash and continues north past the Dimick Farm to a farmhouse beneath a giant pine. Continue another 200 yards into a draw and turn right about 100 yards up its far side. The spot is poorly marked. The side road leads into a large open field that serves as the parking area for the trailhead, as well as for fishermen who try their luck in the branches of Trout Brook.

When you are driving to the southern trailhead, pause a moment to enjoy the view north through Hoffman Notch, to search for bluebirds in the old apple orchard, and to read the sign affixed to a pine: "On this spot in 1845, a sapling of 12 years was transplanted by me. I have watched and protected it in my advancing years. It has given me rest and comfort. Woodsman spare that tree, touch not a single branch. In youth it sheltered me and I'll protect it now. Signed, Paschal P. Warren, June 1, 1920, age 87."

The Trail

The lovely high meadow where you park offers another fine view of the notch. Fire rings show that campers have used the clearing. No signs specifically indicate the trail, but if you head into the woods on the north side of the parking area, beside a WILDERNESS sign, you discover the first of the new yellow DEC trail disks. If you are observant you may also notice here a faint, blue-marked trail heading northwest toward Bailey Pond.

Your route is downhill on an abandoned logging road through a tall and impressive forest with some good-sized white birch. In a hemlock swale, the road has been dug out to a depth of several feet. Within 15 minutes, listen for the West Branch of Trout Brook, which you soon cross.

Continue, now uphill, through a lovely forest of pine and birch with a ground covering of spring-blooming plants. A second bridge and a section of corduroy mark the gentle climb to a very tiny clearing, which has enough clues—apple trees, for instance—to indicate that an early settler lived here.

The woods road continues climbing gently through maple and large aspen to a fork. Bear right on the fork clearly marked with yellow disks. The road descends a second time and then turns to follow a stream coming in from your left. You are now in a big, deep valley, and only a narrow footpath is worn along the route of the abandoned road. You cross the stream twice within 150 feet.

You are now walking in one of the most stately mixed forests in the Adirondacks, making you wonder if it has ever been logged. Huge yellow birch, tall hemlock and ash, and a few large beech stand out. Continuing through a deep, wet glen to the left of the stream, the roadway is filled with lush ferns and wildflowers. You recross the stream on a very slippery log bridge, pass a section of corduroy, and finally hear a larger stream. Flowing from the notch, it is the North Branch of Trout Brook.

You can walk to the North Branch in 40 minutes. As you turn north along the brook, signs point to Big Marsh. Almost no footpath shows on the little-used route that forks right across a bridge over the brook. It is marked for Big Rogers, the local name for Big Pond.

Your route is now almost due north beside the North Branch, but you cross many small streams that flow from Washburn Ridge on your left. The valley is almost level, and your route is joyously accompanied by the many small riffles and falls in the brook beside you. Big boulders fill the valley, which is shaded by a magnificent mix of maple and hemlock.

Beside the third intermittent stream crossing, stop to notice a huge yellow birch. Its diameter at chest height exceeds 5 feet. Next you pass a giant rounded boulder shaped like the back of a sleeping dinosaur and capped with moss and polypody ferns. At one point, a glacial drummond lies between you and the stream, but most of the time you walk close to the water.

For this first hour or so, you have probably been traveling quickly and easily. Now reduce your pace in order to appreciate the details of the deepening valley. There is so much to see. The hillside above the stream on your right, east, rises directly and steeply from the brook. Ledges on the left now crowd the road, and for a time the valley floor is little more than 100 feet across, providing scarcely enough room to walk. The trail continues for 0.5 mile as a narrow footpath through a rich forest floor, threading its way between a jumble of boulders and ledges.

You finally become aware that you are climbing into Hoffman Notch. For a time the valley is more open, filled here with giant spruce and pine, through which you can glimpse the top of Texas Ridge on your right.

After 90 minutes—or more if you have kept a leisurely pace—and a distance of 2.5 miles, the trail climbs above an alder meadow. Giant spruce edge the flow and through them you sense that you are seeing the end of the notch in the distant north. Leave the trail to step out into the sphagnum bog filled with spruce and hemlock stumps and many signs of old beaver work. Look for bear scratches on the spruce.

The trail, carpeted with violets, continues close to the bog's edge, over which are more views of Texas Ridge. The trail continues along a series of drying beaver marshes for more than a mile. As the valley narrows again, you climb over small ledges beside the marshy stream. You are nearly at the top of the notch. Look for a giant tree, felled on your left beside the trail. A typical 13½-foot section has been removed from the butt end, but the rest, stretching over 100 feet, has been left to decay, and now a fair-sized birch and several small evergreens grow from its rotted remains.

Erratics and boulders fill the valley, and a balsam thicket crowds a patch of royal fern close to the bog. After a bit more than two hours of walking, a distance of about 4 miles, you cross a knoll and descend to see the waters of Big Marsh, which is just over halfway through Hoffman Notch. It takes about 10 minutes to walk along the marsh to find a picnic rock with a view of the hills to the east.

Cliffs and ledges extend almost to the water's edge, and huge boulders ring the marsh, where an open flow of shallow water reflects the surrounding hills as well as the tall pine and white birch that border the marsh. Texas Ridge rises to the south, and the steep knob to the north is Hornet Cobbles. East, opposite your perch, is the valley cut by a stream flowing from the flanks of the Blue Ridge Range. The peak of Hoffman Mountain rises above that valley.

As you continue, the valley broadens. The trail turns away from the marsh to hug the western side, crossing several intermittent streams. The trail is very narrow, grown in and filled with witch-hobble and often obscured despite the frequent and necessary markers. It takes at least 20 minutes to cross the rest of the notch and begin the descent, where the old roadway becomes apparent again.

Within 30 minutes you are really descending and can begin to hear Hoffman Notch Brook, which accompanies you most of the remaining distance. You first approach the brook near a wonderful little waterfall. A bridge here across a tributary stream, which flows from the valley between Hoffman Mountain and Texas Ridge, has washed away. So has the bridge farther downstream across Hoffman Notch Brook. You must devise an alternate method of crossing both. In summer, hopping stones to continue on the left bank of Hoffman Notch Brook is no problem. In high water, it is best done upstream from the confluence with the tributary. A short bushwhack along the left bank brings you down to the place the trail used to cross from the east; in fact, a new footpath has been worn along most of the left bank here.

You are in the deepest part of the hemlock-shrouded gorge, walking close to the rapids and little falls. The route is rugged,

the drop is steep, and the ravine is very deep, but the trek is beautiful. Shortly, you pick up the yellow markers again.

Good-sized cliffs and ledges rise on your left, and you occasionally glimpse Hornet Cobbles, which seems to loom incredibly steeply above the trail on your right. When you reach an old logging clearing in a grove of maple saplings, less than an hour's walk from Big Marsh, begin looking carefully to your left. Soon you should catch sight of a 100-foot ledge topped with cedar and birch, over which a stream of water shoots, splitting into several cascades, dropping to pools on ledges on the dark black rock face, and then splitting again into a multitude of fine sprays.

If you are tempted to scramble up the talus slope for a better look at the falls, watch out for the horse nettles that cover the hillside and beware of poison ivy. This may be one of the most remote sites reached by that companion of man.

Continuing north beside the stream, you pass a waterfall right beside a giant boulder, an erratic over 30 feet in diameter and more than 15 feet high. Many other boulders fill the valley. Giant cedar grow among the hemlock, making the stream so dark that photography is impossible. The valley narrows again; it is now scarcely 100 yards across. That horse- and oxcarts once traveled this route defies belief.

Gradually the brook levels, its route becoming more sinuous but its shores still edged with impressive erratics. Gravel improvements indicate the road's recent use. Trees become smaller, and you pass a small gravel pit, some abandoned and rusted machinery, and many signs of a logging camp. Your route is now high above the stream, which is still lovely in the deep gorge below you. The browns, turquoises, and greens of lichens color its light gray rocks.

The trail crosses the stream at a spot that could be difficult to ford in high water. In early spring or after a rain, you will surely get wet. In low water, one good-sized jump may be all that is needed. It takes about 90 minutes to reach this crossing from the notch. Just beyond is a sign indicating that you have left the Hoffman Notch Wilderness Area. The land ahead is owned by Finch, Pruyn, and Company, which permits hiking the continuing trail, but no hunting, fishing, or camping is allowed.

The continuing trail is a chapter in the saga of the struggle to outsmart the beaver, who have built numerous dams on the three streams that converge in the marshy valley that lies ahead and adjacent to the Blue Ridge Road. A stream from the west and the stream from the notch join and intersect The Branch, which flows from Elk Lake. All of the surrounding land is marshy, requiring a number of trail relocations. For at least 20 years, the beaver have been winning, but Finch, Pruyn has recently permitted a more westerly route. This is a bit longer, but it crosses The Branch's two western feeder streams above their juncture. The big bridge across their juncture has been relocated upstream to one of the feeder streams. The trail is generally to the west of previous routes, not only upstream, but on slightly higher ground.

The new trail north into the private land approaches the power line and—instead of swinging east as before—continues straight across the field below the line, heading almost north and back into the woods. A bridge takes you over the first stream, which is the one you have been following from the notch. North of it, the trail heads due north to higher ground, then swings east to intersect the old trail/roadway just a few yards from the parking area on Blue Ridge Road. If the beaver do not flood this last stretch, you can walk it in under a half hour. (If you are reversing this walk, look for the narrow new route shortly after you start. It is not as obvious as the abandoned trail, which followed the old and flooded roadway.)

Along the Boardwalk Nature Trail

47

Bear Mountain and Boardwalk Nature Trail

Distance (total): 8.3 miles–3.5 miles over Bear Mountain loop, 4.8 miles round-trip on Nature Trail

Vertical rise: 540 feet

Hiking time: 6 hours

Map: USGS 7.5' Cranberry Lake

Cranberry Lake, one of the larger bodies of water in the park, lies in the remote northwestern corner of the Adirondacks. Here, the last glaciers of the ice age sculpted the Adirondack plateau before receding to the St. Lawrence Valley. In their wake, long, sinuous rivers formed and great forests arose on the sandy soils left behind. Until the last half of the 19th century, the only human presence was that of transient Native Americans and a few adventurous woodsmen. With logging and tourism coming so late to this region, it can truly be called the state's last frontier.

Before the arrival of civilization, Cranberry Lake was a much smaller lake where the water of several streams merged in a postglacial basin. Later, settlers built a dam at the foot of the flow to control flooding and harness its power for their various downstream mills. This drastically changed the shoreline of the lake, permanently flooding the many flows and drowning acres of standing timber. Today, the old stumps and sun-bleached trunks that remain give character to the bays, which are still referred to as "flows." With its modern dam and large amount of state-owned shoreline, the lake offers many recreational possibilities while providing the water for several downstream hydro plants.

There is no better place to view the islands and flows of Cranberry Lake than from the lookout on the south side of Bear Mountain. Though not as lofty as other Adirondack peaks, it is typical of the handful of modest mountains in the region and dominates the northern edge of the lake. To its east, Bear Mountain Flow merges with Brandy Brook

Flow to form a long, curving bay. Two marvelous trails, one looping over Bear Mountain and the other penetrating the disturbed woodlands near the headwaters of Bear Mountain Flow, are accessible from the nearby DEC campground. In 1991 the latter route was transformed into a nature trail with numbered markers placed at points of interest along its length. Taken together, they offer an interesting introduction to the area as well as a thoroughly enjoyable day of hiking.

How to Get There

Just east of Cranberry Lake Village, Lone Pine Road turns south from NY 3 and leads 1.3 miles to the DEC campground. When you pay the day-use fee at the entrance booth, be sure to ask for a copy of the interpretive leaflet about the nature trail. Continue on through the campground for another 0.45 mile to a parking area on your left, where you will find the trailhead register.

The Trail

A single trail follows red markers southeast for 0.2 mile to a junction where the Bear Mountain Trail continues straight ahead and the yellow-marked Boardwalk Nature Trail turns left, northeast. This hike begins straight ahead.

The ascent of Bear Mountain along the red-marked trail begins immediately, climbing steadily past an intermittent streambed through an old-growth forest of hemlock, yellow birch, maple, ash, beech, and cherry. A lean-to on your left at 0.7 mile marks roughly the halfway point of the climb. It's a good place to catch your breath and shed a layer of clothing. Beyond the lean-to, the slope becomes steeper; the well-worn trail has been rerouted around eroded sections at several points.

At 1.2 miles, the trail levels off on the broad top of the mountain, just at the point where a large, pyramid-shaped erratic appears on your left. The woods now have an almost parklike atmosphere and the walk through the open, grassy understory is most enjoyable. All too soon, the trail begins a slight descent and you may think you have missed any views, but at 1.5 miles a small opening appears on your right. This modest outcrop is actually the top of an extensive rock complex on Bear Mountain's south shoulder and it provides the single dramatic view from the mountain. To the south, Buck Island marks the entrance to South Bay, with round-topped Indian Mountain rising above. Moving west, Joe Indian Island dominates the main body of the lake. Above it and far beyond, the summit of Cat Mountain etches the horizon. Dead Creek Flow stretches away in the distance, fed by the waters of the Oswegatchie River as it snakes its way out of the Five Ponds Wilderness.

There is no better place from which to contemplate the way New York's Forest Preserve has restored our forest heritage. The sea of green before you was all, at one time, heavily logged. To the west, Rich Lumber Company built a railroad as far as Wanakena and used it to strip the surrounding stands of pine in a few short years before 1912. To the east, Emporium Lumber Company took all the hardwoods, while International Paper Company harvested all the softwoods. There was a sawmill at Cranberry Lake until 1927. Emporium's railroad contributed to the rapidity and thoroughness with which the forest was logged. But today, as you look around, you must be impressed with the forest's recovery.

Continuing the loop, the trail descends steeply with zigzags from the lookout, first heading south, then curving west and north. A brief level stretch follows, then a short rise, through a forest of giant maple and beech. After this, the trail descends past a jumble of

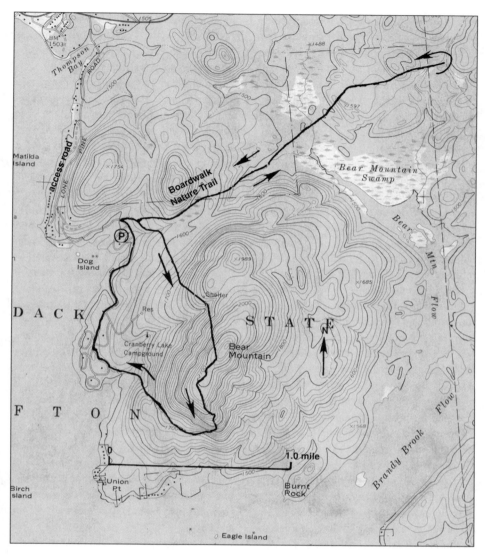

rocks and walls at the base of the southern shoulder. The lake soon appears through the trees ahead. After crossing a stream on a footbridge, the trail ends back inside the campground at a paved loop road. In this mile-long section from the lookout to the road, you may notice several paths intercepting the marked trail. Some of these are used by local people to reach private camps on the lakeshore, and in winter the portions on Forest Preserve land serve as short ski routes. For now, follow the main road through the campground back to the trailhead register, 1 mile away.

The Boardwalk Nature Trail, built in 1987, was initially called the Campground Trail because it linked the campground with the Brandy Brook snowmobile trail. However, the two 250-foot boardwalks through Bear Mountain Swamp are such prominent features that the trail was bound to be referenced by them. In fact, no better terrain for a nature trail can be found in the region. The surrounding forest is in several stages of succession and changes continually with each slight variation in elevation.

Before you start down the trail, it is a good idea to read the introduction in the interpretive leaflet. Some of the features it guides you to will be obvious, others not so easy to see—depending on the season. By taking the time to study the details of each stop along the way, you will get a good understanding of the Adirondacks' natural history.

Start from the register as before; the first numbered stop will be about 500 feet up the red-marked trail on your right. At the junction beyond, turn left following the yellow-marked trail as it begins to rise. You are in the minimally disturbed forest first noticed on your way up Bear Mountain, and it provides a great setting to learn about the midelevation hardwood understory. Since its acquisition in 1926 and the resulting halt in logging, this forest has matured into a handsome woods. Heading just north of east, the trail descends past a wet swale on the right where the slight increase in water allows spruces to grow amid sphagnum-covered hummocks.

Skirting the rocky south side of a hill, the trail enters an area acquired by the state in 1977. Pioneering stands of birch and aspen attest to the more recent logging of this parcel, and the route now follows a fading tote road. As you continue your descent toward Bear Mountain Swamp, cinnamon fern and pink lady's slipper make their appearance and moisture-tolerant spruce and balsam become more numerous. At just over 1 mile, you enter the lowlands of a conifer swamp and encounter the first boardwalk. Although there is no open water to be seen, the ground is saturated, a condition preferred by the large white cedar around you.

A slight rise into a section of mixed tree species follows. Here Labrador tea grows above clusters of bunchberry. It is not long, though, before evergreens again dominate, among them black spruce. Soon, you see a large open bog through the trees on your left; its many tall tamarack are especially beautiful in the autumn when their needles turn orange before falling. Descending again to the level of the swamp, you come to the second boardwalk. This one passes over the main stream carrying the waters of the swamp to Bear Mountain Flow. Because the movement of water is faster here, enough oxygen is present to allow the growth of thick grasses and alders.

Leaving the swamp, the trail climbs back into the familiar, older mixed woods. Spruce and balsam gradually give way to hemlock and white pine, which prefer better-drained soils. In just over 2 miles, you reach an area of past beaver activity. Remnants of dams, a lodge, and several gnawed sticks and stumps indicate that a colony once thrived here. With the woods now regenerating in their absence, it is only a matter of time before a passing beaver decides it is a suitable place to settle in, and the process will repeat itself.

The nature trail officially ends at this point and you may choose to turn back here. The yellow-marked foot trail continues on for another quarter mile to end at a register on the Burntbridge Pond Trail. A left turn at this junction leads 1.4 miles back to NY 3; a right turn takes you deep into the eastern parcel of the Cranberry Lake Wild Forest, where several adventures described in *Discover the Northwestern Adirondacks* await your return.

48

Giant Mountain

Distance (one-way): 6.6 miles

Vertical rise: 3,000 feet

Hiking time: 6 hours

Maps: USGS Metric Keene Valley; USGS Metric Elizabethtown

Giant Mountain Wilderness Area

Giant is in every way an appropriate name for the mountain between Pleasant Valley south of Elizabethtown and the East Branch of the Ausable south of Keene Valley. Several trails lead to its summit, and although the route chosen here, from the west, presents the greatest vertical rise of all the hikes described in this guide, trails from Pleasant Valley on Giant's east side require another thousand feet of climbing. Giant is indeed a giant. It is 4,627 feet tall, the twelfth highest peak in the Adirondacks. The summit commands the best view from the east of the High Peaks; it overlooks almost all of the Champlain Valley and, to the south, the mountains beside Lake George. The climb from Chapel Pond on the west is challenging, and you can descend via the trail along Roaring Brook, also on the west, for a hike as varied as you could wish. If you pause for a picnic lunch on Giant's summit, the day's outing should take at least seven hours.

The trip is fairly strenuous, so be sure you carry enough water. The summit is exposed; bring along extra clothing.

If you plan to hike the two trails as described for this through-route, two cars are advisable. You can walk along NY 73 between Chapel Pond and Roaring Brook trailheads in less than a half hour, but the highway is very busy and apt to be dangerous for pedestrians. If you decide simply to retrace your route, I suggest using the Chapel Pond Trail. The unfolding views on that trail far exceed any along the Roaring Brook route.

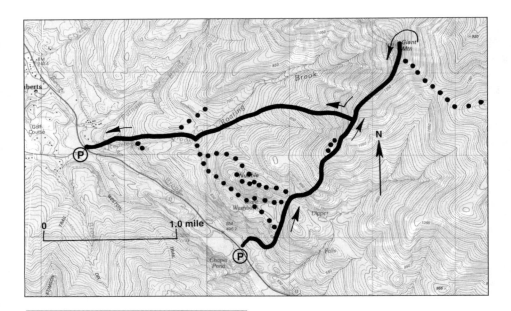

How to Get There

To reach the trailheads, take exit 30 off the Adirondack Northway (I-87) and head northwest on NY 73, following signs for Keene Valley. Chapel Pond is 3.6 miles beyond the road that forks right toward Elizabethtown. The Roaring Brook trailhead, where your hike ends, is 1.4 miles farther, opposite the southern entrance to the Ausable Club. Leave your second car here and return to Chapel Pond.

The Trail

After parking near Chapel Pond, and if you can tear yourself away from the views of the cliffs that rise from the pond, as well as those on the shoulder of Giant, walk south 250 yards to the trailhead, which is concealed in a marsh on the east side of the road. A sign denotes the route to Giant via the Ridge Trail.

Orange Adirondack Trail Improvement Society (ATIS) markers indicate the way. You begin to climb immediately after crossing an intermittent stream. Rocks are tumbled everywhere. At 0.3 mile, the trail angles left and a sign points right to a spring that is not dependable in dry weather. New birch railings guide you to a recently rerouted stretch of trail. Follow the prescribed route, which zigzags across the steep slope. A steeper climb is possible, but it would hasten erosion. The sparse birch cover tells of raging forest fires, and there is no ground cover to hold the thin soil. The mountainside is amazingly bare, brown, and sterile below the tree cover.

Within 15 minutes, as you traverse back toward the highway, a glimpse of Round Mountain serves as a gauge on how rapidly you are climbing. In 0.5 mile you reach a rubble-filled wash, and continue under overhanging ledges. The wash was once the outlet of the Giant's Washbowl, a tiny pond on the mountainside. After walking less than a half hour, you reach an unmarked fork where a footpath leads 50 feet to the left to the edge of a cliff that drops directly to the highway by Chapel Pond. Notice how the cliffs that overhang the western side of the pond have already shrunk below you. The tops of Armstrong and the Wolfjaws are visible to the west.

Continue on the right fork, almost on the cliff edge, to a second lookout and then turn away from the cliff to drop a few feet to a trail junction 0.7 mile from the highway. The left fork leads to Saint Huberts, but you continue straight beside the Giant's Washbowl. Pause to enjoy the reflections of the Giant's cliffs. The trail heads northeast into a spruce and hemlock grove, which indicates the limits of the fires up the mountain. The trail continues through deep woods with huge cedars for 0.2 mile to a second marked junction, where the fork left also heads toward Saint Huberts, via Roaring Brook.

Bearing right, you start up a steep pitch, and the cover quickly thins. After about an hour of climbing, a slide at 1.2 miles yields views across the valley to Round Mountain and Noonmark. You now scramble up bare rock to a second lookout southwest toward Hough and both South and East Dix Mountains. The peaks covered by the Range Trail are now visible beyond the Ausable Valley.

For the 20 minutes you need to ascend the sheer rock face, cairns guide you along the route. The climb continues between view spots, each providing needed respite. Gothics becomes clearly distinguished between Sawtooth and Wolfjaws. The opening south through the long valley shows Pharaoh Mountain's cone 24 miles away and the Tip of the Tongue and Black Mountain near Lake George, 40 miles away.

Cairns direct the trail between the scrubby clumps of spruce, balsam, and blueberries that separate patches of open rock. You come to an overlook east toward Rocky Peak Ridge at about the same time you see a false summit on Giant. Chapel Pond seems no bigger than a drop of water.

The Ausable Club is visible in the western foreground, and the mountains on the north side of Johns Brook Valley appear above the mountains of the Range Trail.

You continue to scramble through low woods to another sheer slope of open rock. The views of only 10 minutes before become even more dramatic, and now you begin to see straight through Hunters Pass, with Dix on the left and Dial on the right. Nippletop is still hidden behind Dial, but Hough, McComb, South Dix, and East Dix now range as separate peaks to the south. Colvin appears on the side of Ausable Lake, and the bare cone of Haystack is apparent between Gothics and Sawtooth.

The trail forks, the way right climbing over and the way left circling a little knob from which the southern end of Giant's summit ridge is visible. The trails rejoin at about 1.8 miles and just under two hours into your hike. You continue across a ridge, looking toward the Giant's cirque, the huge bowl slashed by recent slides, scars that make this mountain recognizable from such enormous distances.

Beyond a relatively level stretch, the trail rises to another intersection, 2.2 miles from Chapel Pond. The left fork leads down toward Saint Huberts, the way you will return. The right fork leads 0.7 mile and 700 feet to the summit, a climb you can make in a half hour. You pass a slant rock shelter and then reach a level stretch around the top of the cirque, with a steep rock ledge on your right. The footpath is narrow, winding through trees scarcely taller than a hiker's head. The summit is still 0.3 mile ahead. One more steep pitch brings you to it. A couple of hundred yards before the actual peak, another trail forks right, leading in 0.7 mile to Rocky Peak Ridge.

Walk along the summit ridge to find overlooks for all directions. Right at your feet extends the new scar of the slide that washed from Giant's summit in a violent series of thunderstorms. Before you, across the deep, scarred valley enclosed by the Giant's arms, spread the Ausable Valley with Gothics beyond, a little south of west, and Mount Marcy finally visible above it. Over the wooded slopes north of Gothics lies MacIntyre, with Colden barely visible between it and Marcy.

On the northern side of Johns Brook Valley, Big Slide is to the left of Cascade and Porter, which appear almost as two summits of the same mountain. To the right of MacIntyre on the distant horizon, MacNaughton, Street, and Nye form a ridge ending over Big Slide. To the right of Porter and Cascade, the long ridge with lots of rock is Pitchoff, and beyond it, the Sentinels and Whiteface are visible.

Now, as you look through Hunters Pass, the summit of Boreas is visible. To its right and 43 miles distant are the steep slopes of Puffer and the heart-shaped top of Humphrey to the left. Farther left, Snowy's peak is obvious, and continuing left, Panther and Wakely are visible with good binoculars.

Hurricane is obvious in the northeast, identified by its tower and rock summit. The eastern horizon is filled with the sweep of Lake Champlain; of the distant Green Mountains, only Camel's Hump and Mount Mansfield are easily identified. The mountains of Vermont seem to range forever north and south.

Retrace your route 0.7 mile to the trail to Saint Huberts. The route is steep enough that you may need 25 minutes to reach the junction. Take the right fork, which heads into deep woods, traversing the steep slopes of Giant, dropping like a rock. The slopes you cross are sometimes pitched at a 60-degree angle, so even the traverse route is steep. No open places distract you as you keep your eyes on the trail to ensure safe footing.

Thirty minutes from the junction, the trail levels out, but you must walk a bit farther before the trees become noticeably taller. As you enter a valley, you sense you are near the edge of the glacial cirque, but new growth conceals it from view. The steep descent continues for the better part of an hour on this trail, covering nearly 1.4 miles before reaching a muddy seep within a majestic hemlock grove. From here you can hear the water of Roaring Brook. You cross two streams flowing from your left in 0.2 mile, and reach a trail junction in another 0.1 mile. The route left is through the Giant's Nubble. You turn right and shortly cross the brook on the pure white rocks amid signs of terrifying amounts of water and fallen debris. The rubble from the slide is now uphill above you. A trail to the right heads up the mountain but is quickly obliterated by the slide. You turn left to follow the valley of Roaring Brook, walking through the prettiest wooded section on the hike, a hemlock grove of tall, straight, towering trees.

A path forks left 3.3 miles from the summit, back to the top of Roaring Brook Falls, a place of beauty and danger. There have been several deaths in recent years. Hikers should not walk out onto the wet and sloping area at the top of the falls. The trail continues on a contour around a deep ravine, running first through magnificent hemlock and then past huge birch, and finally dropping to the valley floor. The entire 3.6-mile descent, with time to pause and study the slide, takes at least 2½ hours.

49

Indian Pass

Distance (one-way): 10.6 miles

Vertical rise: 674 feet

Hiking time: 7 hours

Maps: USGS Metric Ampersand Lake;
USGS Metric Keene Valley; USGS Metric
Santanoni Peak

High Peaks Wilderness Area

In 1836 Professor Ebenezer Emmons was appointed chief geologist in charge of studying the Adirondacks. In the course of this study he visited the Adirondack Pass, which we now know as Indian Pass. Of it he wrote that "in this country there is no object of the kind on scale so vast and imposing as this. We look upon the Falls of Niagara with awe and a feeling of our insignificance; but much more are we impressed with the great and sublime in the simple and naked rock of the Adirondack Pass." Later 19th-century explorers discovered many more dramatic natural features, but Indian Pass remains the most incredibly wild and dramatic spot in the eastern United States.

Indian Pass bisects the Adirondack High Peaks. You can hike through it in one day, if you arrange to leave a car at both the north and south trailheads. I suggest you walk the pass from north to south for both aesthetic and historic reasons. The route is one to anticipate and savor, so set aside ample time to appreciate the marvelous sights and sounds you will encounter.

To heighten the drama, read Alfred Billings Street's 19th-century classic, *The Indian Pass,* before you go. He used every passionate and romantic adjective to describe the pass's awe-inspiring rocks, cliff, and vistas. For example, a typical summer thunderstorm became a dialogue between the echoing voices of the mountains. For all the excesses of his 19th-century prose, you will discover that the pass remains the "magnificent spectacle" he described.

The quirks of sound and echo that as-

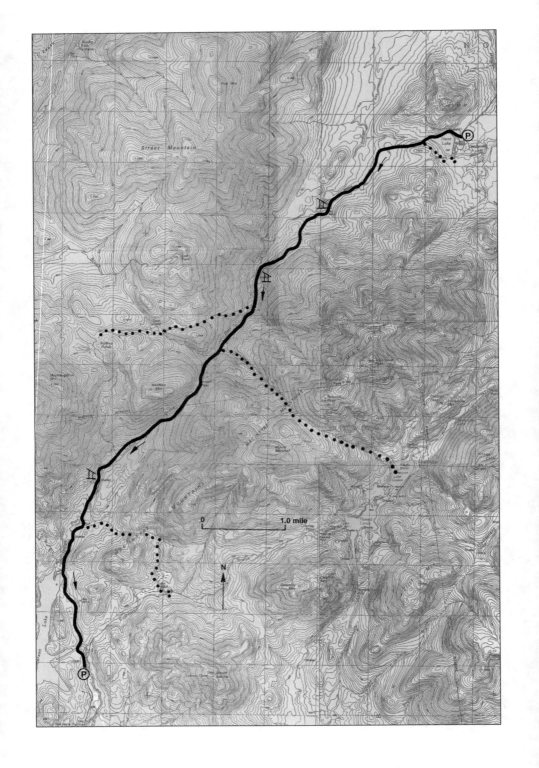

tounded Street will amaze you, for the voices of other hikers seem to reflect from many improbable sources. According to Street, Native Americans called the pass *He-no-do-as-da,* the "Path of the Thunder," or *Os-ten-wanne,* "Great Rock," or *Otne-yar-heh,* the "Stonish Giants."

How to Get There

The southern trailhead, where your hike ends, is the Upper Works Trailhead north of Tahawus, the site of National Lead Company's abandoned titanium mine. From exit 29 of the Adirondack Northway (I-87), drive west 13.5 miles on Blue Ridge Road to an intersection marked TAHAWUS and turn right, north. From Long Lake on NY 30, take NY 28N east 15.5 miles through Newcomb and turn north at the marked intersection. Just south of the entrance to the mine, a road forks left 3.7 miles to the Upper Works Trailhead, which is at the end of the road.

To reach the northern trailhead, drive to the end of Heart Lake Road, which runs south from NY 73 at the hamlet of North Elba, 11.2 miles west of Keene and 3.2 miles east of Lake Placid. Park by the Adirondak Loj, which is owned and managed by the Adirondack Mountain Club. The club charges a nominal parking fee, but parking space may be limited on weekends.

The Trail

The red-marked Indian Pass Trail begins west of the parking lot, circles north of the Loj, swings south beside the Natural History Museum, and continues south along the shore of Heart Lake, following a dirt road that gives access to lean-tos and campsites on Loj property.

In less than 15 minutes, 0.5 mile from the start, you reach the end of the lake, where a side trail forks left to circle it. Continue straight, passing the sign-in box

for the trail, through a birch and cedar second-growth forest over rolling country. Within 0.1 mile you reach the boundary of state land. For the next 1.5 miles, the walking is easy on a good, hard-packed trail. Enormous spruce and good-sized balsam dot the hardwood forest of beech, maple, and birch. A rich forest floor supports a wide variety of wildflowers and ferns. In summer the red berries of twisted stalk and the blue berries of clintonia stand out beside the trail. Openings to the right through the trees give hints of the outline of the valley of Indian Pass Brook. While some guidebooks pay scant attention to these first 2 miles, you should not: You are walking in a very fine forest.

In addition to red trail markers, yellow markers with red numbers at 0.5-mile intervals measure your progress from the Loj. You can easily reach the 2-mile marker within an hour. In another 0.1 mile, on the far side of a stream crossing, a loop trail heads right, past Rocky Falls and a lean-to. This spur is little more than 200 yards longer than the main trail, so take it and enjoy walking beside Indian Pass Brook, with its white stone base and views of the falls that drop into a deep pool from a chute through a cleft in the bedrock. Returning to the main trail requires scrambling up a short pitch, but the entire detour, 0.3 mile long, should take no more than 15 minutes to walk.

Where you return to the main trail, a benchmark records the elevation as 2,160 feet. Turn right, south, passing an intermittent stream and then a second stream in a small gorge. Beyond a rocky section you encounter a mud hole, and you pass the 3-mile marker in the midst of a big stretch of mud and corduroy.

There are interesting ledges on your left as the walking continues easy and level. Along this stretch you may encounter a

Wallface Cliffs from the north end of Indian Pass

howler, or widowmaker, a treetop leaning on a second tree and rubbing against it to create weird shrieking sounds.

Through openings to the right, you should be able to glimpse the shoulders of Street and Nye Mountains and the unnamed mountain that conceals Lost Pond near its summit. You cross one and then another creek, where ledges on surrounding hills begin to enclose the pass. As the valley narrows, you reach the Scott's Clearing Lean-to, 4 miles from the Loj. Ford the creek in front of the lean-to by hopping on rocks. The trail then turns right, and within a few minutes you enter the meadow of Scott's Clearing, which today is filled with raspberries, barrel staves and iron artifacts, and spectacular white birch.

In another 0.3 mile, a blue-marked trail heads west to Wallface and Scott Ponds. Just beyond, a marvelous rock dam creates a flow over which there is a view of Wallface Mountain and Indian Pass. An ancient beaver house stands in the pond, and signs of beaver work abound. A low, water-level trail continues toward Indian Pass, but it can be wet even in a dry summer. I suggest you walk an alternate route, which circles a small hill whose cliff face drops directly to the pond. To find it, angle left at the east end of the dam, almost as if to parallel the trail from the lean-to, and walk to the brook. For about 100 yards the trail follows the brook, whose rock base is strangely colored steel gray. It then swings up a draw. Footing is rough among the rocks and roots. Rounding the top of the draw, the trail crosses a height-of-land in a small ravine, turns toward the valley, and starts down through a steep cleft that cuts the cliff wall.

When you return to the level of the flow, you become aware of how narrow the valley has become. A rock wall is now visible on the east. You cross a stream that enters from the left at 4.7 miles. The next section of trail lies too close to Indian Pass Brook, and footing is apt to be wet until you cross a second brook, 0.2 mile farther. Both streams flow from Algonquin Pass. At 5.1 miles, after about 2½ hours of walking, you intersect a yellow-marked trail that heads east for 3.3 miles to Lake Colden.

Just beyond that trail junction you have a good view of cliffs on an unnamed knob, but then the pass becomes progressively narrower, and vertical cliffs form walls on both sides of the stream. You cross Indian Pass Brook on a gravelly wash, and then recross it to follow a smaller flow from the pass. Just beyond, you see the outlet of Scott Pond, which flows from the west.

The trail now enters the narrow cleft of Indian Pass and begins to climb rapidly. A faint footpath winds up and over boulders and moss-covered ledges, following the small, cold brook that flows from the pass. Steep cliffs face the flanks of MacIntyre to form the pass's eastern wall. Here the pass itself is scarcely 100 feet wide and filled with the rubble of ancient slides. You may often have to use your hands to help yourself along and you will need the one ladder to help you climb the steepest part. The dark, moss-covered canyon with overhanging cliffs ends all too soon. This entrance to the pass is but 0.4 mile long. It should take 20 minutes to scramble up the 400-foot rise into the pass.

As you reach the end of the ravine, Wallface begins to loom high up on your right, its sheer, vertical cliff cut jaggedly. The pass opens wide, and you climb a few feet on the east side, overlooking a precipitous mass of boulders so rugged that the trail could not possibly be routed through the deepest part. As you walk the short distance of the height-of-land, watch for the holes and the mouths of caves among the

➤ The Lost Settlement

Immediately south of the Upper Works Trailhead, a row of deserted houses marks the 1833 settlement of Adirondac, where the laborers of the McIntyre Iron Works were housed. A mile south of the trailhead stands the stone tower of the mine's blast furnace, erected in 1854. The beauty of the precise angles of the tower's cut stone will remind you of European castles. The tower, nearly 48 feet tall, now bears a crown of cedar and huge birch. The iron ore was "discovered" in 1826 by a party who made the trip through Indian Pass from North Elba, led by a Native American guide, Lewis Elijah, who knew the site of the ore bed. The group included my great-great-grandfather's brother, Duncan McMartin; David Henderson; a black manservant; and a dog called Wallace. Within a few years, a company formed by Henderson, McMartin, and Archibald McIntyre began mining and shipping out the high-grade iron ore. Unfortunately, the high titanium content, which made ore-separation difficult, and the problems of shipping the ore from its wilderness location brought an end to the iron mining operation after only a few years.

slabs. On a hot summer day, fog and mist rise in cool drafts from these crevices, where ice often persists well into July. The sharply angular tops of the larger boulders support lichens and mosses and even large spruce and birch. Rising above it all, Wallface creates a dramatic backdrop for the wild scene.

The pass developed as a northeast-trending fault at the same time as many other Adirondack fault valleys from pressures created by the Taconic uplift. But while many of these faults are filled with long, thin lakes, rocks and boulders fallen from the cliff of Wallface and the flanks of MacIntyre have brought the pass to its present level.

By the route you have taken, it is nearly 5.8 miles to the height-of-land in the pass, a point denoted by a DEC trail marker. As you continue south, the temperature rises noticeably when the trail leads a few feet up a ridge on the east side of the pass. As you make a short descent, the sheer cliffs, columns, and hanging ledges on Wallface seem even higher. You walk through a small meadow and within 10 minutes reach a clearing with a fireplace. This is a good stopping spot for viewing the highest part of the cliffs, which rise nearly 1,000 feet above you.

To continue south, find and cross a small stream. It, like the brook on the north, rises from a spring in the height of the pass. The northern brook makes its way to the West Branch of the Ausable, which empties into Lake Champlain. The one you have just met, confusingly also called Indian Pass Brook, flows south into Henderson Lake, whose outlet joins Calamity Brook to form the Hudson River.

Just beyond the meadow, an enormous fallen slab of cliff blocks the trail. You wind around it, climbing slightly before beginning the final descent, which is along a ridge above and on the east side of the gorge. The south side of the pass is drier and more open than the north. Its sides are precipitously steep below you. After a half-hour walk—it takes that long to enjoy this 0.4-mile segment—you reach a sign pointing right up a small ladder to a huge boulder, Summit Rock, which marks the southern edge of Indian Pass. It overlooks the broad sweep of the pass as it falls off toward Henderson Lake, with Henderson and Santanoni Mountains behind. The sight rivals the majestic grandeur of the vista back toward the cliffs on Wallface. You will stand on the outcrop like the tiny figures of the Hudson River School painters, overlooking an awe-inspiring view, completely overwhelmed by the scale of the rocks and forests around you.

A steep descent of 500 feet over 0.5 mile to the southern Indian Pass Brook follows. Within a few minutes you reach the first ladder, a necessary convenience because of the cliffs that rim the pass. The jumble of boulders, caves, and overhanging cliffs continues, with side paths leading to some of the larger boulders that emerge above the trees. Then, in a spot not well marked, the trail turns right, west, toward the gorge around a ledge, at the beginning of a very steep sliding descent into the valley. A pair of ladders assist in the descent. Lovely views accompany you on the precipitous route.

By the time you reach these ladders, the valley has become quite broad. The terrain continues to be rugged. A few openings between tree-capped boulders offer dramatic views of Wallface, which seems to loom even higher than it did before. You continue to look down into the depths of the cleft on your right, with everything on a much larger scale than it was along the northern entrance to the pass.

You pass a waterfall just before you actually reach and cross the brook. Here you have your last view back of the cliffs on Wallface. It will probably take you at least a half hour to cover the 0.5-mile descent from Summit Rock.

The stream crossing marks a real change in the route; the trail now enters a deep mature woods. The descent is gentle for a short time, until you reach a boggy section of trail. Cross it, on slippery logs, looking for turtlehead as you go.

You cross the wash of an intermittent stream, which affords views back east to the ridge that makes up the foothills of the MacIntyre Mountains. The trail crosses a larger stream, the outlet of Wallface Ponds, and then continues beneath ledges on the west side of the valley to the Wallface Lean-to, 1.2 miles and at least a half hour from the stream crossing.

A bridge crosses a small stream just below the lean-to. Within 20 minutes the trail angles left up a small rise, where it meets a freshly painted but ambiguous sign on which is written in elegant script only the word BRIDGE. Turn left to follow the trail 100 yards east to the bridge over Indian Pass Brook. A 10-foot-tall crib of boulders supports the bridge's west end, while a single boulder supports the east end. Beyond, the footpath turns south beside the stream and leads to an old clearing with another bridge sign and an incorrect mileage marker where the trail forks. A blue-marked trail heads back east toward Colden. It is 0.3 mile to the Henderson Lean-to, and 2 miles from the clearing to the Upper Works Trailhead. The trail stays near the stream as far as the lean-to, which is less than 100 yards from the boundary of private lands. The red-marked trail continues through private lands. Permission to cross has been granted hikers, but the lands are posted against fishing, hunting, trapping, and camping.

At a major intersection 0.1 mile south of the boundary, a trail turns right, west, toward the Duck Holes and Coreys, west of Ampersand.

Here you pick up a yellow-marked trail heading south along logging roads improved with gravel. Because the surrounding land is private, you never really see Henderson Lake. After a dull, relatively level stretch, you cross the Hudson River, just below the outlet of Henderson Lake. In another five minutes you walk downhill to the trailhead and your waiting car. The drive south provides several views of the High Peaks. Due east lie the North River Mountains, with Allen to their north, then Redfield leading up to Skylight, with Mount Marcy peeping behind. Just east of north lies Mount Adams, identified by its tower. Northwest stands Henderson, with Santanoni beyond.

When you return home, you will want to relive the pleasures of the hike through Indian Pass by reading Arthur H. Masten's *The Story of Adirondac,* available in reprint. In it you will find a copy of the letter in which David Henderson wrote of his discovery trip through the pass, as well as the history of the mine. And you *will* want to relive the trip, for you will agree it is the most exciting walk in the eastern United States.

50

Algonquin Peak in the MacIntyre Mountains

Distance (round-trip): 8 miles

Vertical rise: 2,936 feet

Hiking time: 6 hours

Map: USGS Metric Keene Valley

High Peaks Wilderness Area

Algonquin Peak in the MacIntyre Mountains is, at 5,114 feet, the second highest mountain in New York State. But in all other respects, Algonquin is second to none. Standing in the midst of the noblest group of mountains in the Adirondacks, it offers an exciting climb and the best view from within the High Peaks.

As you drive toward the trailhead, this hike also offers—on Heart Lake Road—a view of the High Peaks; the MacIntyre Mountains completely dominate the skyline. Adirondak Loj was built near the site of an imposing hotel that the inventor Henry van Hoevenberg had constructed of massive logs in 1878–80. Van Hoevenberg's fortune financed the lodge he planned to run with his fiancée, Josephine Scofield, for whom he named the mountain behind the lodge Mount Jo. Disapproving parents and her untimely death brought an end to the marriage plans, and the forest fires of 1903 brought an end to the lodge. Alfred Donaldson's *The History of the Adirondacks* contains many fascinating details of the development of this northern gateway to the High Peaks.

The MacIntyre Mountains derived their name from Archibald McIntyre, comptroller of the state of New York and partner in the McIntyre Iron Mine, south of Indian Pass. Algonquin Peak was named about 1880 by the surveyor Verplank Colvin after the tribe that once controlled most of New England, the Hudson River Valley, and the St. Lawrence River Valley. The tribe, which sided with the French in the French and

---

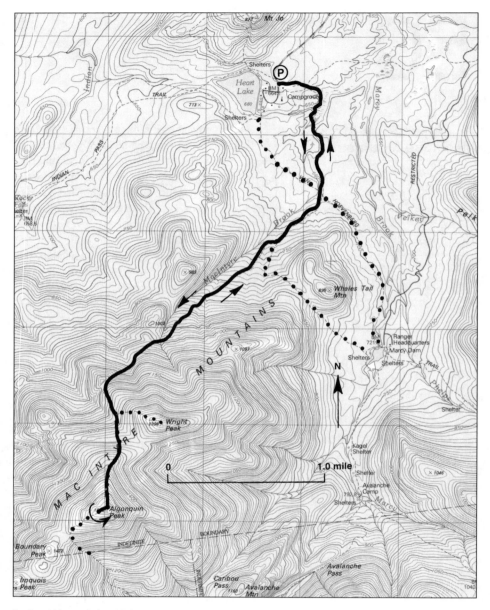

Indian Wars of the 17th century, was gradually overpowered by the Iroquois. Algonquin, according to Russell M. L. Carson in *Peaks and People of the Adirondacks,* "is therefore a monument to the annihilated people, who were the original possessors of the Adirondack Wilderness." (Carson's book is a complete record of the names, early ascents, and trails on the Adirondacks' 46 peaks over 4,000 feet in elevation.)

How to Get There

The trailhead for Algonquin is a historic site at the end of Heart Lake Road, which heads south from NY 73 in North Elba, 11.2 miles west of Keene and 3.2 miles east of Lake Placid. This northern gateway to the High Peaks is owned and managed by the Adirondack Mountain Club (ADK), which maintains a parking lot at its Adirondak Loj at the end of Heart Lake Road. The club charges a nominal fee for parking, but space may be limited on weekends. The trailhead and registration booth are located at the southeastern edge of the Loj parking lot.

The Trail

Heading south from the trailhead, in the first mile you follow the Van Hoevenberg Trail, which is the principal route to Mount Marcy, denoted with blue markers. The route begins down a small incline and crosses a marsh, an alder swamp, and then the outlet of Heart Lake on a log bridge. After climbing the side of a small hill, you enter state land and within 20 minutes, or 1 mile, come to a major trail junction. Here the blue-marked trail to Marcy Dam heads south, left, and the MacIntyre trails, marked with yellow disks, continue straight ahead.

From the intersection it is 3 miles to the summit of Algonquin, with almost all the ascent yet to come. ADK is proud of the work that has been done to repair sections of the trail and to reroute worn areas. Water bars, stairs, and stonework all help prevent erosion. As a result, the lower sections of the trail are easy to walk.

Within 20 minutes you come to a stretch where large stones have been placed through a muddy swale. A ski-touring trail forks left at 1.4 miles, toward Whales Tail Notch. The Whales Tail is a small knob directly northeast of MacIntyre's northern

summit, Wright Peak. Continuing, you walk through a rich hardwood forest whose floor is punctuated by the blooming flowers of understory plants.

Gradually, paper birch becomes the predominant tree. This indicates the extent of the fires that burned the mountainside and all the Heart Lake area in the early 20th century. The spruce and balsam now establishing themselves beneath the birch are your clues to the length of time that has passed. You walk through the birch forest for nearly 1 mile, past ledges on your left, climbing moderately. You will hardly be aware of where you cross the old worn trail. At 2.3 miles, 75 minutes into your walk, a sign points to the summit 1.6 miles away. The gullied wash leading back to your left is the abandoned trail.

A few minutes later you come to a sign pointing left, east, to a camping area. Just beyond, the trail crosses a brook not shown on the USGS map. In wet seasons a crystal sheet of water falls over a high ledge, creating a charming resting spot.

As you climb again, the balsam become thicker, and ledges on your left are covered with a deep moss carpet. Within 15 minutes, in a short level, you cross an almost dry stream. Then a jumble of old blowdowns edges a steep section of trail that zigzags through the scrub. In 15 minutes more, at 2.9 miles, you pass a rock knob on your right, just off the trail. As you turn left away from the knob to scramble up a very steep section, you have views of a wooded summit, the first of many false summits you glimpse as you climb. Two hours into your hike, at 3.1 miles, you reach another trail junction. The way left, marked with blue disks, leads in 0.5 mile to Wright Peak, 385 feet higher than your present location. Continue straight on the yellow-marked trail to begin one of the steepest climbs on a High Peaks trail, an ascent of 912 feet in 0.9 mile. It may take you a full hour to reach the summit from here.

The route is steep, over ledges, with water usually coursing over the bare rock that constitutes the trail. Scrubby spruce and balsam line the route and cling to the sphagnum that makes up the vertical bogs of the alpine summits. The shallow soil is home to many ground covers, including creeping white winterberry, goldthread, and bunchberry, here blossoming at the end of July, eight weeks later than in the Adirondack lowlands. When you reach a stretch of sheer rock trail, pause to look back, for you can now see the summit of Wright Peak, and you appear to be at about the same elevation. Openings permit views north to Whiteface and McKenzie and east to the precipitous rock face of Gothics. Again you have a view of a summit ahead, but it too is false. The blue leaves of dwarf bilberry and the blue-green and white, almost needlelike leaves of bog rosemary show up in the mats of low scrub bushes along the trail. Huge blue crystals of labradorite are embedded in the anorthosite that makes up the rock base of this and all the eastern High Peaks.

Forty minutes from the junction, you reach tree line, with 0.4 mile left to climb. A sign asks that you please stay on the marked trail so that you do not trample the fragile alpine vegetation. From here on, only arrows painted on bedrock or cairns mark the trail. The route is not hard to follow in good weather, but if clouds should roll in, a not uncommon event on high Adirondack peaks, watch carefully for the arrows.

Another false summit looms ahead, but finally you climb over a small ledge and find the true summit. As you climb the open rock slabs, you begin to see the three-leafed cinquefoil of the alpine heights, and in summer you will be surprised to discover bottle gentian blooming at the same time as bunchberry. Adirondack High Peak summers are compressed into a short season.

After you settle in for a picnic, spread out your maps or atlas and orient yourself. The most impressive mountain view is southeast to Colden, the stripes of its slides radiating from the summit like the outflow from some gigantic moonscape eruption. Slides from Colden have changed the outlet of Avalanche Lake, which lies hidden between Algonquin and Colden. Colden's famous trap dyke, a narrow gorge carved out in the sheer rock dome, is clearly visible to the left of the major slides. This view of Colden is my favorite scene in the High Peaks, and one of the reasons is that the mountain was for a time called Mount McMartin, after my great-great-great-uncle, who was one of the founders of the McIntyre iron mine south of Indian Pass.

On the horizon left, east of Colden, lie Skylight, Gray Peak, and Marcy. Continuing left are Hough, the Dixes, and the mountains of the Range Trail, with Giant almost due east. Hurricane, Porter, and Cascade are visible around to the north, with Van Hoevenberg to the northeast. The Sentinel Range is visible over Van Hoevenberg, and to its left, west, lies Whiteface. You will have no trouble spotting the Olympic Ski Jump at Lake Placid.

Moving around to the northwest, Street and Nye form a long wooded range that leads to Wallface in the west. The cliffs on Wallface clearly outline Indian Pass.

Starting again with Colden but this time moving right, or west, you should identify first Redfield. Below you lie Lake Colden and Flowed Land. South of Lake Colden and just to the right of Redfield you can see the cliffs on Cliff Mountain. Next comes a small peak, Little Nippletop, and then Calamity Mountain. Flowed Land points to the valley between Cliff and Calamity, through which the Opalescent River, the outlet of Flowed Land, exits. Over Calamity Mountain and to the right you should see Henderson, with Santanoni the huge mountain behind. Seward and Seymour mark the western horizon behind Wallface, with the Sawtooth Mountains to its north, followed by Ampersand.

You will need binoculars and exceptionally clear weather to see more distant peaks, but it is possible to pick out Blue Mountain and Vanderwhacker as well as many of the outlying summits described in this guide.

Your return will occupy the better part of 2½ hours, with 50 minutes devoted to the first 0.9-mile descent. It is that steep! If you are making a midsummer trip, look for Milbert's Turquoise, an uncommon angle-wing butterfly often seen in large numbers on Algonquin.

Algonquin is a fairly strenuous climb, yet it is much easier to reach than the majority of the High Peaks, which require treks from interior backpacking locations. If the introduction to the eastern High Peaks has stimulated your interest in the Adirondacks' higher climbs, sample a few, but do not neglect the outlying mountains, for which there is the *Discover* series of guidebooks. You will find their climbs and views are more than comparable, but you will also discover a sense of wilderness that is becoming rare in the popular High Peaks.

Books about the Adirondacks

Aber, Ted, and Stella King. *The History of Hamilton County*. Lake Pleasant, N.Y.: Great Wilderness Books, 1965.

Beetle, David H. *Up Old Forge Way and West Canada Creek*. Lakemont, N.Y. and Old Forge, N.Y.: North Country Books, 1972. (One-volume reprint of two books composed of articles published by the *Utica Observer-Dispatch*, Utica, N.Y., 1946 and 1948.)

Carson, Russell M. L. *Peaks and People of the Adirondacks*. Glens Falls, N.Y.: Adirondack Mountain Club, 1973. (Reprint of 1927 edition.)

Donaldson, Alfred L. *The History of the Adirondacks, Vols. I and II*. Harrison, N.Y.: Harbor Hill Books, 1977. (Reprint of 1921 edition.)

Dunham, Harvey L. *French Louie: Early Life in the North Woods*. Saranac Lake, N.Y.: North Country Books, 1970.

Fox, William F. *History of the Lumber Industry in the State of New York*. Harrison, N.Y.: Harbor Hill Books, 1976.

Gallos, Phil. *By Foot in the Adirondacks*. Saranac Lake, N.Y.: Adirondack Publishing Company, 1972.

Grady, Joseph F. *The Adirondacks, Fulton Chain–Big Moose Region: The Story of a Wilderness*. Old Forge, N.Y.: North Country Books, 1966. (Reprint of 1933 edition.)

Graham, Frank Jr. *The Adirondack Park: A Political History*. New York: Alfred A. Knopf, 1978.

Hyde, Floy S. *Adirondack Forests, Fields, and Mines*. Lakemont, N.Y.: North Country Books, 1974.

Jamieson, Paul F. "Adirondack Eskers," *Adirondack Life,* November/December 1978, p. 20.

____. *Adirondack Canoe Waters: North Flow*. Glens Falls, N.Y.: Adirondack Mountain Club, 1975.

____. *Adirondack Reader*. Second Edition. Glens Falls, N.Y.: Adirondack Mountain Club, 1982.

Ketchledge, E.H. *Trees of the Adirondack High Peak Region*. Glens Falls, N.Y.: Adirondack Mountain Club, 1967.

Masten, Arthur H. *The Story of Adirondac*. Syracuse, N.Y.: Adirondack Museum and Syracuse University Press, 1968. (Reprint of 1923 edition.)

McMartin, Barbara. *The Great Forest of the Adirondacks*. Utica, N.Y.: North Country Books, 1994.

____. *Hides, Hemlocks and Adirondack History*. Utica, N.Y.: North Country Books, 1992.

____. *Discover the Adirondacks*. Series of 11 regional guides. Lake View Press (distributed by North Country Books, 311 Turner Street, Utica, NY 13501).

Murray, William H. H. *Adventures in the Wilderness*. Syracuse, N.Y.: Adirondack Museum and Syracuse University Press, 1970. (Reprint of 1869 edition.)

Newland, D.H., and Henry Vaughn. *Guide to the Geology of the Lake George Region*. Albany, N.Y.: University of the State of New York, 1942.

O'Kane, Walter Collins. *Trails and Summits of the Adirondacks*. Boston and New York: Houghton Mifflin Company, 1928.

Pilcher, Edith. "Nehasane," *Adirondack Life,* September/October 1979, p. 14.

Reed, Frank A. *Lumberjack Sky Pilot.* Utica, NY: North Country Books, 2001. (Reprint of 1965 edition.)

Rickett, Harold William. *Wild Flowers of the United States, Volume I: The Northeastern States.* New York: The New York Botanical Garden and McGraw-Hill Book Company, 1966.

Simms, Jeptha R. *Trappers of New York, or a Biography of Nicholas Stoner and Nathaniel Foster.* Harrison, N.Y.: Harbor Hill Books, 1982. (Reprint of 1857 edition.)

Street, Alfred B. *The Indian Pass.* Harrison, N.Y.: Harbor Hill Books, 1975. (Reprint of 1960 edition.)

Van De Water, Frederic F. *Lake Champlain and Lake George.* The American Lakes Series. Indianapolis and New York: Bobbs Merrill Co., 1946.

Van Diver, Bradford C. *Rocks and Routes of the North Country, New York.* Geneva, N.Y.: W.F. Humphrey Press, 1976.

Wherry, Edgar T. *The Fern Guide: Northeast and Midland United States and Adjacent Canada.* Philadelphia: The Morris Arboretum of the University of Pennsylvania, 1972.

Index